The Only Secure Job

The
Only
Secure
Job

Changing from Employee to Entrepreneur

R ICHARD W ORZEL

KEY PORTER BOOKS

Canadian Cataloguing in Publication Data

Worzel, Richard, 1950-
    The only secure job : changing from employee to entrepreneur

ISBN 1-55263-059-5

1. Entrepreneurship. 2. Success in business. I. Title.

HD62.5.W673 1999   650.1   C99-931500-5

The publisher gratefully acknowledges the support of the Canada Council for the Arts and the Ontario Arts Council for its publishing program.

Canadä

We acknowledge the financial support of the Government of Canada through the Book Publishing Industry Development Program (BPIDP) for our publishing activities.

Key Porter Books Limited
70 The Esplanade
Toronto, Ontario
Canada M5E 1R2

www.keyporter.com
www.futuresearch.com

Electronic formatting: Heidi Palfrey
Design: Patricia Cavazzini

Printed and bound in Canada

99 00 01 02 03 6 5 4 3 2 1

Dedication

This book is dedicated to the women and men who invent the future every day of their working lives through the crucible of entrepreneurship, and thereby create opportunity and employment for others; and particularly to the entrepreneurs in my family:

Bill Worzel of Evolution Enterprises, whose ingenuity and tough-minded common sense may well spawn several multibillion-dollar industries through a truly novel technology;

Leslie Sobel, who, while working on a Masters degree in technology, re-invented herself as a successful artist and painter, following her bliss and making it pay;

and Sandy and Adrian Browne, of FieldWorker Products, who have gone through the roughest of entrepreneurial challenges, and may become the first multi-millionaires in the family.

My Thanks

No book is the product of a single mind, and this one is no exception. To those who helped create this one, I offer my thanks. Any errors that remain are, as always, mine. Among many, let me thank:

- Jacky Simmons, my wife and assistant, who helped me keep my feet firmly on the ground;
- my clients, past, present, and future, who have inspired me in addition to feeding my family;
- David Adler, researcher par excellence, who hasn't quite accepted that he is an entrepreneur, but is warming up to the idea;
- Anna Porter, head of Key Porter Books, who has always been the classic case study of an entrepreneur, and who insisted that this book exist;
- Beverley Slopen, my literary agent, who knows—and counsels—the art of the possible;
- David Lavin, Kelly MacDonald, Cathy Hirst, Giselle Robert, Mary-Jo DeCoteau, Derek Sweeney, Diane Chow, Tam Mercer, Lori Brozovich, Kim Hume, Neil DeSouza, and Michelle Taylor, who have been friends as well as allies, and

who have taught me that loyalty comes from friendship as well as from respect;

- Clare McKeon and Diane Broad, who have been fun to work with;
- Steve Wise, the relaxed and professional owner of an Amway distributorship;
- and to you, dear reader, for, as author Spider Robinson once so precisely put it: "When you stop applauding, I stop eating." The opportunity to write books is a privilege, not a right. I appreciate your faith in my work. Thank you.

Contents

What lies behind us and what lies before us
are tiny matters compared to what lies within us.

—Ralph Waldo Emerson

1. Where Can You Get a Secure Job?

"Where can my kids get a secure job?"

As a public speaker and futurist, I speak to something like 20,000 people a year, and this is one of the two most commonly asked questions at my presentations. It reflects a common concern shared by many people today: fear about the future of work. In fact, anxiety about what the job markets can offer young people entering the workforce is at a post-war high, giving parents nightmares about children winding up homeless on the street, or living forever in their childhood bedrooms.

The second most common question is the result of at least as much anxiety, but is asked privately and haltingly: "How can I hold on to my own job until I retire?" As it turns out, the concerns underlying both of these questions are well founded.

The anxiety about finding—and keeping—secure employment affects our perceptions of the future. If you're out of work, then you're constantly worried about money, and suddenly the world seems a harsher, more dangerous place. This is one of the major reasons why, when I ask a large audience how many people expect their children to have a better life than they have, only a small minority raise their hands. Anxiety about the future is high.

Over the past 20 years, the unwritten contract between employer and employee has been scrapped. We used to assume that if we worked hard and were loyal to our employers, we'd be assured of both job security and a pension. This is no longer the case. In fact, many employees feel that employers are now asking, "What have you done for me *today*?" Yesterday's performance seems to count for little in today's corporate world.

The central theme of this book is that job security no longer exists. You can be a hot prospect today, and consigned to the scrap heap tomorrow, as my first vignette illustrates:

RICK WAS A RISING STAR. He had been aggressively recruited by one of Bay Street's top companies as a research analyst with a big future. One of the company's directors had been assigned to be his mentor—to nurture him along and to help him develop. Rick was exceeding all of the goals that had been set for him, and had become the centre of a bidding war between two departments that both wanted him.

Then his company merged with another firm. The merger was handled professionally: within two days, everyone had met with a member of senior management, and been informed whether they were staying with or leaving the company. All of the 180 people who were laid off received generous severance packages and assistance in finding employment elsewhere.

Rick was in the group that got the chop, and he felt cheated. He had left a solid job with an upcoming investment group to explore new territory at this firm. But he had only been there for nine months—not long enough to make an impression or produce any significant results—and now he was out of a job. He had to start more or less from scratch, without much of a track record behind him. It took more than two months to find another job, and even then it wasn't as good as the one he had left 11 months earlier. He was one of the fortunate ones, however, since many of his displaced colleagues didn't find jobs for months, and some of them never really recovered from the loss of employment.

Rick was in a "knowledge industry." He was highly regarded. His superiors couldn't imagine a circumstance that would cause them to want to part with him. Yet, that's exactly what happened, and it's happening more and more frequently. But why? What's causing this change in the world of work?

T he end of jobs, but not the end of work

"We're not at the end of work," explains guru Peter Drucker, the godfather of management writers and theorists, "but we are at the end of jobs."[1] This is, perhaps, an overstatement, because there are still a lot of jobs around. Statistics Canada says that in 1997 almost 11.5 million of us worked for someone else, which is just over 82% of employed Canadians, compared to the 18% who worked for themselves. Yet Drucker's comment captures the essence of current trends, as only 12% of us were self-employed in 1976. The number of self-employed has more than doubled over the last 20 years, making it the fastest-growing sector of the job market.

The world of work has changed, both in the number of jobs and in the kinds of jobs available, and this change has implications for us all. If you happen to have the right skills, and are in the right place—say, as an e-commerce specialist on the World Wide Web and you live in Toronto—then you might be the object of a bidding war between employers desperate to employ you. As a result, you might well see your salary skyrocket.

But if you're 53 years old and have been a middle manager for the same industrial company for the last 20 years, or are 22 years old with a degree in English literature and are just out looking for your first job, the working world for you is vastly different today than it was for your counterparts 20, or even 10, years ago. And if you're fortunate enough to be employed, then you are probably finding that it's not your income that's skyrocketing, but rather the number of hours you're working just to hold on to your job. Finally, if you're unemployed, you are probably having a tough time breaking into the job market.

Regardless of which group you fall into, my point is that you may need this book, even if you don't think you do. Whether you realize it or not, you are at risk—at age 20 or 50.

MAUREEN MACLACHLAN STARTED an unusual business called Age Matters Communications Group Inc. She's a 50-year-old woman who, 20 years ago, recognized that eventually there would be a blossoming market for mature consumers. Accordingly, she set out to learn marketing, business, and gerontology (the study of aging). Today, with Canadians aged 55 and up growing more rapidly than any other segment of the population, she runs a marketing company that specializes in helping companies market and sell to this group. But Maclachlan also watches what is happening to mature employees, and she doesn't like what she sees:

"The corporate world is not interested in an aging workforce. Instead, they are continuing to downsize, especially upper and middle managers in their fifties, and bringing in young people to replace them. Baby boomers haven't felt this yet, but they are starting to edge into the danger zone.

"Companies are not legally allowed to discriminate on the basis of age, but whether accidentally, or accidentally-on-purpose, companies are laying off, downsizing, or forcing into early retirement employees in their fifties. . . . People are being forced out of what they thought were secure jobs, and they're not sure they have enough money to retire. They may have kids at home, aging parents, and their own longevity to contend with. And they may have counted on having another five to 10 years of high earning power left to help them make the transition to retirement.

"What will happen when a significant number of these boomers hit the magic age of 55? They're not, as a group, prepared or positioned to retire. As a result, they'll probably look for alternatives to a job.

"This has happened to two of my brothers-in-law. One had enough saved to make the transition into retirement. The other doesn't, and he doesn't know what he's going to do.

"Some people in this position today look for contract work. But some risk their retirement savings on new ventures. They've worked in a corporate environment all their lives, and they don't know how to go about being entrepreneurial. They don't know what they're doing, and wind up losing the savings they have. This has the potential for widespread disaster as the boomers start hitting 55—and nobody (except me) is talking about it."

W hy is this happening to us?

On the surface, statistics published by the federal government seem to indicate that things are pretty much as they have always been. Permanent layoffs don't seem to be much higher than they were 15 years ago. The length of job tenure appears the same as it has been for the last two decades. But such statistics are deceptive and hide as much as they reveal. Let's consider a simple analogy that shows what's happening in the job market today.

Imagine the job market as a ladder hanging in mid-air, with each rung representing a job (with more than 13 million rungs, that's a very *long* ladder). This is what the Statistics Canada numbers describe: a lot of people holding a lot of jobs. But the statistics don't reflect the dynamic changes that are happening in the marketplace. For example, at the bottom of the ladder, jobs are disappearing, and people are being dropped into unemployment. Meanwhile, at the top of the ladder, new jobs are being created, and added to the ladder. In between, the vast majority of jobs appear stable and seem to offer tenure. But instability has been introduced into the workplace that wasn't there before, and that's what's creating the sense of insecurity.

The new jobs are generally better-paying, more interesting jobs than the ones that are disappearing. The problem is, though, that the new jobs require very different skills than the disappearing jobs, which means that the people who lose their jobs generally don't have much chance of getting the new ones. A 50-year-old foreman for a tire factory, for instance, who has been laid off because his plant closed down, has very little chance of getting a new job as a computer-game designer. It's not impossible; it's just highly unlikely.

Now add the speed with which all this is happening: new jobs are appearing faster, and old ones disappearing faster, than ever before—and not all the jobs that disappear are old nor at the low-skilled end of the spectrum. Indeed, jobs can disappear seemingly at random, as happened to Rick in my earlier example, even though most jobs tend to be stable. This creates an incredible sense of insecurity among almost everyone in the working world—almost as if we were all playing a gigantic game of Russian roulette or musical chairs. The result is that people who have jobs tend to work harder and longer just to hold on to them, and feel burned out and as if they have no choice but to work that way.

But why is this happening? And why is it happening now? The answer is that we are experiencing an acceleration of several long-term trends that are producing radical changes in the job market.

The first force at work is automation, which is eliminating low-skilled and routine work, and producing new, more creative, and better-paying jobs. Wherever possible, employers are replacing workers with machines or computers, which are less expensive and easier to manage than people. Computers are gradually becoming smarter, more adaptable, more capable of making decisions, and are doing things that we have traditionally thought of as jobs for people. And it's not just blue-collar work that's being affected.

The Toronto-Dominion Bank, along with most of the other major Canadian banks, has centralized its personal loan assessments. Today when you apply to the TD Bank for a personal loan, instead of being reviewed by a trained and experienced banker at the branch where you've banked for many years, your loan is assessed by a computer program supplied by a bank in the United States that uses elements of Artificial Intelligence to gauge whether the loan is likely to be repaid. Only in unusual situations does personal judgment enter into the equation. The position of loan officer, which used to require skill, judgment, and experience, has become a much lower-skilled, less secure job that involves data entry, and performing a public relations function with the client.

This pattern is repeating itself over and over again in the working world: any job that involves routine work is likely to be automated—regardless of whether it involves blue-, white-, or pink-collar work.

Moreover, the pace of this change is accelerating, propelled by international competition in the global economy, which is the second major force acting on the labour markets. Foreign producers in developing countries have labour costs that are a small fraction of labour costs paid by Canadian producers. A worker in a textile factory in mainland China, for instance, might earn less than 10 cents an hour, whereas a comparable worker here in Canada might earn 100 times that, plus benefits and taxes. It's easy to see that if Canada competes with China on labour costs alone, we'll lose every time.

Nor is it only low-skilled workers that are being affected. Architects are getting competition from their counterparts in Mexico, who make less than half as much. Computer system design, and software production are being done for multinationals in India, which has a large number of English-speaking, well-educated computer programmers, displacing workers in similar industries here in North America.

In order to stay in business in the face of cheap foreign competition, Canadian companies have to increase the productivity of their workers. They do this in two ways: by pressuring their employees to work longer hours for the same money, which is self-defeating because it produces burnout and falling productivity; and by increasing the use of automation, which either eliminates jobs or limits new employment in boom times.

Moreover, the way the business world works is changing as well, even if you are employed in a stable, prosperous industry. More and more businesses are creating teams of employees to work together on a "project" basis, much as film production companies do. When the project ends, the team disbands. Staying employed in such an environment involves getting rehired for each new project.

So what can you, as an individual, do about all this? Where *can* you find a secure job? There are two answers to the question, but they both boil down to a common attitude: job security simply doesn't exist in the external world anymore. You must create your own job security, and what's more, you have to do it repeatedly.

Your two choices are as follows: you can either look for a job working for someone else, or create your own job by working for yourself. Most of this book talks about creating your own job. The balance of this chapter will deal with working for someone else. If you intend to work for yourself, feel free to move directly to Chapter 2, although you may well identify some opportunities for new businesses here.

How to tell if you should work for someone else

Under what circumstances would you be better off working for someone else? There's no simple answer to this, and it ultimately comes down to what you want out of life and what tools you start out with. To try to help you focus on which choice might be best for you, answer the following true/false questions:

1 I've had less than two years' experience working full-time for someone else.
2 I have absolutely no idea what I could do if I worked for myself.
3 I don't know how to sell things, including myself, and am not willing to learn.
4 I can't think of any kind of work that I would be passionate about doing, or any kind of work that I'd love to do, even if I could do anything I wanted.
5 I've tried working for myself, and I don't want to do it again.
6 I need the stimulation of working in an office surrounded by other co-workers.
7 I have heavy debts and family responsibilities; I can't afford to try self-employment.
8 I work best if someone else guides and supervises me.
9 I give up easily if things don't go right.
10 I could never work for myself; it would scare me too much.

Although there's no "right" score that indicates whether you should work for yourself, if you have more than five "trues" to the above quiz you would probably be happier working for someone else—if you can find a job. But before we leave this list, note that none of these "obstacles" would make it impossible for you to succeed in your own enterprise. Granted, some would make it harder—having little or no work experience, for instance. But all of these obstacles have been overcome by other people who went on to create successful businesses. Finally, it's important to recognize that all of the questions relate to your own attitudes in one way or another. They really don't relate to the outside world or external factors that will determine whether you will succeed or fail. At the end of the day, your attitude has more to do with whether you can succeed in business than anything else, as discussed in Chapter 10.

For our purposes, however, let's assume that you really are best suited to work for someone else. I've got good news and bad news. The good news is that great new jobs are being created all the time. In the 12-month period from early 1997 to early 1998, when we experienced some of the fastest employment growth of the past 20 years, Statistics Canada reported that approximately 400,000 new jobs were created. Of these, 387,000 were new, paid jobs (as opposed to jobs created through self-employment). During this period, Statistics Canada reported that job growth "has been in industries and occupations that tend to pay higher-than-average weekly wages, while the major employment losses tend to be concentrated in low-paying industries and occupations."[2] Hence, contrary to popular myth, the new jobs that are being created are not hamburger-flipper jobs, but rather good jobs paying good wages.

The bad news is that to get these great new jobs you'll need the qualifications that employers want today, and to keep a job, you'll have to continually upgrade your skills and abilities. And pay won't necessarily be based on seniority or even accomplishment. Increasingly, the working world is adopting the "free agent" mentality characteristic of the entertainment and sports industries. That is, the superstars are paid megabucks. The stars get good money. The ordinary free agent picks up the crumbs, working harder and harder for less and less, according to whether she's in demand. And, like a free agent, you'll have to constantly re-evaluate yourself to determine whether your employer will pick up your option next year. In short, you'll have to act as if you were self-employed, and your employer were your client, even if you have what used to be called "a steady job." The days of paternalism are over.

W here are the jobs?

Now, let's consider in which parts of the economy these new jobs are being created. Since 1976, the group of classified jobs that has grown the fastest have been managerial and administrative—despite the newspaper headlines that have lamented the disappearance of middle-management jobs. However, I suspect that most of these new managerial and administrative jobs have been created in small businesses, not large corporations.

Meanwhile, what have been the least secure jobs in that time span? They are mainly jobs in the primary industries, such as farming and logging, and routine processing jobs, like machining and construction. This may be reassuring since you probably weren't considering those kinds of jobs anyway.

Unfortunately, we can't have statistics about where the fast-growing industries will be in the future, because the future hasn't happened. Instead, I've outlined my own projections of the hot industries over the next 10 to 20 years. They are grouped into three main categories, according to whether the growth will be driven by one of three major forces in the business world: technology, demographics, or the global economy:

Table 1-1 **Above-Average Growth Industries**

Driven Primarily by Technology

I. INFORMATION TECHNOLOGY
   A. Internet applications and support
      1. Web site design
      2. Web marketing specialists
      3. Web data mining
   B. Computer software
   C. Communications/computer networks

D. **Hand-held and wearable computers**
  1. Field worker data collection hardware and software
  2. Personal assistant or agent software

E. **Database compilation and management**
  1. Data entry, classification, and management
  2. Sales of databases, including films, music, art works, newspaper and magazine files, stock market databases, vacation destinations, and so on.

F. **Systems analysis**

G. **Systems integration**

H. **Information science**

I. **Artificial intelligence**
  1. Adaptive and genetic programming

J. **Applications of computer technology, especially**
  1. Medical diagnosis
  2. Robotics in surgical procedures
  3. Voice programming of computers
  4. Applications of computers in personal appliances
  5. "Smart" machines and applications that recognize individual needs and customize products and services (e.g., Netscape's personalized browser page, Amazon.com's individually targeted e-mail offerings, "smart" airline gates that recognize individual frequent travellers as they walk through)

II. SCIENCE AND TECHNOLOGY

A. **Environment**
  1. Hazardous waste management and disposal
  2. Reducing waste and pollution
  3. Energy management and conservation

B. **Molecular chemistry**

C. **Biotechnology/genetic engineering**

D. **Nanotechnology**

E. **Robotics**

   F. Materials science

   G. Agricultural research and development (both biotech and mechanical)

   H. Food/nutrition

   I. Lasers and optical technology

   J. Mass-customization products and production (e.g., Levi's "Original Spin" jeans)

Driven Primarily by the Global Economy

I. MANAGEMENT, BUSINESS, AND ADMINISTRATION

   A. Human resources (especially maximization of human potential)

   B. Management consulting

   C. Managing corporate information flows and converting from paper information flows to electronic information flows

   D. Accounting/auditing/financial controls and performance measurement (especially for entrepreneurial and fast-changing businesses, and especially across jurisdictions)

   E. Tax management (especially across national boundaries)

   F. Temporary help

      1. Temporary professionals, including legal, executives, accounting

   G. Professional talent agents for corporate workers (similar to those who book performers)

   H. Businesses that specialize in serving immigrant groups

      1. Financing

      2. Ethnic retailing and service industries

II. MANUFACTURING

   A. Civil aviation

   B. Telecommunications

   C. Robotics, plus machine tools

   D. Instrumentation

III. ENERGY
    A. Offshore petroleum industry
        1. Geophysical services
    B. Alternative energy sources
        1. Fuel cells
        2. Hydrogen
        3. Wind power
        4. Solar power (from space as well as on earth)
    C. Local energy generation (such as single building fuel cells)
    D. Energy storage (including, but not limited to, battery technology)

IV. EDUCATION
    A. English as a second language
    B. Foreign-language translation and training for business applications
    C. Adult education/training/skills upgrading
    D. Cross-cultural training

V. MARKETING
    A. Data compilation and mining of personal information
    B. Identifying new niche markets
    C. Direct marketing
        1. Direct appeals based on detailed knowledge of the actual purchases of specific individuals: "assassin marketing"

VI. CONSUMER TRENDS
    A. Religious and spiritual products
    B. Unhealthy indulgences
    C. More cosmopolitan foods, including exotic fruits and vegetables
    D. Cross-cultural cooking and eating trends

Driven Primarily by Demographics

I. HEALTH CARE

    A. Fitness/wellness

        1. Sports, especially for baby boomers; "master" and "mature" sporting groups

        2. Dietetics/nutrition

        3. Alternative health management techniques

    B. Most medical specialties, including "second-tier" health services for well-heeled patients, especially, but not exclusively, including

        1. Geriatrics

        2. Oncology

        3. Osteopathy

        4. Dentistry

        5. Ophthalmology/optometry

        6. Proctology

        7. Gynecology (but not obstetrics)

        8. Podiatry

    C. Veterinary services

    D. Medical supplies and instruments

    E. Private medical insurance

    F. Nutri-ceuticals (i.e., food as medical therapy)

II. FINANCE

    A. Personal financial planning

    B. Investing and investment banking

    C. Savings/trust services

    D. Personal service premium banking services

    E. Consulting for small business/home offices and start-ups

III. HOUSING/REAL ESTATE

    A. New supportive living developments for the elderly

    B. Home renovation

    C. Second home/vacation home construction

IV. PERSONAL SERVICES

    A. Home services, especially for the elderly

        1. Companions, housekeeping, physiotherapy, paramedical and nursing, shopping, house maintenance

    B. Anti-aging products

    C. Child care (until the baby-boom children mature)

    D. Funeral homes

    E. Direct sales

    F. In-home sales

    G. Home-delivered services and products

    H. Professional errand and "concierge" services

    I. Repair services

V. ENTERTAINMENT

    A. Fine arts

    B. Graphic arts

    C. Magazines and newspapers (electronic and print)

    D. Desktop broadcasting (television and radio) over the Internet

    E. Performing arts

    F. Films and videos

    G. Music

    H. Computer games/virtual reality

    I. "Edutainment" games and software

    J. Spectator sports

VI. HOSPITALITY INDUSTRY

    A. Travel

        1. Adventure travel

2. Travel with religious or spiritual themes
3. Educationally-themed travel
B. Hotels
C. Restaurants

VII. OFFICE EQUIPMENT
A.   Home office/small office suppliers

There's a catch in looking at this list, though; even if you get a job in a fast-growing industry, that doesn't guarantee job security. Statistics Canada reports that "industries with rapid employment growth do not necessarily have low layoff rates, and those with declining employment do not necessarily experience high rates."[3] Furthermore, rapidly growing industries are typically also rapidly *changing* industries, which means that they experience the ups and downs of other industries.

All of these points lead me back to my central thesis: you must take the leading role in managing your own career. You can't simply hop on a conveyor belt that will carry you smoothly through your career and deposit you safely in a snug retirement. The only job security is between your ears, and the only secure job is the one you create for yourself.

2 What's It Like Being in Business for Yourself?

"THERE'S A HUGE DIFFERENCE between working for yourself and working for someone else," says Sandy Spicer, owner and president of NICs Garage (which stands for "Non-Intimidating Car Service"). "Now not only does my business have to be successful enough to pay my own bills, but I have a staff as well. I'm responsible for them, and that pressure is added stress."

Sandy is right in the thick of the transition from employee to entrepreneur. She started her business 18 months before I interviewed her, and had already weathered a couple of major crises, dealing with problems she never expected. And she found that the experience wasn't quite what she thought it would be:

"When I worked for other organizations, I never thought twice about who cleaned the office and what went on as far as cleaning up. Yet, when I was leaving work last night at midnight, the last thing I did was take out the garbage. I wouldn't have thought of that before—when I came to work in the morning, the garbage was just automatically emptied."

Sandy also acknowledges some of the other difficulties associated with running your own business.

"There is a negative side, and a huge negative side. Before we opened, there were all the long hours we put in doing renovations, but there was still an excitement about it. You don't realize the full impact until the business is up and running. You get busier and busier, and the workload is piled on until it gets to the point where you're making enough that you can hire another person. Then it sort of gets relieved again until it starts to build up again as your business grows."

And she admits to being physically exhausted because of such pressure. "I'm usually the last one to leave work at night, often around midnight, and usually the first to get here in the morning. Except Mondays—that's my morning off each week."

But, despite these challenges, when Sandy is asked whether she has any regrets, she cheerfully responds, "Not at all. I love being an entrepreneur. There's the ability to know that what you're building is yours, it belongs to you, not the company you're working for. In many ways, it's like raising a child. There are a lot of things that are hard about raising a child when it comes to temper tantrums and so on, but there's also a sense of pride.

"When we see things we've done right, when our customers say, 'Wow, I don't know what I would do without you,' those are things of immense pride. It makes you glad that you're there.

"What you put into your business, you get out. When you work for someone else, you can put in long hours, you still have the stress of work, and you can still try very hard. But when it's your own business, it's a one-to-one correlation with what you're going to get out. When you put more in, you get more out, and it's yours. It's not just a pay cheque, it's an asset, something that will have real value when you're finished. And I love it, I just love it."

"**Y**ou become unemployable"

Sandy's comments echo those of many other people who run their own show: it's hard work, some of it unwelcome. There are things you have to do that you won't enjoy doing, from cleaning the floors and emptying the garbage, to disciplining or firing an employee, to calling a customer and being tough enough with them to get them to pay, to doing the accounting, and making sure the nickels all tally for the tax collector. It's hard work, and it's often no fun. But almost without exception, people who have left the corporate world to become entrepreneurs say they could never go back.

You will become a different person, and you will probably enjoy it more than being who you are now.

KONRAD TITTLER, WHO CREATED two businesses selling industrial chemicals, says this about what effects running your own business will have on you:

"Once a person has chosen to be an entrepreneur, he becomes unemployable. You're not a corporate person any-more. The process of creating your own business forces you to succeed, partly out of fear—that was a big part of my moti-vation when I started—and partly out of a determination to show you were right.

"If you stay in business more than a year, then you are looked at differently by potential employers. If you're succeeding, then people have a hard time imagining you working for them. You're somehow larger than life, and not a worker any more. If you've failed, then there's the stigma of failure to deal with, along with a tacit acknowledgment that you at least tried."

Tittler didn't have to deal with the stigma of failure, because he never admitted to it: "I was the only guy in the world who went bankrupt every year, but I was also the only guy who didn't accept it. You've got to persist through the hard times. If you don't have that persistence, then stay employed; you won't like doing this."

And when asked about the differences between traditional employment and self-employment, Tittler responds, "The major difference between the corporate world and the entrepreneurial world is that here you can devote all your energy to getting stuff done. In the corporate world, you can't do that because you've got to devote part of your energies to succeeding internally, to playing corporate politics. It's a sad waste of energy.

"Aside from this, dealing with all the details of running a business took some getting used to. There's always so much to do, and so much of it is necessary, but not particularly interesting."

And what caught Tittler by surprise about running his own business?

"Asshole bankers. I thought bankers were like other people, that there were good ones and bad ones, and they had good days and bad days, but they're not. They're run by a system, and if you're not careful, their bad judgment will seriously damage your business.

"They'll say something like, 'We have lost confidence in your industry, and can't lend to you.' That's hogwash. Even in bad times, and in declining industries, there are winners. But they don't want to know about that. It doesn't fit their formulas."

E mployee versus Entrepreneur

The comments of the entrepreneurs highlighted in the accompanying vignettes underscore an important point: if you've never run your own show, then you don't understand the differences between working in a traditional job and working for yourself. I've studied these differences for the past 20 years—first out of a sense of personal curiosity, and eventually out of professional interest, both as a consultant and as a futurist.

Some of the differences are not as sharp now as they were in the past. As we discussed in Chapter 1, the world of work has changed, and the demands on employees more nearly match those on entrepreneurs. If you've read my book, *The Next 20 Years of Your Life: A Personal Guide into the Year 2017*, then you already know that I foresee a definite shift towards entrepreneurship in the future. It's not merely a coincidence that most of the new jobs are being created by entrepreneurs and small businesses. To succeed, all businesses must be agile, quick to change, and responsive to innovation and customer needs. Successful entrepreneurs, because they have everything at risk, are sensitive to these things.

As a result, the qualities that companies need in their employees are becoming more and more like those that entrepreneurs must have to succeed. In fact, companies are increasingly forcing the people who used to be employees into becoming entrepreneurs by hiring them as consultants, contract workers, or part-time workers. And even those who are still full-time employees often find themselves behaving as if they were entrepreneurs.

One of my friends works for IBM—a company that used to be known as a cradle-to-grave employer. Mike is a team leader who bids on consulting contracts for IBM. When he succeeds in obtaining a contract, he assembles his team, flies out to the client's city, and spends weeks or months there working on the contract. When the project is complete, the team separates, and he returns home and starts all over again.

Although Mike is a long-time employee of one of the world's great multinational corporations, he actually has more in common with an entrepreneur than he does with his own working lifestyle of 20 years ago.

The following table summarizes many of the most significant remaining differences between today's employees and entrepreneurs. Although none of these points may be surprising in theory, they will come as a shock when you experience them.

Table 2-1 **A Comparison between Employees and Entrepreneurs**

Entrepreneur	Employee
Income	
• Income fluctuates dramatically	• Income is stable
• Initially earns much less than worth	• Usually paid close to market value, less cost in benefits and payroll taxes
• Has the potential to increase income and net worth dramatically over time	• Unlikely to increase income and net worth dramatically
• Can wind up with a major ownership position in a significant company, go bankrupt, or anything in between	• Unlikely to wind up with significant ownership of the company, unlikely to go bankrupt except through mismanagement of personal finances
Control	
• Tremendous freedom of action	• Limited freedom of action
• Big frog in a little pond	• One member of an organization
• Has significant control over establishing company goals	• Has little control over establishing company goals
• Can often have a significant impact on the company	• Rarely has a significant impact on the company
• Responsible to the business' clients and creditors	• Reports to more senior employees of the company

Entrepreneur	Employee

- Has reasonable freedom to change clients and creditors
- Has significant medium- and long-term control over choice of work

- Has very limited freedom to choose superiors
- Has significant long-term control over choice of work

Lifestyle

- Accepts personal risks as a necessary evil to achieve established goals
- Often feels tremendous anxiety concerning actions taken
- Immediate personal exposure to all the problems of the business

- Almost never accepts direct personal risks to accomplish corporate goals
- Often feels some anxiety concerning actions taken
- Can be personally exposed to some of the problems of the company, but usually insulated from many others

- Must work extremely long hours to keep business alive

- Works relatively regular hours, depending on ambitions, demands of the job, and expectations of superiors

- Forced to learn and do all types of necessary and unpleasant tasks for the welfare of the business
- Rarely has regular vacations
- Short of a business failure, likely to remain with the business for five years or more

- Usually performs a narrow range of tasks, according to job description and expectations of superiors
- May have regular vacations
- Short of being fired, likely to change companies at least every five years

Entrepreneur	Employee
• Company failure likely to be a devastating personal financial loss	• Company failure would be an emotional blow, result in a loss of income, and may result in loss of pension rights, but unlikely to be devastating to personal savings
• Odds of loss of income are moderate to high due to business failure; otherwise, job security very high	• Odds of being fired due to personal shortcomings are low to moderate; odds of losing job through downsizing or merger are moderate
• Generally perceived as low-status employment because of small size of business	• Generally perceived as moderately high-status employment
• Office likely in home or low rent area with cheap furnishings	• Pleasant office surroundings are part of the benefits
• Usually does office cleaning and maintenance	• Never empties own garbage

So, the question remains, should you become an entrepreneur? Unfortunately, there isn't one simple answer that applies to everyone. One thing is clear, though: self-employment is difficult. It involves long hours—probably longer than the hours you are working now. It means living with fear of failure. It means placing strain on your relationships, particularly if you're married and have children. It involves learning new skills—often skills that you have no desire to learn, such as bill collecting, or selling, or accounting, or dealing with irate customers or unreasonable employees. It means doing menial tasks as well as the flashy, ego-boosting ones. It involves discovering that there is no glamour in business, and that excitement wears off, just as an excited kid eventually gets bored with his birthday presents. It means smiling and saying "yes" to a customer when you'd rather drop-kick him out of your office. Self-employment means all of these things.

But what entrepreneurship requires more than anything else is the willingness to change. You must be willing to become a different person—to grow, improve your skills, accept new values, and become both more disciplined and courageous in the face of fear. Yet, having warned you of the obstacles ahead, let me offer you reassurance as well: no entrepreneur whom I've met wants to go back to working for someone else.

If, despite my warning, you still want to start your own business, then read on. But let me end this chapter with a prime example of the kinds of changes you're going to have to go through, based on the journey of Sandy Spicer of NICs Garage:

"I'VE ALWAYS HAD A STRONG desire to open my own business. I was a single parent when I moved from Saskatchewan to Alberta. I had a two-year-old daughter, and an old car, and no money. My mechanic was someone I put a lot of trust in—someone I knew personally. When I moved I was kind of scared; what was I going to do if my car broke down? I had had some previous bad experiences, and I thought that 'Wow, wouldn't it be great to open a garage that was more focused towards women, is not as intimidating, and people can ask questions?' But I was a single parent, and had no money, so there was no way I could do it.

"I left school quite early, and didn't finish my grade 12. After a number of years of managing a clothing store, I took night classes to upgrade my math and my English to grade 12 level, then I entered university as a mature student and took my commerce degree. It took me five years to do a four-year degree as a full-time student. Then we moved to Vancouver.

"I worked for a number of years, but still wanted to open my own business. That was one of the driving forces to go into commerce. But just out of university I had a huge student loan, and still had a child to support, so I worked as a financial analyst for a good five years for B.C. Transit. Then it was time to move on, so I took a year off. During that time, my partner had been to Calgary to visit his sister. She had an old car, and had run up over $5000 worth of repair bills. He said, 'They should have just told you to get rid of your car and get a different one.'

"So he came back and said, 'Remember that idea of yours about the garage?' and I said, 'Yeah.' And he said, 'Let's do it.'

"So we spent a year researching, and then opened NICs Garage. In a way, it's named after my father, who was a mechanic whose name was Nick, and he died when I was six. And my daughter's name is Nicole, so I shortened it to Nic. But then I was laying in bed one night, and I thought 'Wow! What it really stands for is Non-Intimidating Car Service.' NICs Garage is dedicated to that."

NICs Garage opened in 1997. Sandy went back to school in the mid-1980s. It was a long journey, and a story I'll come back to again, but the point I want to make now is this: Sandy started as a high-school dropout, with no money, an old car, and an infant daughter. But that's not the life she wanted. She wanted to run her own business, and realized she was going to have to become a different person before she could make that happen. Now, almost 15 years later, she's making her dream a reality.

The experience is much different than she thought it would be—harder, grittier, with much more to think about and do than she ever expected. But remember her final conclusion: "I love being an entrepreneur."

3 — What Kind of Business Could You Start?

When you ask most people about the possibility of starting their own business, you are likely to get one of the following three responses:

1 "I have no idea what kind of business I could start."
2 "I've got a really terrific idea for a business."
3 "I've heard about a really great idea for a business."

Each response poses different problems, so the first step is to take your time before deciding on a business. Once you start, you're committing time and resources that you will never be able to recover, so you want to be *really* sure that you've chosen the best idea. And, perversely, the key to finding a good idea is to remember that a good idea means nothing; execution is everything. Ideas are a dime a dozen, so take the time to consider lots of them, carefully and thoroughly research the best possibilities, and then choose the one that plays to your strengths and gives you the best odds of success.

If this process sounds tedious and difficult, stop for a moment and consider how much more tedious and difficult bankruptcy and failure would be. According to the Canadian Federation of Independent Business, only one in five new businesses survives past its third year. That means you are more likely to fail than succeed—unless you work hard at improving those odds.

Let's start by dealing with each of the three responses identified above:

1 Don't worry if you have no idea what business you could start. It's possible to generate hundreds of ideas, and then sift through them to find the ones that offer you the best odds of success. I'll talk about how to do this a little later on.

2 If you're sure that you've got the best possible idea, terrific. But consider other possibilities and ways to improve your idea before you leap into implementing your idea.

3 If you've heard about a really great business idea, stop and consider alternatives before committing your time and talent to a path defined by someone else. Consider the case of Mike and Carol, described below.

MIKE AND CAROL WERE LOOKING for a new business. Mike was a very successful dentist, but was tired of dentistry, and thought of it as a treadmill where he got paid for piecework, like workers in a sweatshop. Carol's background was in marketing, although she had put her career temporarily on hold while staying at home to raise their two kids. Now that her children had reached school age, she wanted to return to the workforce.

One night at a cocktail party, a friend, hearing that they were looking for new opportunities, introduced Mike and Carol to another friend, Tom, who was starting a new business making a new kind of metal garage door with an automatic door opener. Mike and Carol spoke at length with Tom, an engineer with an auto-parts manufacturer, who explained his product and marketing strategy.

Tom also expressed his need for start-up capital, as well as for someone with administration, accounting, and marketing expertise. His computer spreadsheet projections showed a healthy business turning a small profit within the first 15 months, and then becoming solidly profitable as the product was distributed across Canada. The company's three-year plan reflected his intentions to expand in the enormous U.S. market. Tom offered Carol and Mike 35% of the company for $250,000, and offered Carol the position of VP Marketing and Administration at a salary of $45,000 per year. But Tom wanted to move quickly, because he had already negotiated his manufacturing arrangements and needed to commit by the beginning of next month.

For Mike and Carol, this opportunity seemed to fit their needs perfectly: the potential to make a profit through something other than Mike's dentistry, and with great long-term potential; a decent-paying job for Carol that could grow as the company grew; and the possibility of eventually going public with the modest fortune that could come from selling their equity stake.

Mike and Carol made a counter-offer to Tom, and after some haggling agreed to pay $300,000 for a 50% share of the company, with a $40,000 salary for Carol to start, rising to $60,000 once the company turned its first monthly profit.

These negotiations became irrelevant nine months later, however, when the company went bankrupt. The invested capital had run out, and while the partners had produced a very nice garage door, they couldn't interest enough retail outlets to carry their product, and were unable to gear up marketing through other channels fast enough to sell sufficient product to stay alive.

Mike and Carol had been mesmerized by the glamour of the proposition, the possibility of a job for Carol, and the impressive financial projections, but had never asked the simple question: "What do we know about making and selling garage doors?" They had jumped at the first idea that came along without checking whether it made sense for them and whether it played to their strengths.

Tom hadn't deliberately misled them; he had merely seduced himself. He had taken a neat idea and run with it. He figured that his strengths in design and manufacturing, coupled with Carol's expertise in marketing, and added capital from his new partners would somehow overcome any obstacles.

There were no villains in this piece—merely people who overestimated the value of a good idea.

Opportunity doesn't just knock— it pounds relentlessly

Let me deal with two of the most dangerous statements on this subject:

"Opportunity only knocks once."

Wrong. A given opportunity may only knock once, but lots of other opportunities will come along if you simply remain open to them. The trick is knowing which ones to respond to, and which ones to ignore.

"If you build a better mousetrap, the world will beat a path to your door."

Also wrong—and very dangerously so. Consider that Apple Computer still offers a far better operating system than Microsoft Windows, yet Microsoft ate up Apple's market share, to the point where it appeared as though Apple would eventually go bankrupt.

Similarly, Sony's beta videotape recorder was clearly superior to VHS, yet VHS rules today. Being better doesn't determine who wins. Execution does.

"What most entrepreneurs don't understand," explains Bob Shoniker, an experienced Bay Street financier and an entrepreneur himself, "is that ideas are common and plentiful, but money is hard to come by. In and of itself, a great idea is *worthless*, and a large part of my job is to educate the people who come through here that ideas are not terribly important. It's management and execution that pays the bills."

Ⓚ nowing where to look for ideas

So if you need an idea, here's where to start looking:

1   **Look for a market where you are the expert.** This usually means going into an industry that you already know a lot about, one where you know the consumers, buyers, pricing, regulations and restrictions, competitors, and strategies of that industry. If you intend to enter a market that's new to you, you'll need to spend a lot of time researching that market.

2   **Choose something you love doing.** Since you'll spend many, many hours creating your business, make sure you enjoy it. Passion for your business will carry you long after the initial excitement has worn off.

3   **Look at ideas with new eyes.** "New ideas don't come out of your head," says entrepreneur Konrad Tittler. "Ideas come through your ears, by listening to your customers, suppliers, and employees, by reading everything you can find about your market and your industry, by talking to everyone who might have the germ of an idea, or a thought that's of relevance. The problem is that some people just don't see a new idea when it presents itself."

W here do ideas come from?

Ideas can be found and invented on demand, in almost any quantity desired. So rather than pounce on a weak idea because you think it's your last chance at financial freedom, pile up the ideas, go through a few dozen until you find three or four that fit you. And if you don't find one you like, keep looking. *You'll do yourself a tremendous favour by avoiding booby-trapped ideas. And in the long run, you'll be much farther ahead by taking the time to find a good idea than by settling for one that doesn't work!*

But if ideas are so plentiful and cheap, why can't you see them?

Part of the answer is: they're hiding right out in the open. You don't see them because you've walked right by them a hundred times. In fact, you'll know you've found a great one when you describe it to someone and they say, "That's so obvious I'm surprised nobody's thought of it before!" There are two major places to look for business ideas: where you work and live right now, and way out in the wild blue yonder. We'll begin with those ideas that are all around you.

Let's start by thinking about where you work, where some of your best ideas may be staring you in the face, but pass unnoticed because of a process that psychologists call "habituation." If you've ever been at a friend's house where there's a grandfather clock, you've probably noticed how loudly the clock ticks and chimes at first. Yet, within an hour or so, you probably don't hear the ticks anymore, and within three or four hours you may miss hearing the chimes as well. Your nervous system has figured out what the clock does, and then filters it out so it doesn't interfere with new sounds. This is a survival trait gifted to us by evolution.

In the context of work, habituation means that you tend to stop perceiving the things that you see and deal with every day. Consequently, a great idea can walk past you, jump up and down in front of you 15 times a day, and you'll simply ignore it because it's familiar.

Think about some of the most annoying things that happen to you in any given day at work. Maybe it's the lousy coffee you get, or the supplier who's always late with his shipments, or the division that can't seem to get its act together. Your greatest annoyance could represent a golden opportunity by finding a way to improve it. Wouldn't all the other people who also find it annoying be willing to become your customers? Quite possibly—because it's happened before.

T o boldly go where someone has gone before

CLAYTON WORKED FOR A MULTINATIONAL company for years before he finally decided he'd had enough. Instead of starting from scratch, Clayton looked at unprofitable divisions of a number of businesses, searching for ones with good potential. He discovered such a "diamond in the rough" in a division that made communication and support-system panels for hospitals— the kind that are located at the head of each patient's bed, and through which the buzzer for the nurses' station, the oxygen lines, and the emergency alarm systems all run.

The division was a perennial loser—never making much money, just barely paying the bills. After examining the department's budgets, Clayton decided that the division could make good money if it were run entrepreneurially instead of bureaucratically. Once he'd worked through the figures, he submitted a proposal to buy the division with part payment in cash, and the rest in an earnout. In effect, he bought the division with the company's own money, paying the profits that the division would have made if it had been run properly, but in instalments spread out over several years.

Then he worked hard to make his new company function the way it should. He fired several of the workers, including the general manager, and took on many of the jobs himself, including secretarial and reception tasks. He went through the customer base to determine which ones were valuable and which ones should be "fired." Then he personally visited the valuable customers, told them what he was doing, and promised to improve what they were getting.

It turned out that there were a lot of things Clayton didn't know as well as he had thought. For example, the bank lost confidence in him and started to make threatening noises. But he went to his outside shareholders and convinced them to put up enough additional money that the bank was willing to let him ride for another six months before they considered pulling the plug, by which time he had the situation under control again.

Clayton eventually went into a much more glamorous hi-tech business—using the hospital division as a cash cow and a base. He didn't have to start from scratch—and avoided a lot of the pitfalls as a result.

🅣 en questions that will lead you to opportunity

Now let's go through some of the questions you can ask that will help you find opportunities. As you find ideas, *write them down*. Also, don't quit looking when you find a good one. Your goal is to generate *lots* of good ideas, and then to choose the best ones.

1 **Look at your suppliers or your company's suppliers.** Which ones do a poor job of serving you, either personally or professionally? How could they improve their service? Do they have employees who really don't seem interested in helping you? Does the supplier sell what you need or what they make? This is a subtle, but vital, difference. One type of supplier serves the customer; the other serves themselves. Companies that serve the customer make more money.

Now ask the same questions about your customers—and your own employer.

2 **Look at the management of your suppliers, customers, and employer.** Is anyone approaching retirement age, and possibly looking for a way to sell out? Are they considering expanding into new areas, and need cash to do so? Are they fed up with a particular part of their business? If the companies you're examining are owned by a larger corporation, does this part of the operation integrate with the overall operation, or is it kind of a poor relation? Is it a winner or a loser in their portfolio? Do they pay much attention to it? For the moment, don't worry about whether you could persuade the owners to sell. All you're doing now is looking for possibilities. Practical considerations come later.

3 **Look at the products or services sold by your suppliers, customers, and employer.** Could you go into competition in one or more of these lines and offer another source of supply? Often buyers do not like having only a single source, and will give business to a second supplier just to keep the first one honest. Is there a market where customers would like to have an alternative? Or, at the other end of the spectrum, is this a highly fragmented market where buyers would like to find a reliable supplier?

4 **Can you change an existing product or service, or change the way it's marketed?** Can you sell it packaged up with related products or services? Could you unbundle it and sell it separately from other products? Make it a different shape, colour, size, or give it an additional function? Can you develop a premium product? A stripped-down, discounted one? Can you sell it by phone rather than in stores, or sell it to stores that carry related products? Can you put a product and a service together, or take one apart? Can you make a product into a service, or a service into a product?

5 **Are there any new products or services recently introduced that you could sell locally or duplicate quickly?** In most product categories, there's usually room for two, and sometimes three,

suppliers. If you can be the second supplier to offer a successful new product, then you cut down the risks involved in guessing whether people will buy it or not, and save a bundle on R&D as well. But you must act quickly. Being fourth, fifth, or sixth into a market is usually a good way to go broke.

6   **Have any old products or services been discontinued because there's not enough demand to be worth it to a big company?** If so, then you'll have a built-in market that wants the product and will be frustrated that it can no longer get it. Or, in a related question, has your industry, or that of your suppliers or customers, changed its ways of doing things? If so, it may be that you can set up a business offering things the way they were "in the good old days." Remember: you don't need as big a market niche as a large company. Seeing someone abandon an old niche means it's unlikely that someone else will jump into it.

7   **Have buying patterns changed?** Are products that used to just roll off the showroom floor now sitting idle? If so, what are buyers interested in now? Companies often can't respond very quickly to changes in the market—but you can.

8   **Is there an industry that is dominated by one major company?** If so, they may have a "one size fits all" philosophy, forcing their clients to buy something that doesn't quite fit their needs. Could you target one segment and design a product specifically for those customers? If so, you may be able to steal that segment. If that works, you could design another product for another segment, and nibble away at the market your big competitor has already created.

9   **Can you do someone's dirty work for them?** Is there some part of your industry, or that of your customers' or suppliers' industries, that is awkward or difficult or inconvenient for them to do themselves? If so, could you do it for them? Although the idea of deliberately choosing an "ugly" business sounds strange, it's a great way to avoid competition. In fact, one of the biggest problems with hi-tech industries is that they're glamorous, and therefore invite competition.

10 Can you transport an idea that has already succeeded somewhere else? If oxygen bars (i.e., places that offer doses of pure oxygen) are popular in California, will they work where you live? Can you take a fashion item in Europe, bring it home and sell it locally, before the major retailers catch on? Is there a service being offered in a trendy part of the world that you think could catch on where you live? The nice part about this idea is that you get to travel. Go somewhere where people do things differently and look for ideas to take home.

B lue skies and new ideas

Now let's go out into the wild blue yonder, and look for new ideas as well.

There's no reason for you to grasp at ideas when you can produce them at will, in any quantity you want, at any time you want them. And, best of all, you can produce ideas that play to your strengths, then sort through them until you find one that you really like, and can get excited about.

Grasping at ideas is like trying to snatch up a school of minnows—they slip through your fingers and vanish. And if you focus on what's already been done in the world it can seem like all the great ideas have been used up. I mean, as Duddy Kravitz remarked, someone has already invented Kleenex, right?

Where, then, are you expected to find all these "great" new ideas?

To answer that, we're going to take a detour through your brain, to examine some of the assets you may not use as much as you could.

In 1981, Dr. Roger Sperry shared a Nobel Prize for his research on split-brain activity. His results seem to indicate that the left half, or hemisphere, of the brain usually handles most of the logical, rational, reasoning behaviour, as well as our ability to talk, write, and use words. The right brain, meanwhile, seems more involved in athletic coordination, music, art, intuition, and creativity generally.

What this means is that the part of our brain that is good at coming up with ideas is not the side that is good at describing them. Worse, our society pivots on words, logic, and reason (at least in theory)—none of which are related to intuition or generating ideas.

And *this* means that in our society, intuition and creativity take a backseat—except in places such as concert halls or museums. Indeed, in the business world, there are few putdowns more damaging than to say someone is behaving "irrationally" or "illogically."

It is only when a paradigm-buster like Edward de Bono comes along and disguises creativity in rational attire by labelling it "lateral thinking" that intuition can creep quietly up to the boardroom table.

So let's see how to do it.

Brainstorming, step by step

Although brainstorming is not a logical process, to describe it clearly I'll have to resort to a logical presentation. To do otherwise might be very creative, but I doubt if it would be very understandable.

1 This is where ideas come from

Although psychologists might disagree with me, as far as I'm concerned, new ideas come from rubbing two previously unrelated ideas together. Putting two unrelated ideas together, especially if the combination seems slightly weird, takes you out of your normal, "business as usual" way of looking at the world.

Once free from the straitjacket of everyday thought, your right brain is free to enter into your efforts, and will likely toss out some interesting thoughts for you to consider. You then take these thoughts, let them grow and develop, and the result is an interesting idea that you can then set aside and think through more carefully later on.

2 Brainstorming works best with a small group of friendly people

Coming up with new ideas is a bit like a pin-ball machine: you rack up points as your thoughts bounce off things. With more people, you have more mental bumpers to bounce off. And if you get stuck, as sometimes happens, someone else can often get you moving again.

If you've got the right people, the group takes on a glow of warmth and excitement, much like the feeling of a party that has jelled properly. This excitement encourages you to take chances, and suggest something really outlandish—which is where some of your best ideas will start.

One of my favourite outlandish ideas is the edible poker chip.

I was once facilitating a brainstorming session with a group of hopeful entrepreneurs. Somehow we were relating the words "gamblers" and "nutrition," although how we got there I can't recall. Someone suggested making poker chips out of potato chips—which gives you some idea of where our minds were.

Being a faithful facilitator, I chalked "edible poker chip" on the board and managed to keep a straight face while suggesting that that way you could always eat your losses. Someone else said this made them think of poker games, which made them think of long nights. This led them into long winter nights, which made them feel depressed (it was February at the time).

Someone else jumped up and said, "Why don't we run a gambling school during the winters, ending in a junket to Las Vegas for the graduates?"

"And how about approaching one of the Vegas casinos to sponsor it as a promotion so we don't have to use our own money for things like gambling chips and equipment?" someone else piped up. "We could probably get them to give us a couple of promotional videos to use to advertise the course!"

And the idea just sort of snowballed from there: an integrated package of something interesting to do on long winter nights, the glamour of travel to an exotic location, and the sex appeal of hitting the tables and coming home with a bundle. All from the edible poker chip.

But be careful: a successful session needs the right-sized group. Large groups tend to intimidate people, who become afraid to speak out "in public." Normally I find that groups of six to eight friends work best, but it really depends on who is involved.

If everyone is warm and encouraging, then you can get away with groups of 10, 20, or more, and there will easily be enough ideas to go around. But if the people involved are critical or defensive, then even three is too many. Which brings us to point #3.

3   Criticism in any form must be completely banned

This one point can make or break your whole brainstorming session. Everyone *must* understand that you are deliberately trying to come up with unconventional, silly, off-the-wall ideas, which you will then critique later. As a result, sarcasm, snide comments, and even so-called constructive criticism are off-limits. This is harder than it sounds. Most of us make small, cutting jokes, or barbed comments and never notice it. These everyday comments are sudden death in brainstorming.

What kind of comments do I mean? Things like, "Do you think that'll work?" "That's been done." "What have *you* been sniffing?" "Where on earth did you get that one?" "That's a pretty good idea—from a woman." "Trust you to come up with something like that." "It'll never get off the ground."

What these kinds of comments do is eat away at your participants' willingness to speak up. So stay away from criticism in any form—and don't let the others in your group practise it either.

4   Get the setting right

Brainstorming works best when everyone's relaxed. So it's best to do it at a time and place that sets people at ease. For this reason, it's often better away from an office—although someone *else's* boardroom or conference room might be fine. For the same reason, someone's living room is fine except that the person who owns it may feel the need to "host" the participants.

If possible, use a blackboard, flip-chart, or something else to record any ideas and keep them in front of the group. A paper flip-chart is particularly effective because it can also provide a permanent record of what you've discussed, and may inspire new ideas when you review the earlier ones.

Make sure everyone has paper and pencil. Ideas evaporate if they're not recorded. Schedule your session when there's no time pressure. If possible, set aside a whole day for brainstorming, preferably on a weekend. Everyone should wear comfortable clothes. And, if possible, don't let anyone wear a watch.

5 Here's what to look for

And what are you looking for in all this? You'll know it when it happens. It's the "Ah-ha!" reaction that everyone has experienced at one time or another when they finally think of, or find, the thing they've been seeking. It's not the clever idea you want, but the obvious one that no one has thought of yet. The one that provokes the "Of course! Why didn't I think of that?" reaction. Another way of knowing when you've struck gold is when you find yourself thinking, "I wish I could hire someone to do that for *me*."

But as you hit this kind of idea (and you will if you've followed the steps up to this point), remember that in the end you want something that people will accept quickly, without a lot of convincing. That means that it must be an idea that makes immediate sense—not something so new it takes half an hour of explaining. I'll come back to this point in a few moments.

6 Record all the ideas that come up

Don't judge any of the ideas that emerge. Write them all down. The time to judge, weigh, and sift is later, after you've got a nice

long list of ideas to choose from, not now when you're simply trying to generate ideas. With dozens of exciting ideas to choose from,
not only will you find it easier to make the choice, but you'll also
find that the ones that seemed so-so when they came up may turn
into real winners when you start thinking how you can use them.

7 Have somebody lead the discussion
This is the final point, and, along with the rule about no criticism,
it's the most important. You need an effective leader—someone
who can stop one person from hogging the floor, someone who can
get things moving when everyone has run out of steam. The facilitator doesn't have to be charismatic—just someone whom everyone else is willing to listen to. It might even be you. Or you might
all agree to take turns.

T he opportunity matrix

Now that you know *how* to brainstorm, it's time to look at how you
start. This is where the opportunity matrix comes into play. The
opportunity matrix is simply a mechanical way of joining unrelated
ideas. I guarantee you'll never exhaust the possibilities it can produce. That's important because you may need to use it two or three
times before finding the idea you want to exploit.

Here's how to build yours:

Before your brainstorming group gets together, ask everyone to
write down all their talents, skills, abilities, and interests, both past
and present. When you assemble for your session, merge your separate lists into one long list that represents the collective strengths
of the group. This list we will label "skills" for reference purposes.

Next you will draw up a list of what I call "targets." On this list
you will divide up all the potential times, places, and groups of people or companies that your venture might serve. For instance, you

might start with a target like "the first five minutes of the day." With the edible poker chip, our first target was "gamblers."

The following are some possible targets.

Potential Targets

Times or events

Just before wake-up

First five minutes after wake-up

Snooze period after alarm

Time spent in the washroom

Time spent dressing

Breakfast

Just before leaving for work

Commuting time

Arrival at work

Morning at work

Just before lunch

Lunch time

Just after lunch

Afternoon at work

Just before leaving work

Commuting home

Arrival at home

Just before supper

Supper time

Evening activities

Preparation for bed

Bed time

Night time— early hours

Night time— pre-dawn

Weekday nights

Friday nights

Saturday nights

Sunday nights

Saturday mornings

Saturday afternoons

Sunday mornings

Sunday afternoons

One-day holidays

Sick days

Vacations

People

Newborn infants

Babies

Toddlers

Pre-schoolers

Primary school kids

Junior high school kids

Senior high school kids

University and college students

Graduate students

Post-graduate students

High school dropouts

Apprenticed workers

New workers

White-collar workers

Blue-collar workers

Salespeople

Sales clerks

Restaurant workers

Entrepreneurs

Millionaires

People (cont.)

Young men	Middle-aged	Stockbrokers
Middle-aged men	women	Bankers
Older men	Older women	Housekeepers
Men, pre-retirement	Unemployed people	Gamblers
Retired men	Photographers	
Young women	Criminals	

Organizations

Manufacturers	Television stations	Photography
Retail sales stores	Radio stations	studios
Variety stores	Newspapers	Insurance
Car washes	Cable TV	companies
Customer service	companies	Banks
organizations	Cleaning	Brokerages
Religious	companies	Real estate agencies
institutions	Grocery stores	Hardware stores

Obviously the list of targets I've presented are only examples. Add as many more as you want. Be sure to include your current employer, suppliers, customers, clubs you belong to, events you attend—everything that you can think of.

Now take these two lists—one of skills and one of targets—and put the skills across the top of a gigantic spreadsheet, and the targets down the side. Obviously you could only do this if you had an enormous piece of paper, which is one possibility, especially if you get a big roll of paper. Or, you could do it on a computer spreadsheet, which is a virtual big sheet of paper. If you want to do it this way, go ahead. It's not necessary, but if you feel it would help, do it.

With the lists across the top and down the side, you've created a matrix or table. One skill plus one target is one box in the matrix—and the jumping-off point for brainstorming.

A sk the right questions

Hence if your first skill is "organizing," and your first target is "just before I wake up," then you will use this pair as the starting point for brainstorming. Specifically, you will try to imagine that you are someone who needs something organized, and you are just about to be woken up. Once you've imagined what someone in this situation is feeling, ask the following three questions:

1 What would I like if I were in this situation and had this skill available?
2 What kinds of things do I dislike, or dislike doing, that I could have someone do for me if I am in this situation and have this skill available?
3 What could we do for people in this situation that they would pay us for?

Then, as you answer these questions, just throw out any thought that comes to mind. Remember that it doesn't have to make sense—and probably won't at first. It's just to stimulate you to connect two previously unconnected ideas. Keep trying different possibilities, remembering to come back to the skill and the target and trying to see how they would work together.

As ideas start coming out for any given pair, see if they connect with anything else. You don't have to stay strictly within the skill-target box. That's just a jumping-off point. If the discussion rambles on in other directions, let it ramble as long as ideas seem to be popping out.

Once you get some ideas from a skill-target square, think about ways to enlarge or embellish them. Remember how I described the thoughts that developed from the edible poker chip. Look for directions that an idea can take you, not just what occurs when you start.

If you start to run out of ideas from a given skill-target pair, or if this pair hasn't produced anything, choose another pair. You don't have to follow any particular order. If you're interested in exploring a specific pair, then by all means do so. In fact, you might go around the room and ask participants to take turns choosing pairs.

If at first you're not having much luck, especially if brainstorming is new to you, then suggest anything that comes to mind. Try competing with each other about who can come up with the most outlandish idea, or the silliest idea, or the least practical idea. Although it will seem artificial at first—and you should be willing to feel a little silly when you start—it will get the ball rolling. Once you've started, you'll find it's fairly easy to keep going if you're following the brainstorming rules.

B roaden your ideas

Once you've got the beginnings of a few good ideas from a given skill-target pair, take one of them and see if you can broaden it. Ask yourself, what different methods could you use to sell this? Could you make it bigger? Smaller? Could you sell a cheap version? An upscale edition? Could you sell it over the Internet, or advertise it electronically? Is there a particular group of people that would have a special interest in it? Could you bundle it up with a related good or service and sell it as a package? Could it be sold in an unusual way—one that might be surprising with this kind of product of service? If it's a service, could you make it into a physical product? If it's a product, could you make it into a service?

In other words, keep thinking of ways you make it different from products or services that might be similar.

R emember: nobody wants products or services

Finally, remember that you are trying to look at the world through your customer's eyes and feel his or her emotions. After all, nobody really wants a quarter-inch drill when they go to the hardware store and buy one. What they want is quarter-inch holes. As a result, if you're trying to sell drills, you'll probably fail. If you sell holes, however, then you've improved your chances immeasurably. The grandmaster of management science, Peter Drucker, discussed this concept specifically when he said, "Anyone who is willing to use marketing as the basis for strategy is likely to acquire leadership in an industry or a market fast and almost without risk."

4) Choosing the *Right* Business

So far, you've thought about what type of business you might start, and thought about what you really want in a business. Now let's look at how you choose the *best* business from the ideas you've collected.

It's true that the world pays off on execution, but this starts with giving yourself every possible chance of succeeding by choosing the right idea. Granted, you may be able to take a bad idea and make it succeed through sheer grit and determination, but why do so when you could work at something that you'll enjoy, that will make your life easier, and the chances of winning higher? This is what you want to consider when you evaluate ideas: which ones will offer the best chances for success?

Let's discuss some of the key criteria that can help you achieve this.

"How long can you tread water?"

One of comedian Bill Cosby's classic routines was a clash between God and Noah over the building of the ark. When Noah balked at doing all this work and suffering the abuse of his friends and neighbours, God asked him a simple question: "How long can you tread water?" And when a friend, client, or casual acquaintance asks me for my opinion of their wonderful idea for a business, I often find myself thinking of that line.

The moment you commit to operating a business, a clock starts ticking. It doesn't measure time by hours and minutes, but by the number of dollars it'll take until the business generates enough cash to keep itself alive. To survive, you have to finish everything necessary before your money runs out.

Which leads us to the first criterion: *the more quickly a business can become self-supporting, the greater its chance of success.* Let me give you an example of how choosing the wrong business can kill you because you can't hold your breath long enough.

ALTHOUGH THE PEOPLE INVOLVED in this case weren't clients of mine, I knew the vice-president, and watched their progress with interest. They had been engineers for a well-known multinational electronics company until the company decided to abandon its research efforts. Believing in the work they were doing, they bought the rights to the intellectual property and set up their own firm, which we'll call TechniTron.

These men were all research engineers doing work in an esoteric field, with little immediate application in consumer electronics. Their customers were either large corporations or the military, which meant that the company had to produce reliable products to a tight set of specifications.

Their product was in the R&D stages—it needed another five years of almost pure research before the first commercial prototype could be built. After that, they still had all the problems of marketing, manufacturing, coping with competition, and providing customer support.

TechniTron eventually failed because it ran out of money. Now, the vast majority of ventures fail because they run out of money. That's like saying people die because their hearts stop. It's true, but it doesn't explain much.

When I asked my friend what he would do differently in retrospect, he offered some thoughtful, worthwhile comments. He said they should have hired a first-rate manager to run the company while they got on with the research. They should also have set up some sidelines, either in less ambitious products or in outside consulting work, to bring in some cash until the "Big One" finally came in. And they should have avoided working with an underwriter who promised money from the stock market, and then failed to deliver.

But from where I sat, I thought they were pretty well doomed from the start—for a number of reasons. First, they were working on something that had no established market, and yet required lots of R&D money. Second, they were years away from reaching the break-even point that means survival. They had to do everything right *and* be lucky for a long time in order to succeed. They were counting too much on luck, and not enough on skill.

There's no doubt that TechniTron could have made the device and could eventually have been successful. But it would have taken time, many different kinds of skills not normally possessed by engineers, and more money than they would likely have ever been able to raise.

If they had done the things that my friend said he wished they'd done, they might have made it. But I believe they complicated their lives enormously by choosing the wrong idea in the first place. It wasn't a bad idea, nor was the product a waste of time. It would undoubtedly have been great. But it didn't do anything because it was never produced.

"So it's been done before? So what?"

For counterpoint, take the example of Marci Lipman, founder and president of Marci Lipman Graphics, which used to sell Canadian art, prints, and graphics, and Marci Lipman's Collectible T's, which sold silk-screened T-shirts and sweatshirts. Marci has since closed her companies and is doing other things now (although still working for herself), but she's been through one of the toughest businesses around: clothing. Marci's products were ones that everyone immediately understood, and for which there's an established market.

Before she started her first business, Marci Lipman Graphics, Marci would *not* have been voted the person most likely to succeed. In her own words: "I'd got out of college and I still didn't know what I wanted to do. I went from one menial job to the next until a friend asked me if I'd like to sell art.

"I started by making cold calls to architects and designers. Mostly they were interested in Canadian art and Canadian artists, and since I knew where to get it, I became an art consultant. I bought some posters from New York and opened a wholesale showroom. I had no business background, I failed the only economics course I ever took, and I was on unemployment at the time. I took out the lease on my store for one year, but I only expected to last for three months. I was lucky, I was in the right place, and I followed my instincts.

"Pretty soon I had people banging on the windows, asking to come in and look around, people calling me up, wanting to buy my prints—and I wasn't set up to sell retail!

"But [when I finally opened to the public], I cared a lot about what I was selling and the people I was selling to. I knew their names, their phone numbers, and how they had had their prints framed."

Little or nothing about the concept of her businesses was original. So, is it important to have a unique idea?

"One of the worst things you can say to yourself is 'It's been done before,'" comments Marci. "Well, so it's been done, so what? Do it in a unique way! Everybody brings a different personality to business. You have to constantly be changing. It's that constant creativity that will keep you ahead of your competitors."

Marci's sentiments are echoed by someone on the other side of the country, and in a completely different industry: industrial chemicals.

"You don't have to be revolutionary," comments Konrad Tittler of Vancouver. "If you can deliver a new benefit that customers want, you can create a new market niche around it." And that's exactly what Tittler did with his first company, Diachem Industries. "The product we were making [chemicals to treat lumber] was identical with the product everyone else was selling. It was priced the same, and sold to the same people who had established supply relationships. But everyone in the industry was selling these chemicals in 45-gallon drums, which meant that the buyers had to have their employees pour the chemicals out of the drums when they needed them.

"All we did was offer to put in storage tanks, then deliver the chemicals by tank truck so that the buyers could draw the chemicals straight out of the storage tanks, eliminating the need for their employees to handle them. It wasn't a big difference, but given that it cost them exactly the same amount of money, they liked the service.

"This enabled us to take a significant share of the market. By the time our bigger competitors caught on to what we were doing and started imitating us, we were established."

These cases underscore my point: you don't need a revolutionary idea. All you need is something that will make your customer's life better in some way, and one that lets you sell successfully against established competition. This leads to my next two criteria: *You don't have to do something radically new—in fact, a proven business idea increases your odds of success—but you do need to offer a benefit that will attract customers away from competitors, and you need to stay ahead of the competition as it adapts to you.*

Ⓐ slow success instead of a fast failure

When I say you should choose the *best* ideas, I'm referring to the ideas that offer the best chance of success—not the ones that you like the most. This may mean that you choose a less glamorous business. As a result, one of my key criteria for selecting an idea is: *the less outside financing your idea needs, the better your chances of success!*

Perhaps you have some really nifty ideas for your new venture—sexy, exciting, and innovative ideas that draw "ooh's and ahh's" from the adoring multitudes. But if these ideas require heavy financing, your chances of owning the company when they make it to market (if they ever do) just nose-dived.

Why? Because, as financier Bob Shoniker explains, "What most entrepreneurs don't understand is that ideas are common, but money is a scarce resource. There will always be more ideas than money to finance them."

And from this sentiment flows the golden rule of venture capital: "He who has the gold, makes the rules." The keepers of the gold guard their hoards as jealously as any dragon out of Tolkien. They part with it grudgingly, and only on usurious terms. So the more money you need from others to make your idea into a successful, self-financing business, the more you'll have to give up. Eventually, you'll either own so little of the company that you'll be nothing more than an employee with a profit-sharing interest, or the company will fail before you can raise all the money it needs.

If, however, you choose to try to do things without outside financing, your progress will be slower—but much more certain.

"START OUT WITH VERY LITTLE MONEY," cautions Konrad Tittler. "Hone your skills, prove out your ideas, and then raise the stakes. There has to be a humble beginning to enable you to make small mistakes without losing a lot of money."

Tittler and his partners took this slower boat to success. They formed Diachem Industries in April 1975 when Tittler was 42 years old, with a wife and five children in school. His friends still talk about how he got his start "barnstorming" around the West in a truck with some chemicals stored in the back. Yet, Diachem became the largest Canadian-owned producer of specialty chemicals for the resource industries, until it was eventually sold to a multinational for a nice piece of change. But he didn't build the company with a lot of other people's money.

"Banks or outside investors," explains Tittler, "have expectations that put constraints on what and how you do things. If you don't take in that kind of money, then the only interest you have to pay is your living expenses, and you can spin that out for as long as you're prepared to put up with the discomfort.

"You're better off taking in an investment of skill rather than money—money gets eaten up pretty quickly. And there's always a way to do whatever it is you want with very little money.

"In fact, I'd say it's *always* dangerous for a fledgling operation to have too much money. The guy who leads the operation may be highly skilled in one area and not very skilled in others. If he's got too much money, he's going to do things to a different scale, and probably waste a lot of what he's got. I've never seen anyone take investment money and keep it in the bank until they've needed it.

"Businesses rarely fail because they didn't have enough money to begin with, but I've seen a lot of companies fail because they have too much money—although that's not the way people see it. If a venture fails, the principals always say it's because they needed more money. I think it was probably because they had too much—and used it unwisely, setting up overhead they couldn't support.

"Most people have a lot of false pride. They've had a secure job, a title, a certain kind of car, a nice office, and so on. Then they think that because they've become entrepreneurs, it's some kind of promotion that should carry with it all the perks they had, plus some more. They think they have to keep up some sort of image for the neighbours. But the real promotion is being able to choose your own direction, even if you do it from a hole-in-the-wall office with second-hand furniture.

"Being an entrepreneur is like some form of guerrilla warfare. The successful people are the ones who go in and change the rules of the game. If you do things the way the big companies do, you're going to fail. You haven't got the money to beat them at their own game. Only by playing a different game can you win out."

So look for ideas that require little or no outside financing. That keeps your risks lower, and your chances of success higher.

And if you must have outside financing, then be aware of the risks that such financing brings with it. We'll talk about raising financing in Chapter 8.

E mployees or no employees?

One of the most important decisions you will make as an entrepreneur is whether to have employees. After all, employees are expensive, and can become your greatest risk. In fact, I've known many entrepreneurs who say, "Employees don't *solve* problems; they *create* them." So if you choose an enterprise that is bigger than you can run alone (with or without your partners), and need employees, then this becomes one of the biggest dangers that you take on—legally, financially, and economically. Employees can also be your biggest headache, as entrepreneur Deborah Sawyer put it in a *Globe and Mail* article:

> [So] decidedly one-sided is current labour law in favour of employees that owners of small businesses are virtually defenseless, another disincentive to job creation. In my experience, employment law does not exist to protect employees from their employers but from themselves. They can walk out on a moment's notice and retain their rights while an employer has to give notice or pay in lieu. They can break your equipment and waste your supplies, but you are rarely able to deduct from wages as compensation.[1]

Sawyer's sentiments are echoed by Sherry Orr, who owns and runs a trucking firm in Alberta: "I believe your employees can be your biggest asset, or your worst nightmare. A [bad] employee can wreck your equipment, fail to deliver things to your clients, and destroy your reputation, yet you're not allowed to charge him for the cost of the damage he's done. You may not even be able to fire him, even if the damage was deliberate."

But if, despite the drawbacks, you decide that you'll need employees, what's the best way to approach it? "Well, when I hire someone," Orr explains, "I not only go through all the routine things, like job applications, but I rely very heavily on my gut instinct, and when I realize I've made a mistake, I fix it by getting rid of the person quickly. But beyond this, you have to work with your people, and help them grow. That keeps them interested and involved."

JONATHAN STRAUSS, PRESIDENT OF Strauss Publishing of Winnipeg, faces an unusual problem when hiring employees: he's 19 years old, and has only recently finished high school. He notes, "When I interview someone for a job, the first thing I do is look them straight in the eye, tell them how old I am, and ask them if they have a problem with that. You can't discriminate [in hiring] on the basis of age, but you can't hire someone who isn't going to respect you, so I haven't hired anyone who won't respect my age."

Beyond this, Strauss believes that hiring the right people creates a working environment that's enjoyable, which makes it easier to come to work. And part of the way you do that is by valuing the people you hire.

"Part of the challenge is for the employer to make it possible for the employee to stretch and accomplish things that make them feel good about what they've done. And then you need to reward them for it, so they know that you know. We have a revenue-sharing agreement based on business brought in beyond their salaried responsibilities. I think of this business as more of a partnership than some place where I'm the boss.

"This is a fun place to be."

Lloyd Segal of Caprion Industries of Montreal takes this concept even further. He and his two partners, Clarissa Desjardins and Martin LeBlanc, created a real Canadian success story—Advanced Bioconcept—and recently sold it to a multinational pharmaceutical company for enough profit that they could probably retire, even though they're all in their thirties. They don't see employees as a burden, but as an enormous opportunity:

"We run this company very much as a partnership with our employees. We probably spend more time interviewing and screening prospective employees than anyone we know, because we know that a bad fit can be disastrous to a young company.

"But having terrific people around is a big part of what makes us love to come in here and work the hours that we do. It also increases our odds of success."

Desjardins adds, "We give a lot of thought to the psychology of people. We treat them the way we want to be treated. We don't hide any conflicts, and we let people know that we appreciate it when they come to us with problems or complaints."

Segal continues, "Martin and I worked for people who gave us room, and also for people who wanted to micro-manage everything we did. We vastly preferred those who gave us room, so we resolved that that was how we wanted to run our business: hire good people, give them the tools they need, then leave them alone. This creates an environment where we get maximum achievement with minimum direction.

"We judge people by how much they get done, not by how many hours they're here. Sometimes we come in [during a working day] and *nobody's* here—and that's fine. It's always about the objective, never about the appearances. And when you do that, you create an environment where people hate to let you down.

"We've had times when our stated objective is to come out with four products this month. Well, once, when the people responsible knew by mid-month that what they were working on wasn't going to be ready in time, they went off in a completely different direction on something they knew would fit our product line, and that they knew they could finish in time. They were ingenious, and came up with a real winner. Those are the kind of people we hire and that we enjoy working with. People who need a lot of task-based direction wouldn't enjoy it here—and we wouldn't enjoy having them."

So, the next principle is: *employees can be your greatest asset, or your biggest problem, and having them raises your risks but can increase your potential.* Think carefully about how well you manage people, at how much money you have to support a workforce, and whether you should "own" the workforce or contract out for the support you need. The lower-risk option will almost certainly be not to have employees—which doesn't automatically make it the right choice. It just means you should consider it carefully.

H ow high is your overhead?

I was once interviewed by a university student as an example of a successful entrepreneur. When I explained that I'd been self-employed since 1978, he commented on the longevity of my success. I looked at him and said, "You need to realize that by selling my own services, I'm in the low-risk end of the business. People who sell products or have a large staff of people whose services they sell take much bigger risks."

If you're selling your personal services, then you own the means of supply, and your costs are merely your cost of living, which you would incur anyway. But if you're trying to start and run the classic widget factory, and sell widgets, then you also have to pay for the factory, distribution system, sales force, customer service, and all the other things that go with it. Or, at least, that used to be the case. Today, the concept of contracting out has become much more widespread, which makes it much easier to create a business without the enormous overhead of the past.

PERHAPS THE BEST ILLUSTRATION OF this concept involves Myra Sable, president of Sable & Rosenfeld Foods. Sable & Rosenfeld was founded in the 1980s, and blossomed into a company employing as many as 100 people. "I had fancy offices, and spent a lot of money on looking like a big company," she explains. "Then, five or six years ago, the market changed, and the way people shopped changed completely. I had two choices: change the way I was doing business, or go out of business.

"So I closed the fancy offices, the plants, the warehouse, and let go the dozens of people who were working for me, and started contracting everything out. Today I have three employees, and do you know what? I spend all of my time doing what I love doing instead of worrying about all that overhead.

"There's so much talent out around. You can create a business with really good people, and still not have to employ them.

"What I learned," concludes Sable, "is that you have to think like a big business—after all, you're competing against them—but just don't spend like them. I compete with General Foods, and so I have to think like they do. But they have lots more money than I do, so I beat them by finding the places where I'm better, and pushing those."

So in planning your venture, think carefully what you have to spend money on, and then don't spend money on anything you don't need to until you can afford the luxury. If you succeed, you'll be able to spend money. But until your success is assured, think cheap, keep the overhead down, and only worry about appearances when they will influence your clients' buying patterns.

In choosing the business you want to run, think about whether you're better off selling services or products. Think about whether you can contract out the things you want to sell, specializing and focusing exclusively on those things you are best at. And use this criterion to design your business: *never spend a nickel you don't need to spend, unless spending it will bring in two*. Remember: as an entrepreneur, money is your life blood. Don't shed it without a fight!

P lay to your strengths, not your weaknesses

SO, WHY DID YOU START YOUR OWN BUSINESS? **Greg Blagoev,** one of the twenty-something founders of Snug Industries, a Toronto manufacturer of streetwear with roots in the underground rave scene, popular with young people, but overlooked by the major marketers, explains, "When Tony [Elston, my partner] and I worked for other people, we had to do what they wanted us to do. We weren't known as professionals in the clothing trade; we had no reputation or credentials. But what we wanted to do was to express our thoughts and our ideas. There was no way, with our background, that we would have had as much control over what we were doing working for someone else."

How did you decide on clothing? "My dad was in the clothing business since the 1950s, so I'd been around clothing all my life. I also went to Ryerson and Sheridan College and studied design. I apprenticed to a tailor, and learned as I went along. I had summer jobs in the business.

"Tony and I met at a party, and he was working in the business, too. We were both fed up working for other people, and we kind of clicked. We started with a concept and a fabric— motorboat vinyl—and we worked in my attic. It was really hot and stuffy, and carrying everything up four flights was a real drag, but it was the only way we could start.

"We each put in $100 to start, making two designs, producing as many clothes as we could out of the material, and sold them. With the $2000 we made from that, we made some more clothes, and just kept on going until we outgrew the attic, and had to get our own studio."

What enabled Greg and Tony to succeed is that they knew what they were doing. Not only did they both know the clothing business, but they also knew their target market. As they told *Report on Business* magazine in November 1998, "'We actually live in the culture and cater to it. We understand it.' ... They're not leaning on market research firms to tell them who their demographic is either. 'We're part of the culture, we attend parties; these people, in a sense, are us.'"

At first, it's tempting to attribute their success to luck—but with a business that now grosses well in excess of $1 million, it's simply not true. None of their success was accidental. Their cheap start-up costs are one tip-off. Their move to what Greg describes as their first "really raw, open concept" studio in an unfashionable part of town underlines this, as well as their continuing ability to stay on top of the market. While they throw rave parties and invite the top DJs in, they also research the market and focus on upcoming trends. But Greg and Tony's recognition that they lacked certain business acumen is the final clue to their success. Consequently, they sought administrative and financial support from another entrepreneur.

Is this the story of two lucky guys, novices in their trade, who just happened to hit it big on their first try, then stayed lucky long enough to build up a million dollar business? I don't think so. Their story reflects the recipe for self-employment success: they knew their market, knew their product, and, perhaps most importantly, recognized what they didn't know, and got help for it. And their success shows—they now have imitators, companies like Le Chateau, Stitches, and the Gap, which are attempting to emulate their designs.

So when you sit down to plan your grand strategy, remember the words of Erwin Rommel, one of the ablest generals of World War II: "The only purpose of strategy is to make the tactics work." *If you design your business and your business plan to pivot on the things you do well (your tactical strengths), then you will vastly improve the probability of your strategy succeeding.*

K ISS and don't get clever

The next criterion is widely known, but often ignored. *If you keep it simple, and don't rely on being clever, you will dramatically improve your chances of success.*

The "KISS" principle ("Keep It Short and Simple") is known throughout the business world. It isn't usually *practised*, mind you, but it's widely known.

You are managing change in building a business, and you don't know the eventual outcome. The more things you try to change, the more you'll have to watch. Worse, the complexity *multiplies* rather than just increases. Hence, managing change in two areas is *four* times as hard as managing a single change. Changing three areas is *nine* times as hard.

In order to manage events, you've got to be watching them. So keep the complexity down, and focus on the key events.

As for being clever, well, it often happens that an idea will sound slick, but not work well when you try it. This usually happens when you try to fool customers into believing that you're offering them something different and worthwhile, when in fact all you're offering is the same old stuff wrapped in fancy words. For example, one entrepreneur started a business called "Dining Out," and convinced himself that "a practical incentive for diners to try new gourmet dining experiences" was different than "two meals for the price of one." It didn't work. Either the clients saw through his ploy or they just didn't understand what he was talking about. In either case, he had to change his whole marketing thrust.

To put it in the colourful phrasing of ad men Al Ries and Jack Trout: "Advertising is a seduction, not a debate." Let's generalize on that: all marketing is a seduction, not a debate. You'll never get an opportunity to argue with enough prospective customers to sell much product. Your approach must seduce them quickly or the opportunity is gone. So choose an idea that's simple and offers the customer a valid reason for dealing with you—not just a clever slogan.

Y ou can't be nimble if your feet are bolted to the floor

The next criterion may take a bit of explaining: *Your odds of success will depend on how quickly you can adapt to change. Choose a business that doesn't hog-tie you to one fixed way of doing business.*

LET'S GO BACK TO THE entrepreneur who started "Dining Out." He had planned his business as a national and international operation that would expand rapidly through a franchising-type concept. He had planned to license a given city or territory for his marketing system. Then, in exchange for the business plan of how the business should be run, he would receive a percentage of all sales. And that's how he wrote all the contracts. However, he soon discovered that the only way his business would grow quickly was by getting the different centres to recognize one international card rather than selling several local cards. But since he was tied into contracts with different centres, he couldn't change the overall strategy without renegotiating all the individual contracts. Although he tried this approach, he had to give up so much in the process that he couldn't make any money. He had to run hard just to avoid bankruptcy.

In contrast, let's look at Patrick Bird of Isolation Systems in Etobicoke, Ontario. Patrick purchased a business in a fairly straightforward industry. He sold products to the health care industry, and discovered that margins generally weren't meeting his expectations.

In the process, however, he became aware of the need for accurate, synchronized clocks in hospitals—as well as other areas, such as broadcast corporations, airports, and the like. So he started up a new division to sell such clocks, based on computer and communications technology.

Here, again, he found that the market was not what he had expected. But in the process he became aware of the need for ultra-security in microcomputers. He started dabbling in this field, and then found a way of making microcomputers uncrackable. After a lot of work (and money), Isolation Systems finally won the approval of all the government cloak-and-dagger types, and developed a protected niche in that market.

But he had to change directions three times to find a niche that he could fill and defend. Had he been less flexible, he would have gone bankrupt very early on.

When you bet your whole strategy on a fixed way of doing business, then you may make it—if you prove to have perfect foresight as to how things will work out. But chances are you're going to have to change your plan to fit the circumstances. If you've invested in machinery that only allows you to do things one way, or tied yourself up in contracts that make change and adaptation impossible, or bet the farm that no one else will be able to duplicate your research, you may be right. But heaven help you if you're wrong.

Do you know where your customers are?

So far, we've discussed your needs, your financing needs, your potential competitors, and so forth. But what about your customers? Do you know who they are?

Who's the first person or organization you will sell to? Do you know? What about the second, the fifth, or the twentieth? If you know who your customers are—down to the individual who is making the buying decision—then your chances of succeeding increase dramatically. Why? Because you then know exactly what you're going to sell, which eliminates a lot of the fuzziness.

It also means you know what they will buy—and how much they will pay for it. And you will know whether you can make a profit selling it. Finally, you then have a pattern to use to look for more customers. If you don't have any idea who will buy your product or service, then you'll have to start from scratch. However, if you *start* by knowing someone who's prepared to slap down their hard-earned cash for what you've got, then you at least know that you're not the only one who's crazy.

So my last objective criterion is: *If you know who your first customers are, you will boost your chances of success.*

 o something you love!

And in all these marvellous, impersonal criteria for success, don't forget your own preferences! Let me repeat Lee Iacocca's point, and make it my final criterion: *Your chances of success go up when you get into something you really like.*

THE TRIO OF PARTNERS AT Snug Industries got into it because they really wanted to make their own clothes, in their own way.

Jonathan Strauss, the 19-year-old owner of Strauss Publishing, puts it very bluntly: "I wouldn't be doing this if I wasn't having fun! I wasn't out there looking for a business. I'm working while my friends are at school—this has to be something you enjoy doing, or else there's no point."

And Strauss goes further than this: "If you want to be an entrepreneur, do something that you want to do, where you feel you can accomplish something you want to accomplish, and not just because you want a job. If you do, your odds of success are much higher."

"I found that because I hired the best people I could find," adds Konrad Tittler, "and challenged them to grow the company, that in almost all of our departments we were at the forefront of the industry, we were excited, and that there were new ideas flowing all the time.

"We all had a sense that we could contribute ideas, and that those ideas could become a reality, so we each felt that we could make a difference. This allowed us to recruit the best people. In fact, as soon as we knew that there was a winner around, we went and offered them a job. Pretty soon we were perceived as a collection of all-stars. And the proof was that we were able to attract people to come on board without a healthy pay cheque. People will give up a lot to have fun doing what they love."

You'll be spending an awful lot of time working at what you choose to do. If you have to force yourself to do it, you'll likely find that it is not only tiresome, but it is also tiring. Eventually, you're more likely to run out of energy—and that means disaster. So, having fun, doing something you enjoy doing, and doing something that makes you feel you're making a difference in life will all make it easier to do the work, and increase your odds of succeeding. It's not just good fun you're after—it's good sense.

R emember: Ideas are cheap!

Remember the fundamental principle underlying this systematic approach to choosing a business: *Ideas are cheap! If you haven't found one that fits, keep looking until you do!*

Don't compromise what you want in a business and build your life around an idea that won't get you where you want to go. Don't do things that don't work! Don't choose an idea that doesn't have what you want!

Instead, go back and generate some more ideas—keep looking, reading, talking to people, and listening. It's worth the effort. This is the cheapest part of the whole process of being an entrepreneur, so don't stint.

And now it's time to evaluate

So now that we've got these various objective criteria and your own personal preferences, what do we do with them?

The following quiz lists the different criteria we've been discussing as statements. If you work your way through it, it should give you a rough idea of each idea's likelihood of success. You'll still be subject to luck, but we can't really measure that.

Note that the highest possible score is 100%, and that's only possible if an idea gets a "10" from every criterion. Without that, the odds go downhill very quickly indeed. This is not to say that such an idea can't succeed—it's just not as likely. Whether you try with a low scoring idea is up to you. Personally, I prefer to bet when the odds are in my favour.

Now, as to the personal preferences, here I would give a rating of either "yes" or "no," depending on whether the idea fits your personal preferences. That means, if an idea doesn't fit every personal preference, it gets dismissed automatically. Life's too short to put up with your business. You should enjoy it.

Gauging Your Chances of Success

Based on the factors you control

Instructions: Grade each statement from 1 to 10 based on how well it describes your situation or idea. Use the scale indicated below. Then add up the totals for the whole column.

Completely Wrong				Partly Right					Perfectly Correct
1	2	3	4	5	6	7	8	9	10

1. I don't need any employees to carry out my business plan. _____
2. There are no luxuries in my plan; my overhead costs are as low as they can possibly be. _____
3. I'm selling only my own services. _____
4. I don't need any outside financing to make this idea a success. _____
5. I know this market and the competition, and this business plays to my strengths. _____
6. This is a simple idea that already works in the marketplace. _____
7. The way I do business can be changed dramatically if necessary. _____
8. This business will support itself and me within a very short period. _____
9. I know who my first 10 customers will be by name and phone number. _____
10. I really love working at this. I'll look forward to going into work every day, even when times are tough. _____

Total Score _____

Notes: Your total score represents your odds of success out of 100%. Hence, a score of 70 means you have a 70% chance of success based on the factors within your control. There is also the element of luck, which you don't control directly and which cannot be gauged.

Your score is also based on how good your judgment is. For instance, if there is more potential competition than you thought, then your real score is obviously lower than you believe it to be. Also, if you convince yourself that your scores are higher than they really are, then you'll make the score unrealistically high. Remember that this assessment is to help you, and you should make it as honest as possible. Specifically, it can point out weaknesses in a particular idea.

Finally, note that these points contradict each other to some degree. Sorry; life's like that. No idea will be perfect.

Up on the high diving board

Thinking about starting your own business is like standing at the top of a high diving board—higher than you've ever ventured before. You look down and get an uneasy thrill that runs from your toes up into your groin. Perhaps your mouth is dry and your heart is pounding. This is the reaction of your autonomic nervous system, letting you know that you're in the presence of danger. You face a decision: take the plunge or climb back down the ladder.

I have no great advice about whether to attempt the dive or to leave it untried. What I *will* say is if you go for it, then you owe it to yourself to execute the dive with all the skill and technique you can muster. *Don't change your mind in mid-flight—that spells disaster!*

Now, taking this analogy one step further, if you were learning to dive and had a coach teaching you the fundamentals, you might dislike or disagree with some of the things being taught. You might prefer to do things differently. But once you're in the air, your personal preferences make no difference at all. Gravity will pull you down, like it or not, and your entry into the water will hurt or not, without any regard to whether you like the skills that go into successful diving.

As an entrepreneur, you will have to do any number of things you find distasteful, difficult, or even downright nasty, including staying up nights doing bookkeeping or collecting money from your customers. But you know what? Your company's bank account doesn't care how you feel. You've either done what was necessary or you haven't. So, if you decide to jump off that high board, then do so with all the skill and technique you can muster, or don't do it at all.

Does all of this scare you?

This book is intended to be encouraging—to give you that nudge to get you to go into business. I believe that your chances of success are good if you do it properly, and that you will find the experience of being an entrepreneur worthwhile and fulfilling, *even if you fail.* But perhaps you find this cold reality harsh and unappealing. Make no mistake; parts of being an entrepreneur are like that. So, if you decide not to take that leap because of anything I've said, then this book will have been the best investment you've ever made. By helping you decide to climb down rather than take the plunge and then change your mind in mid-air, I've saved you tens of thousands of dollars and endless hours of work, pain, and headaches. And, by choosing to live and fight another day, you may have improved your chances of success when you do decide to try.

T he next step

Now that you have a better understanding of what you need to look for in an idea, I'd suggest that you go back through the whole idea-generating process again until you come up with two or three strong, qualified ideas. These two or three you'll take to the next—and final—qualifying stage: the business plan.

But beware! The temptation is to fudge your ratings on some ideas to make it easier for them to qualify. Don't do it—or at least, if you are going to do it, do it with your eyes open. Don't fool yourself that an idea is better than it is.

And remember: ideas are cheap!

5 Plotting Your Own Success

The rule of thumb is that 80% of new ventures fail but 90% of proven, properly structured franchises survive. Why? What makes the difference, and what can you do about it?

The major differences between a proven franchise and a new venture are obvious. A franchise is selling into an established market using a proven business plan that includes proper financing. New ventures, on the other hand, often try to create a new or previously untapped market, or establish themselves from scratch against entrenched competition. They typically lack a well-thought-out business plan and their financing is rarely complete.

So if you're willing to buy someone else's marketing position and business plan, and you're willing to work hard to make their business plan work, then you should be able to tell when to order the Ferrari before you ever sign the franchise agreement (we'll talk about franchising as an opportunity in Chapter 6). But if you can do that with someone else's plan and someone else's market position, then you can probably do it with your own as well. The question is: will you?

Planning is cheap, failure is expensive

"ONLY ABOUT 20% OF NEW businesses survive to their third year," notes 35-year-old Lloyd Segal, one of the principals of Caprion Pharmaceutical. "You always start off with the odds stacked against you, so it's vital to do everything you can to improve your chances."

Segal and his partners, Clarissa Desjardins and Martin LeBlanc, certainly did that, starting their original company, Advanced Bioconcept Ltd., in 1995 and then selling it off to a major international pharmaceutical company for a hefty profit three years later. They started with an idea—a good one, admittedly, but still just an idea—but then did the things necessary to make it work.

Clarissa incorporated Advanced Bioconcept Ltd. in 1992, when she was a student studying for her doctorate at Montreal Neurological Institute. She and a friend came up with a way to follow the path of a drug in the body without using radioactive isotopes, which is a problem that pharmaceutical companies and medical researchers had wrestled with for many years. "When we made this discovery, I knew that this was a unique opportunity, and I just had to pursue it. I was very scared, but I couldn't let it go. We see a lot of technologies—good, worthwhile technologies—developed by scientists, but nothing ever comes of them because they don't know how to create a business to go with them. I have a lot of pride in my work, and I didn't want that to happen to me. It became a mission for me—something that I had to prove. I didn't do it for the money, although I didn't turn away from the money either."

However, although she's an intelligent and talented biotech researcher, Clarissa knew she lacked business expertise. Although she managed to bring the company to a certain level, incorporating it, bringing in a group of outside investors, and creating an active board of directors, she couldn't take it to where she knew it needed to be. "I spent 18 months writing a business plan, and trying to secure investors. I reached my low point just before Lloyd and Martin came into the picture. I don't think I could have gone on if they hadn't come in."

Martin and Lloyd were intrigued by what Clarissa was doing. They both had good jobs, working for McKinsey & Co., and were slated for a big future in this prestigious, global consulting firm. But Clarissa turned to Martin, a childhood friend, to be responsible for the business side of things so she could focus on the science.

"We really loved working at McKinsey," says Lloyd, "and it was tough to leave. But Advanced Bioconcept appealed to us for three reasons. First, working for McKinsey, we were always counsellors to kings, but never kings ourselves. . . . I didn't want to give somebody advice anymore; I wanted to get out on the front line and do it. The second motivation was money. What we saw in Advanced Bioconcept was an opportunity to make some real money. Third, we saw an opportunity to build something significant. Bioconcept was in an industry that was going to go through a massive change in the way it did things, and we were going to lead that change.

"The last thing we thought about was job security. We had a ton of job security at McKinsey, but the day we left we had none—zero, negative job security, and we did it anyway. But we were quite disciplined in researching the market in depth. We also worked out a good relationship with Clarissa, so that we were three equal partners. We all agreed that in the worst-case, Armageddon scenario, we could at least sell off the business for an amount that would pay us for the year or two we put into it. Of course, the upside was what we were looking for."

So, did they dive in? Nope. Lloyd continues, "In order to ensure that we were not just kidding ourselves in the excitement of doing an entrepreneurial deal, we actually hired a Philadelphia-based, scientific due-diligence firm to conduct an independent evaluation of the science, the technology, and the intellectual property, which Martin and I knew nothing about. I think that was a discipline that I would encourage anybody getting into any business to do because you can get carried away with an opportunity, and get so excited that you ignore some of the foundation principles that need to be behind any kind of business. We were dogged about making sure the market we thought was there was actually there.

"I think it's very important to have a fact-based, numbers-based business plan, even if you just make up the numbers. Anybody thinking about going into business should be able to say, 'I'm to get into a market that's worth \$X in terms of sales, and I think that within Y years I can deliver Z% of that market.' If you can't complete that sentence, don't get into the business. You're not prepared.

"We didn't know how to get to those numbers, so we made them up, and that what's you need to do. I mean, we were trying to come up with a market for a product that didn't even exist. So we told people what we thought the number was, although we were guessing. We played it across 10 different people in the industry and the combined intuition of that number of people in the industry was enough to help us correct it.

"I worry about people who say, 'Ah, I know there's an opportunity there, but I have no idea what it is.' That's not to say that there haven't been plenty of people who have succeeded by doing that, but when you start a business by guessing instead of doing research, you've got to be luckier than you are smart. I'd much rather be as lucky as I am smart than *depend* on being luckier than I am smart.

"We consulted everyone we could who we thought could teach us something. We even listened to those people who said, 'You'll never make it.' We wanted to hear *why* they thought we'd never make it. Then we could decide if there was anything we could do to make sure that they were wrong."

So that's when they plunged in, right? Not quite.

"Once we had our business plan, we hired a respected research scientist in the States to look at what we'd done and pick it apart. We paid US$4,000 for what was a pretty basic study of the feasibility of our plan, essentially for four days of a PhD professional. I would have spent three times that. We were taking a much bigger risk than that. It would have been idiotic not to have spent the money.

"One of the things that we learned during our market research is that it's not enough to build a better mousetrap; you have to deliver the service and the solution to the customer. We didn't know that before we did our homework. We thought we were going to be shipping boxes of biochemicals, when in fact we had to deliver A-to-Z solutions to pharmaceutical companies, so we changed the structure of the business plan."

The results prove the value of their preparation. Once they started, they knew what to do, and went right to it.

"Our target market [pharmaceutical research scientists] had the highest penetration of Web use in the population—something like 99.4% of these scientists have an Internet account, and use it more than twice a week—so it was a 'no-brainer' to use the Web as our marketing tool. But it was very important in this community to project an image of quality and reliability, because that's what's necessary in pharmaceuticals. Before the Web, or without the Web, that would have meant impressive offices, legions of well-educated sales people, and an expensive advertising campaign. With the Web, if we did it right, we could project all of these things, and take the orders, all on-line, and still work out of our tiny offices here in Montreal.

"We spent $60,000 on our Web site. That was 20% of our total capital, and it seems like we took quite a gamble. But it worked out just as we expected. We tapped into the power of the Web—which was just starting to emerge at that point—and created a very impressive corporate image. We think it's cool to have a Web site that makes people think you have 50 people working for you.

"And when the company that bought us out came in to negotiate the purchase, they couldn't believe it! They thought we were a much bigger, better-financed company.

"But we spent the money where it counted—just as we'd planned."

L essons from Advanced Bioconcept

Let's look at some of the key points made by Segal and Desjardins:

"You always start off with the odds stacked against you, so it's vital to do everything you can to improve your chances."

The depressing truth is that most new businesses fail. I believe that the major reason new businesses fail is that they haven't planned properly or researched carefully enough before they start. They jump in, make avoidable mistakes, then make unavoidable mistakes, run out of money, and have to fold. In short, they don't do their homework.

You must do everything possible to move the odds in your favour before you start. You will save yourself pain and heartache, and you will dramatically increase the odds of success.

"We see a lot of technologies—good, worthwhile technologies—developed by scientists, but nothing ever comes of them because they don't know how to create a business to go with them."

It's not enough simply to have a good idea. You must also have a clearly defined product or service and someone to buy it. You need to differentiate yourself from competing businesses and present a compelling case why customers need to buy what you're offering. You need to fulfil your promises, and support your sales so your customers stay with you, and become real fans. And you need to run the business effectively, which means doing the accounting, paying the bills, collecting monies due to you, doing the filings with the governments, hiring (and firing) employees, filling out *their* forms for the government, cleaning your offices—and anything else that must be done. All of this takes an incredible amount of time and the ability to juggle different (and sometimes conflicting) priorities.

But you'd better think these things through ahead of time so that you know how you're going to handle them. Having a great idea is only the seed; it's a long, long way from the harvest. You need the complete package to survive and thrive.

"I would encourage anybody getting into any business to do [extensive market research] because you can get carried away with an opportunity, and get so excited that you ignore some of the foundation principles that need to be behind any kind of business."

Having a good idea for a business is intoxicating. But, like a new love affair, the intoxication inevitably wears off in the face of everyday reality, and when it does, you'll need more than just the excitement, you'll need to have a plan, know the numbers, and be prepared for the hard times as well as the good.

And that carries through into your initial successes as well. A lot of businesses meet with initial success, the principals decide, "Hey, this is easy! We've got it made!" and they take their eye off the ball, start making sloppy decisions, and fail. There are no glamorous businesses. If you want excitement, go to an amusement park!

"I think it's very important to have a fact-based, number-based business plan, even if you just make up the numbers. Anybody thinking about going into business should be able to say, 'I'm to get into a market that's worth $X in terms of sales, and I think that within Y years I can deliver Z% of that market.' If you can't complete that sentence, don't get into the business. You're not prepared."

Making projections about a business is an almost impossible task—but it's also a necessary one because it forces you to accept a certain mental discipline. Creating numbers out of thin air is not easy to do well—but doing it, and then checking the market to verify those numbers, forces you to think things through and confront your own ignorance about your business.

"You've got to be as lucky as you are smart. When you start a business by guessing instead of doing research, you've got to be luckier than you are smart. I'd much rather be as lucky as I am smart than depend on being luckier than I am smart."

Luck is inescapable—both good and bad. But the less skill you put into your business, the more you are depending on luck. And if you are depending on luck, you might as well skip the business, and spend your money buying lottery tickets.

"It's not enough to build a better mousetrap; you have to deliver the service and the solution to the customer."

Remember what I said earlier: nobody wants a quarter-inch drill—they want quarter-inch holes. You have to provide *solutions*, not widgets. In fact, you can build extraordinary businesses around really ordinary products or services if you can make them into solutions.

The value of a business plan

Aside from your own talents, your business plan is your greatest tool and weapon. It brings order and harmony to your efforts. It provides a clear direction for everyone in the organization. It allows everyone's efforts to lead to your final corporate goal, even if each individual can't see the forest for the trees. It keeps you on track, doing the most important things first.

A business plan is also important outside your company. If you ever seek outside financing, you'll need to present your business plan, because it gives a bank or other investor some idea of whether you know where you're going and how you intend to get there.

Properly created business plans fill one other purpose as well: they provide contingency plans for the problems that will inevitably crop up. "The only guarantee one can make," says one successful entrepreneur, "is that things won't turn out the way you expected." So when they don't, you must be ready to wade in and make things happen anyway.

There are two tendencies in doing business plans, which reflect the qualities of different kinds of people. The first tendency is to rush through a plan, if one is done at all. These people want to get started. If you're that type, you've already had more than enough of all the detailed planning I've discussed so far. You want to get on with it.

To you, I say, by all means get on with it. But do it so the odds of success are in your favour. It won't pay you to mess up your first try. True, you can always try again. But you'll be better off if you get it right the first time.

I REMEMBER ONE CLIENT WHO was a "take charge" type, with very little patience for paperwork. He had never held a job, having started his first travel agency in university and seen it grow straight up from there. Yet, I remember a couple of long nights, stretching into the wee hours, during which we worked and reworked a business plan for a new venture.

When I asked him why he was making such an effort to develop a business plan in a field that he already knew quite well, he said, "Rich, I know the travel business cold, but I've never tried to market it this way before. I've fallen flat on my face enough times to know that if I don't plan for it, sooner or later something's going to come up I hadn't thought of. If I don't have a plan at that point, I know I'm either going to get distracted by the problem, and forget everything else, or I'm going to concentrate on the things I know I can do. If I do either of these things, I might just as well stick with what I'm doing now.

Besides, I know I'm eventually going to have to go to outside investors. I'm practising up on the language so I can pitch it right when the time comes. I'm not spending time; I'm investing it."

F or those who are ducking the moment of truth...

The other group of people are those who are not only comfortable doing plans, but they actually prefer making plans to taking action. Often, they'll work on elaborate plans partly to ensure that they have all the bases covered, but also to delay having to act. To these people I say: you'll never reach your goals if you don't start.

So here's how to create your plan:

There are several ways of using this technique, but my favourite requires three things: a felt-tipped pen, a big supply of square Post-It™ notes, and a large blank wall. If you don't have a blank wall handy, then use a roll of three-foot-wide, heavy, white paper and lay it out on a table or the floor. Here's what you do with them:

1 Write down everything you can think of that needs to be done to get your business up and running. Use a Post-It™ note to record each task. (Write the task in the bottom of the Post-It™ note, leaving space above for later.) Don't try to put things in order as you think of them. It's only important that you write down as many things as you can. Your goal is to identify specific, bite-size chunks of things to do. In theory, you should be able to take one of the Post-It™ notes, and tackle that task as a separate job in a short period of time, preferably less than a working day.

   Involve anyone else who is responsible for overseeing any part of the process in creating this planning wall. You may even want to include everyone who will be working with you. Just remember that having too many people involved can make it a cumbersome process, creating more confusion than clarity.

2   Draw two lines on each Post-It™ note, with the following headings, so that each one looks like this:

Figure 5-1

Time Required	Estimated Cost
Description of Task	

For convenience, we'll call each note a "node." In the large space at the bottom, write the task to be done. In the small, upper left box, estimate how much time it will take to do the task (in hours, days, or whatever other unit is most appropriate) and write that on the node. In the upper right box, write the estimated cost of performing the task, including personnel costs.

3   Place each node on the wall in about the order you think it'll go in the scheme of things. To do this, think about what other tasks each node relates to, and place it with those tasks. If it helps, organize the tasks by subject matter, such as "sales," "manufacturing," "marketing," "accounting," and so on. Don't worry whether you've got each task in exactly the right order or the right category. You'll straighten all that out later.

4   Now organize each of the tasks in the correct order. To do this, think about what each person, or group of people, will be doing, and in what order. So, for instance, if your marketing efforts will be to identify potential groups of clients, then find them geographically, then figure out how to reach each prospect, organize the steps involved in that sequential order. Your goal is to be able to hand over the chain of steps to the person or group involved (or work on it yourself) and be able to say "Here, do this in this order." So mentally walk through each chain to confirm that you've got all the steps and that they're in the right order.

As you do this, two things will happen. First, you'll remember steps you've left out. When you do, write up the missing nodes and tack them up in the right places. Next, you'll think of things that relate to other areas.

Let's go back to our marketing example. Once potential prospects have been identified, you can't start contacting them until you know your advertising and promotion budget. This means that you'll have to wait until you've created a budget for marketing. To show this on your wall, create a node stating "Get advertising budget from management" and put it into your marketing sequence at that point. Then write up nodes for the accounting and management projects saying "Prepare advertising budget for marketing," and put them up in the right places. This will show you the interactions between different areas of responsibility—or between different tasks, if you're doing everything alone, or with only a few other people. It ensures that everything gets done, in the right sequence, and at the right time to keep everything moving along.

5 Once you have everything in the proper sequence, estimate how long each step will take and how much it will cost. If necessary, simply approximate times and costs, and write them in pencil on your Post-It™ notes. You'll probably change them several times as you progress.

6 Now, along the top of the wall or roll of paper, place a series of time marks. For example, post signs for each week that read something like "March 17-23." Place them equal distances along the top of your planning wall so that you can see the full span of your plan, from start to finish. This means you may want to put up months instead of weeks, or days instead of months, depending on how far ahead you're planning.

7 Now move the nodes forward or back, so that each task is located in the proper time slot. Nodes that show jobs to be done by a single group simultaneously should appear within the same time slot. Once you've done this, you should be able to step back and see what needs to be done, and when. You'll also be able to see how the various groups need to relate to each other, and where the bottlenecks in your planning are.

Figure 2 gives an example of what your plan might look like.

Figure 5-2

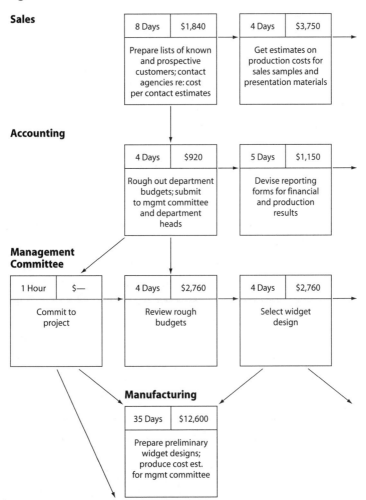

Sales

8 Days	$1,840
Prepare lists of known and prospective customers; contact agencies re: cost per contact estimates	

4 Days	$3,750
Get estimates on production costs for sales samples and presentation materials	

Accounting

4 Days	$920
Rough out department budgets; submit to mgmt committee and department heads	

5 Days	$1,150
Devise reporting forms for financial and production results	

Management Committee

1 Hour	$—
Commit to project	

4 Days	$2,760
Review rough budgets	

4 Days	$2,760
Select widget design	

Manufacturing

35 Days	$12,600
Prepare preliminary widget designs; produce cost est. for mgmt committee	

You should also be able to run through a given horizontal line (say for marketing) and estimate the total costs for marketing, just by adding the estimated costs of each step.

You can also tell if it will be possible to meet any deadlines you've set or that have been set by others. If you find your chains run beyond these deadlines (and they almost always do), you'll have to go back through each chain and see where you can speed things up. You'll need to keep working back and forth between chains until everything balances. But don't simply force the numbers to fit, because you'll only be fooling yourself.

If you can't make your plans fit either your deadlines or your budget, you'll have to decide if the project is doable, the deadlines can be extended, or more money can be raised. And remember that it's better to find out about such problems *before* you start.

T he benefits of using a planning wall

Once done, using the planning wall makes life easier. It becomes simpler to estimate overall funding requirements because you can see all the needed pieces to be financed. You can tell how long things will take, and where you need the most people to get stuff done. And you can monitor your progress.

As you finish each step, you can either put a bold stroke through it with a thick felt-tip pen or simply remove the note from the wall. This makes it easy to see what's moving and what's stopped, and to focus your efforts where they're most needed. It also allows you to revise time and cost estimates as you go along, and see their overall effect.

Various software packages perform the same task on computer. I haven't recommended them for this exercise because I believe it is easier to identify any problem areas by physically moving them around. However, a computer definitely makes revisions easier and faster, and is especially useful for keeping deadline and budget numbers up to date. So by all means look into critical path, project management, or precedence-planning software packages—but you might want to do it by hand first anyway.

Once you've finished the planning wall, discuss the chains of responsibility with the people involved (if it's not just you). Confirm that nothing has been overlooked and that everyone can live with the cost and time estimates. Your groups should take a special interest in this step, because they'll be responsible for executing their chains of responsibility.

H ow do you forecast sales?

Regardless of whether you hate or love this step, inevitably you'll have to try to accurately forecast sales. Why? To ensure that you have enough money, people, and time to do what needs to be done. And this applies whether sales die on the floor or go through the roof, as either one is a major challenge. However, if you want to do more than guess, then go to where your potential customers are, watch what they do, and ask them what they want. This was the approach Myra Sable and Carol Rosenfeld, founders of Sable & Rosenfeld Foods, used when they first started out.

MYRA AND CAROL INITIALLY WANTED to set up what Myra Sable describes as a "a kiosk, a sophisticated soup kitchen, selling soup and quiche" at Toronto's St. Lawrence Market. To find out whether this idea made any sense, they visited St. Lawrence Market, counted the number of people who went by, and figured out how many people would have to buy from them in order to make a profit. Once they had the results, they discarded their original idea as unprofitable, and eventually went on to start Sable & Rosenfeld as a specialty food manufacturer.

"I don't understand people who fall in love with their ideas," remarks Myra. "I recall one time I had two teachers who wanted me to mentor them. They wanted to start a business making and selling apple pie from a family recipe. Personally I thought the apple pie was pretty bad, but not wanting to be discouraging I asked them what research they'd done—and they said they hadn't done any!

"Again, not wanting to be a wet blanket, I suggested it would be tough to market apple pie the way they wanted. I suggested that they look into selling apple pie by the slice at donut shops—I'd never seen that done, and at least there was an existing market. But they didn't want to do that—it wasn't their idea of what they wanted to do.

"I never heard from them—or of them—again. I have no idea what they eventually did, but it seemed like if they couldn't do it their way, they didn't want to do it at all."

When you are trying to estimate your sales, go to where the customers are. Look at what they buy—and what they don't. Talk to them. Count them—and multiply by the amount they'd have to buy to produce enough sales to make it worthwhile.

But beware: first estimates are often (always) optimistic. Save your enthusiasm for your customers, employees, and investors. For forecasting purposes, you need realism mixed with a dose of gloom to counteract your natural excitement over your business. And you must know the industry you expect to compete in, and the other suppliers that you'll compete with.

Virtually every entrepreneur I interviewed emphasized that you must be exceptionally knowledgeable about the industry in which you are going to compete, because you'll be competing against people who are experts. As Konrad Tittler, who twice bought and created big successes out of businesses other people didn't want, says: "You *have* to know the market you're in. Why would someone do business with you? If you don't know the answer, then your customer is not going to find out on his own! It doesn't happen."

How, then, do you make forecasts? Well, if you know your industry well, and have some working experience in the area in which you will be operating, you'll have a pretty good feel for what's possible. If your product is new, or one in which you have little experience, the task is much, much tougher, and your chances for success much lower.

However, the process is pretty much the same. In essence, you need to "guestimate" four things, based on what you've seen and discovered about the market:

1 The number of customers;
2 The quantity that each customer would be likely to buy in their normal operating cycle;
3 How fast you will gain market share; and
4 The price that your customers would be willing to pay.

Let's look at each of these components.

1 The number of customers

In many ways, this is the hardest thing to estimate. Will they love you or hate you? To estimate this, identify the following facts:

- What kinds of people would use your product? How many of these people are there? If your universe of potential clients is small, you must convince a large percentage of them to buy. If your universe is large, you may only need a fraction of a percent to buy.
- How hard and how expensive is it to reach your customer base, either in whole or in part? Do your customers use the Internet, and can you reach them on-line? Or do they dislike technology,

so you have to reach them in more conventional ways? Can you place an ad in one magazine or will you need to advertise on national TV to reach even a few of them? How tightly focused are they geographically? Are they all together or spread out? How easy is it to find people that fit your customer profile?

If reaching your clients is easy, fast, and cheap, then you can justify a higher rate of sales than if it's tough to find or reach them. If there's a lot of competition to sell your kind of products, then customers will be bombarded with competing messages, which means they're more likely to ignore yours. This also means that the clearer your picture of who your customers are, the more likely you are to be able to reach them, and the more product you'll likely sell.

- How hard is it for your customers to reach you? Can they stop in on the way home from work, or do they need to write to you to place an order? Can they order from you over the Internet, and if so, can they find your Web site easily, or is it drowning in a host of similar sites? If it's simple for them to order—and receive— your product, you should have higher expectations of sales.

- How many words does it take to describe your product? The longer it takes you to describe your offering to a potential customer, the more likely you are to lose their attention before you finish. This is especially true in consumer products. For example, 7-Up's classic slogan, the "Uncola," is about as good a product description as you can get. Not only is it short, but the desired marketing concept is immediately understood. In comparison, "a practical incentive for diners to try new gourmet dining experiences," stands an excellent chance of being completely ignored by consumers.

2 How much of your product will each customer buy?

Once you've estimated how many customers might buy from you, you need to figure out how *much* each one will buy, on average. To do this, think about a typical cycle that they would go through between purchases of your product. Some things, like ice cream or newspaper delivery, might be purchased daily in the right seasons. Some, like automobiles, might be bought every four or five years, leading to an average purchase of a fraction of a car per customer per year. And some, like baby carriages, might be purchased only once in a lifetime.

So look at the proper time period, and determine how often a single customer might buy from you. Then decide how much they'd buy per purchase. Customers are unlikely to buy 10 ice-cream cones at one time, for instance, but they might buy a dozen roses.

Once you've determined the potential volume of sales if everyone in your target group could be persuaded to buy from you, move on to the next step.

3 How fast will you gain market share?

Here you'll have to guess, based on several factors. How well known is your product or service? How well known are you? What's your advertising budget? How much competition will you have, and how strongly and quickly will they react?

It would be unusual if you gained most of the market in a short time. Instead, expect to gain a small percentage of the market in the first year, and estimate that it will grow, slowly at first, and then more rapidly as you become better known. Only estimate increasing market share if you have something to offer that will cause your customers to change to you from what they're using right now. Remember that consumer behaviour is difficult to change. It's easier for people to keep doing something than to change to something new.

4 How much will your customers be willing to pay?

If this is a new product, you'll have to make an educated guess about the price. Ask people how much they might be willing to pay for the things you're planning to sell. At what price would they jump at the chance to buy? At what price would they not even consider buying? Is there a price at which they'd try it as a novelty?

Pricing is largely an art—the art of guessing what will prompt your customers to reach for their wallets. If similar products already exist, you'll have to set your prices in relation to them. Your prices may be higher or lower, but they must bear a relationship to competing products, based on the combination of value, quality, and price, because your customers will surely compare to decide if you offer good value.

And remember that quality isn't based on your opinion, but on how useful your customers find your offering. It's easy to fool yourself into thinking your product or service is more attractive than it really is. Instead, you need to be highly critical of your own offerings, questioning everything, and looking for a way of getting unbiased, outside opinions of every aspect of your "guestimates." Otherwise, you will fool yourself into failure and bankruptcy.

P utting these variables together

With these four things, you can develop an estimate of sales. Take your estimated number of potential customers and multiply it by your estimated market share. That gives you the number of customers per period. Multiply this by the average quantity that each customer will buy to give the quantity of product sold. And multiply that by the estimated price to get the dollar value of sales, which is your revenue. (See the following formulas.)

1 $$\frac{\text{potential \# customers}}{\text{period}} \times \frac{\text{percentage of}}{\text{market share}} = \frac{\text{\# of your customers}}{\text{period}}$$

2 $$\frac{\text{\# of your customers}}{\text{period}} \times \frac{\text{amount purchased}}{\text{customer}} = \frac{\text{amount purchased}}{\text{period}}$$

3 $$\frac{\text{amount purchased}}{\text{period}} \times \frac{\text{price}}{\text{purchase}} = \text{dollar sales volume}$$

If you have more than one product, go through this process for each one.

I s all this really necessary?

Will this process guarantee good estimates? Not necessarily. It depends on how accurate your guestimates are. Do you have to estimate sales this way? No, you can use whatever approach will give you the best results. But the fact remains: you need hard estimates of your potential sales, for the following two reasons.

First, you need hard-nosed, hard-headed estimates to let you know if your business is likely to create the kind of success you want and need. Remember the advice of Lloyd Segal of Advanced Biotech: "Anybody thinking about going into business should be able to say, 'I'm to get into a market that's worth $X in terms of sales, and I think that within Y years I can deliver Z% of that market.' If you can't complete that sentence, don't get into the business. You're not prepared."

Second, you need to track your actual sales against your original estimates. If you find that reality is much worse than your estimates, then knowing it early gives you at least a fighting chance to change direction or make corrections in time to survive. Otherwise, you'll run out of money, and be surprised when it happens, because you won't know how badly you've done.

The result of your estimates will change as you test them against people who know the business or do further research on how the business worked, and will change again as you enter the marketplace and learn more about your customers and yourself. Don't be afraid to revise your estimates. That'll help you stay on track. But never lie to yourself; that leads to disaster.

P olishing your crystal ball

Now you should prepare financial projections of your business to help you cope with financing, and to ensure that money is coming in fast enough that you can survive. And as things change—and they will—you must update your plan to reflect what's happening. Remember that your projections are your navigation charts to keep you in safe water. Don't erase the rocks and shoals simply because you think the picture looks prettier that way.

If you've followed the process I've outlined so far, you already have most of the pieces you'll need to put your projections together. Your revenue projections will come from your sales forecasts. Your costs will mostly come from your planning wall. Remember that each node contained an estimate of the costs attached to it. This will give you most of your operating costs.

The things likely to be missing are overhead, or administration costs, salaries, and the cost of the materials needed to produce your products or services. Estimating overhead costs—which are costs you must incur that don't produce revenue directly—can be done by deciding what kind of head office you'll need. This includes things like secretarial and clerical support, record keeping, inventory control, accounting (especially accounts receivable!), shipping, purchasing, and anything else you need to make your business function.

If you know a little about accounting, or if your business will be small and fairly simple, you may want to wade through this by yourself. Virtually all of the drudgery can now be done by various software packages; whenever possible, use them rather than relying on paper and pencil. If you're not sure what software to use, ask whomever will be doing your financial statements and tax filings for you—probably your accountant.

If, however, you neither know nor want to know anything about accounting, or if your business is fairly complex, hire an accountant to work with you to prepare your financial projections.

Mind you, relying on an accountant doesn't necessarily mean you'll get more accurate projections. I had one client who hired an accounting firm to help him create financial projections and a business plan, and wound up with expensive nonsense.

JACK WAS RAISING MONEY FOR a worthy project—his own. When a couple of potential investors had asked to see his business plan and projections, he decided he'd better have one, and so he contacted an accountant to prepare it.

Unfortunately, the accountant knew nothing about the business that Jack was proposing to start. That didn't matter, because Jack didn't know much about it either. So the two of them spent a day sprawled over a table in the firm's conference room, picking numbers out of thin air.

"How much do you think you can sell in the first three months?" the accountant would ask.

"Oh, lots." Jack would reply.

"What does that mean in dollars?"

"I dunno—what would you think it meant?"

"Right; we'll put down $153,750 for the first quarter," the accountant would conclude. (Notice the nice, unrounded number—that adds credibility.)

"Now how much will you pay people?"

"What people?"

"Your employees."

"How many do I need?"

"Oh, I should think four in head office and three in each branch office. Let's put down $86,500 for salaries for the first quarter. Now about office rental...."

And on they went, until they came up with some very solid-looking projections. They showed the company turning a profit in the fourth month of operations—and paying the original investment back after 14 months. It was very exciting.

It was also very wrong. I've kept the original business plan in my files as a magnificent example of self-deception. It initially projected investment needs of $500,000, which is what Jack raised. However, the company ultimately needed *four times* that amount and six additional years to reach break-even—and the original investment was never paid back, even when the business was eventually sold, almost 10 years later.

How did they survive? Jack is a very, very persistent and resourceful man who doesn't take "no" for an answer. He was also eventually forced out of the company he sweated bullets to start. Did his projections get him the money he needed to start out? Yup. Did they put him in the position he wanted to be in? Nope. Was it a good idea putting the projections together that way? You decide.

A short course in accounting

This is not an accounting textbook, but there are some key concepts you will need to understand. The descriptions below are undoubtedly too brief if you're unfamiliar with the concepts, and too long if you already know these things. Make sure, though, that you understand what they mean, even if it means paying your accountant to teach you.

The first concept is that of accrual accounting. This is the essential difference between cash flow and profit and loss. Both a cash-flow statement and a statement of profit and loss count how much money you've received and paid out. But cash accounting means you count the money when you get it or pay it out. Accrual accounting means you count money when it's owed to you or when you owe it to someone else. The difference is important.

You may have shipped products to a customer, but not yet received payment. Under cash accounting, you wouldn't count that money until it was received. Under accrual accounting, you would count it once the products were shipped and the customer had been invoiced because you've earned it. It's legally yours, even though you don't have it yet. This difference is crucial because *you can't spend money that isn't in your hand, even if it legally owed to you.* If you confuse "profits" with "cash" you will find that you don't have the money to pay your bills.

Another major difference between these cash-flow and P&L statements is that the P&L statement includes depreciation, which represents the cost of your major assets (cars, equipment, buildings, and so on), spread out over their useful working lives. Hence, if a piece of equipment cost $10,000 and could be used effectively for five years, one method of calculating depreciation would be to take the $10,000 cost, divide it into five equal parts, and subtract $2,000 from your income each year. This way you recognize that you're using up, or depreciating, that piece of equipment.

In comparison, a cash-flow statement would count the cost of a piece of equipment when you paid for it. If you paid $10,000 in cash the first year, that's when it shows up on a cash-flow statement. If you borrowed the money from the bank, the $10,000 appears in three places: as money received from the bank; as money paid out for equipment; and as interest payments and principal repayments as you make them.

You will generally use the cash-flow statement for running your business. The P&L, or income statement, is more for investors and the tax collector but is also useful to check whether you're really making a profit or just slowly selling off your assets.

For example, one business that's famous for bringing in cash but losing money has been health clubs. In the past, such health clubs would sell a five-year membership in advance and bring in a lot of cash, but still lose money. (I believe this is now illegal, but the example is instructive.) The first year the club would fill their membership list with new members, taking in all their money in advance, and using it to buy the fancy facilities they need. The problem was that they then have to run the club for four more years without *any* money coming in to pay for operating expenses or new equipment.

If they looked only at the cash-flow statement, it would show a terrific business in the first year, and a disaster after that. An income statement, on the other hand, only shows the money they've earned when they've earned it by giving service (i.e., month by month as members have access to the club), and compares it with the operating costs and the equipment they've depreciated.

Hence, if they sold their memberships too cheaply in order to get cash up front, that wouldn't be evident from the first year's cash-flow statement, but would appear as a loss on the first year's income statement.

 he balance sheet

The balance sheet gives an overall picture of your financial health at one specific moment, and is, therefore, a key statement demanded by any investor or banker. Your balance sheet shows three major things about your company: how much it owns (assets), how much it owes (liabilities), and how much belongs to you (shareholders' equity). The amount that belongs to you is computed by subtracting what you owe from what you own.

One important aspect of the balance sheet is that it's a snapshot of your company's financial situation taken at a particular time, whereas the income statement and cash-flow statements show what changes have taken place over a period of time, like a month or year. Balance sheets are connected from one period to the next by the income and cash-flow statements. The changes in the balance sheet generally result from the purchase of goods and services, and the sale of products shown in the other two statements. Hence, for example, profit earned in a year as shown on the income statement may appear as an increase in cash on the asset side of the balance sheet, and a matching increase in shareholders' equity on the liabilities and shareholders' equity side. The depreciation for a piece of equipment subtracted from revenue on the income statement will be deducted from the value of that equipment on the balance sheet.

If these accounting concepts are unfamiliar and make no sense, or seem unduly complicated, then you should probably seek professional help in preparing financial projections and dealing with your bookkeeping, financial statement preparation, and tax filing.

W hy you need financial projections

Having explained a little about these financial statements, let me now tell you why you need them. Along with your business plan and personal and corporate track records, your financial projections are the first things that potential investors and bankers will want to see. But these projections also show you what kind of future you're expecting in concrete terms.

And you'll need more than a single year's statements. If you're creating them to show to possible financiers, then you need to show at least three prospective years of results, and possibly as many as five. They'll want to see how you expect your enterprise to unfold, and, if you're taking over an existing operation, how you expect it to change.

If the financiers are experienced at reading financial statements, they'll quickly pick up unrealistic assumptions ("How come you show sales doubling in the first three years with no increase in salaries?") or outright mistakes ("You don't seem to be showing any purchases of raw materials to make your products.").

We'll discuss more about how to make presentations to investors in Chapter 8.

For your own use, you'll probably want to show your cash-flow projections monthly, and possibly weekly, at least for the immediate future. The purpose is to identify any major problems, such as running out of cash, so you can prepare for them.

I remember receiving a panicked call from a friend who was looking for some financing. Alan was trying to start a magazine aimed at upscale travellers, and seemed to have all the necessary ingredients. But, being essentially a salesman by nature, he was good at the big picture but tended to be weak on the details. His immediate problem was that he had just looked at the costs he'd be facing over the next 90 days, and found that the revenue he was expecting wouldn't cover it. Accordingly, he was scrambling for additional financing.

Now, finding financing is tough at the best of times, but when you're desperate for it and need it immediately, it's almost impossible. So it was with Alan. His magazine foundered on what I call the "90-day gap." Every business, at one point or another, seems to get into a bind where they're expecting money to come in, but it's still a ways off. Meanwhile, the bills are right here, right now, and they have to find some way of bridging the next 90 days. If they can do that, paradise seems to be open to them. If not, they're out of business.

Finding the cash to span that 90-day gap can be the most expensive money you ever raise. The best way to survive it is not to allow it to happen in the first place. You can only do that if you can see it coming, and have planned for it in advance.

A nticipating versus forecasting

Forecasting is easy, I always tell my clients. It's being right that's tough. And the best way to be right is not to plan for only one set of circumstances.

The future can unfold in many ways. And there's no way to tell in advance which way it'll happen; that's not under your control. What you *can* do is anticipate the different possibilities, and be ready to cope with them. So the difference between anticipating and forecasting is whether you've allowed for the universe to unfold in ways other than those you expect.

For instance, you know that everybody will love your product. They're going to want one for themselves, and two for the rest of their family. And you plan for that expectation. But what happens if they want *three* for themselves, and one for every single member of their family—*and* start giving them away to strangers. You won't be able to keep up with production, you won't have enough inventory, you won't have enough capital to finance expansion. This kind of unexpected success could put you out of business. How? Well, first, you can find that you've got so much money tied up in materials in production that you don't have enough cash to pay the rent or salaries. Or a bigger competitor may see what you're doing, and jump in because it looks so profitable.

But suppose no one buys *any* at the price you've set. What do you do then? Close up and go home?

If you've only planned for things to go exactly as you expect, that's probably what you'll be forced to do. By the time you can react to conditions dramatically different from what you expected, you'll be dead.

If you anticipate several of the most likely possible futures, though, you'll have contingency plans ready to go. Hence, for example, if you see sales going through the roof, you've got a presentation all ready for the bank, and immediately run down to see them to arrange for an expanded line of credit. Meanwhile, you exercise the option you took to have your product manufactured by a third party on a cost-per-unit basis until you can expand your own production facilities.

If you see that product isn't moving, you go back and figure out what's happened that you hadn't expected. It may be that this "failure" is the greatest thing that will ever happen to you. Why? Because it tells you that conventional wisdom about the buying public is wrong. They may want something very different. If you can figure out what it is, you may scoop all of your competitors.

It may be, for instance, that customers don't see this as a luxury, and so they want a discount approach. If you're the first to try a "no-frills" approach aimed at a low price point, you may capture a significant amount of market share before your competitors wake up to what you're doing. But you have to be sensitive to what's happening. If you think only in terms of your forecast, then you won't pick up important information until late in the game because it doesn't fit the pattern you're expecting.

So prepare for the future by anticipating different possibilities.

A nd the winner is...

Remember that the primary purpose of this long, and rather complicated, chapter was to help you make your final choice from among the best ideas you were considering. If you go through the steps of producing a business plan for each idea you are seriously considering, using the steps outlined in this chapter, you will have wasted a lot of effort on the ideas you *don't* choose. But you will also have learned a lot about them. Choosing the best one should be easy now. The best idea will have the fewest snags, pitfalls, and dangers, and the greatest potential and simplicity.

And when you've chosen the idea that's going to be a winner for you, use the plan you've prepared. Make sure it all hangs together, and that you've figured out everything you need. It's cheap to make mistakes now. It'll be very expensive once you've started.

Once you're satisfied that you've covered all the bases, then turn around and walk through your business plan, just as you've laid it out. And keep adding onto and changing it, so you never run out of a plan to follow. It'll have to change as you find things are different from your expectations, so make that part of your plans. Remember, "The only thing one can be sure of is that things won't go the way you expect."

6 Alternatives: The Internet, Franchises, and Network Marketing

It should be evident by now that starting a business from scratch is hard work. It requires imagination, access to a broad range of talents, self-discipline, and lots of research and preparation. Not everyone will feel comfortable or confident doing this, especially if they've never done it before, and the process alone may be daunting enough to stop you from trying. There are, however, alternatives that can make it easier to get started.

These alternatives are not shortcuts because there are no shortcuts, and each of these options requires just as much hard work and discipline. But they can provide more guidance, and fill in some of the gaps in your background while allowing you to learn some of the skills you need. Moreover, they may allow you to do things with less capital or easier access to investment capital than you might otherwise have, and, as we've discussed, finding capital is usually the toughest part of starting your own business.

The three alternatives outlined in this chapter are the ones I am asked about most frequently: creating a business through the Internet; buying a franchise; and network or multi-level marketing.

All three are legitimate alternatives, although all three present their own significant challenges.

T he Internet

The Internet is not properly an alternative, because starting a business over the Internet is much like starting any business from scratch. Indeed, another way of looking at electronic commerce (or "e-commerce") is that the Internet is merely another marketing and sales tool.

Although this is technically true, it misses a major difference: the Internet is so different from traditional forms of marketing that it is a little bit like describing a hurricane as a strong breeze. The Internet is transforming marketing. More, the Internet is transforming all business, including both franchising and network marketing. To see the truth of this, check back on the story of Advanced Bioconcept in Chapter 4, which built a biotech business almost entirely through Internet marketing, a process that would have been impossible even five years ago. Remember, though, that the company's product was uniquely suited to this medium. Your business might not be suitable to the Internet.

In the discussion below, I've assumed a certain degree of familiarity with the Internet and have not stopped to explain everything. There are two reasons for this. First, the details are much less important at this time than getting the overall concepts, and if I stopped to explain the details, I'd spend all my time doing that. So if you are unfamiliar with a particular term, pretend you're reading *The Brothers Karamazov* and have hit a Russian name that you can't pronounce; just buzz right over it and go on with the story. Second, if you're not familiar with these concepts, then you will have to invest some time, most of it on-line, learning them from a much longer description than I am providing here. Using the

Internet is like learning to ride a bicycle: someone can explain it to you until they're blue in the face, but it really won't mean much until you're actually trying to do it.

EARL EPSTEIN IS THE VERY PERSONABLE and highly intelligent president and CEO of Passport Online in Toronto, which, among other things, helps people create Web sites and e-commerce businesses. Passport is an Internet service provider (ISP), and one of the earliest entries into this field in Canada. With all the shakeout that has gone on, and with the competition from the biggies in the industry, it says something about their operation that they've been able to survive and thrive. I asked Earl how someone would go about getting into an Internet business.

"E-commerce segments according to the role the Internet plays in your business," he explained. "Are you selling something to an end-user that exists in the real world? Is it a service or a product? If it's a product, is it a piece of hardware, and does it have to be shipped? Or is it a piece of information, which can be a product, too? So there are many, many different things that can be e-businesses, or Internet-based businesses, ranging in complexity, in the likelihood of success, in the capital required and the start-up costs, and the amount of technical capability you need to have. Let me illustrate the simplest form for you.

"I have a friend in Chicago who calls herself 'Hope.' She likes to do horoscope readings and tarot cards, and stuff like that. She's not running a scam—she has been paid in the past in the real world to read tarot cards and tell fortunes and so forth, and although I'm a skeptic, if I were going to believe anyone could do this kind of thing, it would be her. She's now running an Internet-enabled business, albeit on a very small scale. What she did is this:

"She registered a domain for herself, 'hopes.com,' which I think is kind of catchy, and she built for herself, in very simple HTML [the Internet standard programming language], a Web site. She put up there general horoscopes month by month, and some tantric stuff, and some good herbal remedy stuff; a nice kind of holistic, slightly psychic site that was very straightforward in its information delivery, and didn't need any tricks or bells and whistles. She started off by saying, 'If you would like a reading, please e-mail me and I can contact you by phone, and you can send me a cheque, and I can do your reading.' That was very cumbersome.

"But then she found a company that would allow someone like her to have the ability to take credit cards on her site. She gives the information to them on what she wants to charge, and sets up a link so that when the person on her site is ready to buy, they click on the link, it takes them to this other company's site. They then collect all the needed information, and the customer's credit card is billed $X. Then it returns a validation to her through e-mail so that at the end of the day, she sees that someone has gone to her site and paid for a reading via this third party, who takes 10% off the top.

"I don't know how she does the reading, whether it's by phone, or by Internet chat, but it's pretty straightforward. So this is not sophisticated at all, it's very simple. Her investment of time was 20 hours in learning HTML, and the cost of registering the domain was US$100, and hosting her site cost her US$100, which is nothing, and she's up and running.

"This is now sort of hobbling along—she's doing two or three readings a week. It's not self-sufficient by any stretch of the imagination, but on the other hand, she's not trying to promote it. But it's a real simple thing. She could promote it more successfully within the Net using a number of free, simple promotion techniques, and she could be doing a lot more readings within, say four weeks.

"Very simple, no real capital upfront, and a very minimal technical knowledge required—and very little money comes in from it.

"Now there are some problems she can't overcome because she's done this in a minimal configuration. Number one, she's not clearing the credit card and doing the reading in real time, and that drives away a lot of people. People are impulse driven [on the Internet], and a small purchase is often an impulse buy. So if you can't get instant gratification, you're going away. So she's lost some traffic there.

"And her site could be embellished in a lot of ways to get more repeat traffic, get more references, and so on. There are a lot of things she could do if she had better technology and more money. In the current configuration, she could be doing more than she is, simply by investing her time.

"So that's level one: the home-brew, simple, do-it-yourself business. And it's nice, but look: not everybody can be a psychic on the Internet. It's good to be a psychic first. Hope's site has one great virtue: nothing has to be shipped in the real world.

"Suppose instead that you built a site like hers, but you sold your own homemade dog biscuits, for example. How much inventory do you keep, how quick is your turnaround, how long will it be before the customer gets mad, what third party are you now passing part of your revenue on to buy the raw materials and to ship this stuff and to package it, what regulations and inter-state rules and laws are there that might prevent you from shipping food products? Obviously, the very simplest type of Internet-based business is to sell information, insight, or consulting, where you're giving something that's unique because it comes from your mind, and where somebody's prepared to attach value to that.

"That's the easiest one, but not one that everyone can do, because it relies on having something that people might want and that you can sell almost as a novelty. That's the nice thing about fortune telling; people are surfing around, looking for some kind of mystical stuff that appeals to them, and they come across your site, and say, 'Oh, I could do this for $10.'

"I guess the next level is something that does involve the physical world, but doesn't have the need for instant satisfaction. And maybe you do make something. Maybe you're a pet enthusiast, and you've come up with a really cool collar for your cat that's reflective, and has a little bell or something, and people can't find them in a pet store. And you sell these things for five or ten bucks a pop. So you make 'em in your spare time, you've got a bunch sitting around, and a pet person finds your site and orders it. They're not gonna die if it takes two weeks to get to them. They'll be happy when it arrives, but probably they'll have forgotten about it ten minutes after they place the order. This is one of the nice things about low price-point stuff on the Internet.

"So you could be making something in your back yard, or your garage, and using the same model, you could be offering people the opportunity to purchase the things you've made over the Net. You can get your stuff out there.

"Having said that, 'out there' is getting bigger every day. There's so much noise, and so many of these small sites, that someone might use a search engine to search on 'pets' and get 60,000 hits, and if your site's a tiny, little one, it may take longer to get listed, it may be way down on the list, etcetera, etcetera."

W hat sells best over the Net

It should be clear from Earl's comments that running a business over the Internet may be no simpler than running any other business. It delivers an enormous advantage—being exposed to people around the world, rather than those just in your geographic area—but it comes at the cost of requiring the technological and marketing smarts to exploit it, an understanding of the mentality of Internet users, and the ability to make yourself heard above the enormous babble that the Internet has become.

AT THE CORE OF YOUR Internet business you still have to offer something for sale. "I would say that that's a truism in any business," says Epstein. "You need to be able to deliver something that doesn't just have value, but that it has the kind of value that would make someone want to choose you over the competition, or that by virtue of its uniqueness would make it difficult for anyone to compete with you. These are all marketing/mix questions.

"The Internet is like anything else in that respect. If it's not easier, or more desirable, or cheaper to buy it over the Internet, there's no point in trying to sell it over the Internet. Selling milk over the Internet, when it's available 200 yards down the road at your corner store, probably isn't a great bet. You have to use your head! Why would you use the Internet to sell? Is it just because the Internet's sexy? Or is it because the Internet lets you do some things that other media won't? When you're making this decision, that's what you need to think about.

"Like, consulting comes out of your brain, so it doesn't require shipping, but by the same token, there are many other media that are better suited to carrying it. Written stuff doesn't tend to be very sexy over the Internet, either.

"Really, when you go to a Web site and are going to do a transaction, you're looking for one of two outcomes: first, the Web site is going to deliver something to you immediately that is reasonable to be delivered over the Internet; or two, you're going to order something over the Internet that is delivered in the real world.

"The first set of things fall into three categories. One would be textual information that can be instantly delivered, maybe a document that can be used as a boiler plate [i.e., routine legal language] for contracts, for example. We've done that over the Web, by the way, for contracts. You go to a site, you find a boiler plate contract that's similar to what you're trying to do, you pay ten bucks, and you print it out. That's great! It's a two-second transaction, and everybody wins.

"The other one that is less effective, but maybe sexier and getting more effective as time passes, is delivering a piece of software. That could be a computer program, or it could be some type of multimedia. What's happening now, for instance, is that people are selling music in MP3 format, which is an audio compression protocol, and such recordings are pretty good. They sound great, and they're bandwidth efficient. If you have a 56K modem connection, it's not unreasonable for you to buy and download a five minute song, which you can keep on your hard drive, copy onto a floppy, or, if you have the capabilities to do it, copy it onto a CD-ROM. And that's a new thing that's happening.

"Can't get a record distribution contract? No problem. When you've finished with the music in the studio, throw up a simple Web site and put these MP3s on there, and when someone pays you, they can download an MP3. It's actually becoming part of marketing and promotion for established bands, too, where they get the single out, pre-release, and everyone gets excited and hungry for the record.

"The third thing is a service that you can sell in real time over the Internet. But unfortunately, the only two services that you can sell in real time that people will pay for are sex and horoscopes.

"So all of these things so far are instant access things: you get the money, you deliver the product electronically, it doesn't need to enter the real world at all.

"In the second category of things sold through e-commerce, you either ship the product from your own inventory, or you play the role of a VAR [value-added retailer] or a distributor or something, and you have it drop-shipped from somewhere else. So the order enters via cyberspace and exits via the real world.

"If you're going to sell products, volume may not be necessary if your margins are good, and it's a product that really sells well over the Internet (like if the person doesn't need to try it on) and how hard it is to find locally, and how many people are competing with you, there may be a big enough margin in selling products that you don't need to do a mass volume.

"Like if you need some kind of specialty food, and you find this place in North Dakota that makes it and will package it up and ship it, Bingo! That works! If your margins are high enough, and you've got a specialty product so that people are looking for you, you don't need to advertise to find them."

ⓣ he TV and radio model

"The other way things are sold through the Internet is the TV and radio model: provide something interesting for free so that enough people will want to visit your site that advertisers will want to sponsor it.

"Pick a hobby, it could be anything. If you're in the know, if you're connected, if you're a good communicator—and that covers a lot of people—then there are ways you can get traffic, and sell advertising. This is all elusive stuff right now, but I saw a statistic on TV about how a big, national [American] study concluded that memory retention of particular product names from a banner that was seen on a Web site was massively more effective at making a lasting impression than a 30-second TV commercial. I don't know who the study was done by or where, unfortunately.

"Pricing right now for banner advertising is ridiculously low because nobody believes in it yet. If it's true that it's effective, and if you have a site that gets a lot of eyeballs, and especially if they're targeted eyeballs, psychographically, then that's worth a fortune, right? But this is kind of emerging. Right now it's hard to sell banner ads because nobody knows if they're worth anything, and they're hard to track. But if the initial information is correct that a good banner ad is insanely effective, then unlike mass media where you can't really control demographic and psychographic exposure—meaning that they're reaching the wrong kinds of eyeballs who don't qualify for what the advertiser wants—then it becomes clearer that the Web becomes a great place for this.

"Again, if you're doing, I dunno, a dog-groomer's site, and someone who sells dog grooming products or equipment and wants to get to those people, they're going to do a lot better and they're not going to waste any money with your site compared to putting it on the football game on Sunday afternoon. The cost-per-thousand of *qualified* eyeballs is way, way less.

"So there are opportunities out there. It's kind of too early to tell just how big they are. But to make them work you need content that's of interest. It doesn't need to be interesting enough that people will pay for it, and that's a good thing. There's a difference between what you'll pay for and what you'll take for free. But it does need to be (a) interesting and valuable, and (b) *current*. There's no point in having someone come to your site and discover that it's a great site that has great information, see the banner ad one time, and say, 'Ha! I've read this, now I can leave and never come back!' Any time you're doing something on the Web, you try to build community. That's a real key to success.

"A free site that has content has to be interesting to a specific sort of person, it needs to be delivered in a way that's interesting to read or interesting to browse or interesting to look at. If you've got a lot to say, but if you can't communicate it very well, you're dead. Motion video is still a no-no because it takes too long to download, but audio, as long as it's not downloading to a lot of people concurrently, works.

"Another way to sell traffic and get advertising when you don't have the content is to be a portal. You be the guy who knows how to find the content. You go out there and sift through all the crap that comes back when you do a search on Yahoo!, and out of the 6000 sites, you pick the 25 best ones and organize them nicely. Then people will read that banner ad, and find the site they want because you just saved them five minutes, and that's the value you've added.

"It's kind of weird how many ways there are to add value to someone's Internet experience and to get paid for it."

T he power of the Dark Side

"Beyond this, the game then runs an infinite number of different levels of sophistication and complexity. Where these different layers start to define themselves are dependent on questions like: How much will you spend to develop the site? How much will you spend to support the site on an ongoing basis? How much will you spend to continue to promote the site? And the back end becomes: Are you now so sure you can sell widgets over the Internet that you know that you need 100,000 square feet of warehouse and a very sophisticated internal order processing system to make it work?

"I don't know, for example, how Amazon.com works on the back end. I know what their interface looks like, and if you want to look at them as an example of a biggie at the other end of the scale, what do they have? Well, an incredibly sophisticated site that's very fast, must use masses and masses of Internet connectivity, which is a monthly billing issue that gets very expensive. They probably have a huge server farm because they have to support many concurrent users very quickly. They probably need to be constantly updating the technology in their site because they've got competition hot on their heels, so that's got to be a full-time, ongoing process. And then there's the back end, and I have no idea how that works. I mean do they send the order directly through EDI [electronic data interchange] to the publisher, and it gets drop-shipped from the publisher? Or does the order go to the publisher, and then they ship it? Or do they warehouse things, or do they refer the order to the local bookstore and have it shipped from the local store? I mean, these are all different schema that you can use when you work at that level."

The Internet, then, doesn't make life simple or complex in and of itself. It opens up enormous opportunity, but it demands great technical and marketing sophistication. Or at least a great deal of planning and thought—just like any other business. And if you don't have the technical sophistication that you need to do this yourself, but believe you've got the right kind of product, service, or system for e-commerce, where do you get advice?

"Ohhh," groans Epstein, "enter the spin doctors, and the witch doctors, and the guys that sell snake oil. I think that's the hardest problem to solve. How do you find somebody, and assess their qualifications from your perspective as a novice? Who will be your guru? There's no certification that anyone can get. There's no university degree that even *suggests* to you that they know what they're doing. Everyone can be a consultant. So I'm not sure, because this is still so new, that it's not just a question of *caveat emptor* on the part of the person that wants to set up an e-business.

"What we try to do [at Passport] is to avoid Internet buzz-words and explain things in simple, direct terms. Terms in the Internet business are like standards in the computer business;

everyone sets their own standard, and the only thing that's good about them is that there are so many to choose from. There is this sort of unspoken, secret alliance among 'Internet marketers' where they come up with a new buzzword every two weeks to make sure they continue to have apparent value to the people who are paying them. And a lot of Internet stuff is either really straightforward and doesn't need a buzzword, or very, very complex, and can't possibly be properly defined by a buzzword. And yet, there are buzzwords galore."

So one of the biggest downsides of working on the Internet is finding a reliable guide, or guru. And that's not the only problem, according to Epstein:

"The downside of everything I've said is that this is the Gold Rush, the American Dream, and the thing about the Gold Rush or the American Dream is that you only hear about the success stories. There's no point talking about the failure stories; you want to emulate a success. But you're still entering an arena with 40 million other people who all think that they can be the big success. Who knows if there was a Web site that came out the same day as Amazon.com that happened to have a name that didn't sound good? Or that crashed for the first two weeks while everyone was finding Amazon?"

So just because someone can order from you instantly from halfway around the world, doesn't mean that the Internet is easy. Don't underestimate the Dark Side of the Net.

 **K**eys to starting well

As is clear from Epstein's discussion of Amazon.com, you can spend any available amount of money on an e-commerce business. But, as I've said before, money is hard to come by, and financing may be the hardest part of being in business for yourself (although the sex appeal of the Internet may help you raise financing more easily). So how can you start simply, and do things that don't cost a fortune?

"Obviously, if you have no time and no money, then you're not getting very far," says Epstein, "but if you have time and you have Internet access, then the first thing to do is something most people overlook, because they're thinking Web, and they're thinking e-mail. This is to get involved in the 20,000 active discussion groups that are going on over the Internet all the time, which are referred to as Usenet or newsgroups. In Usenet, most likely you could find, oh, 10 discussion forums that are active, all of which are being read by the kind of people that would be interested in what you're trying to sell, author, broker, or whatever you're doing in e-business.

"If you approach it the wrong way, you'll get bad will. If you approach it the right way, you'll get goodwill. So there are do's and don'ts. But to become involved, it's a simple value-value thing. You know: you're not putting any money out, we're not putting any money out, our value is that we get the benefit of your interesting insights into things, your benefit is you get the value of the goodwill of the people who are listening who say, 'Ah, Richard Worzel's a great guy!' And when they see your book, they probably pick it up, okay? Usenetwork is the same way. If you have something to contribute to the group, contribute it without asking for anything other than goodwill. And if you're subtle and polite about it, you can certainly mention in your conversation in the group, that if they'd like more information, or if they'd like to get involved in this project that you're doing, they're welcome to check you out at www.your-site. It's really easy to do, it takes a minimal amount of time if you know what you're doing, because you know your product. People always appreciate the value of having an expert around if you're not obnoxious about it. That's easy, free technique number one.

"Easy, free technique number two that is often overlooked is to find any and all Web sites that are similar but not in competition with what you're doing. Then contact the owner, or designer, or Webmaster and politely say, 'I have a site that would probably be of interest and value to people who are visiting your site. I know you have a site that, conversely, would be of interest to my visitors. Can we exchange links?' And again, this is the way the Internet has worked for the past five or six years, but people suddenly get big ideas about bulk e-mails because they think that's going to work. Like, if a party was going in before you walked in the front door, you wouldn't just walk in and try to dominate the conversation. Yet that's what's happening with the Internet today, and it's causing problems.

"So, these are established, polite ways of doing things, and they work. And you can have crossed links with sites that have much higher traffic than yours, particularly if your site has some free value. So, again, it's a question of giving something away to get something back. If the only thing your site does is sell something, there aren't a lot of people that are going to want a link to it. But if your site sells something, and also has some extra added value, a site with much, much heavier traffic than yours that doesn't have the insight or the information that you give away for free as part of your site, might be very interested in linking to you. Suddenly you funnel massive amounts of traffic to your site, for free.

"And I guess the third one is to keep in touch with the people who have visited you in the past. Make sure that your site—and this is a simple thing to do—has the ability to capture from a visitor, if they're interested, their e-mail address and their name. Then routinely send out a newsletter. Again, this is simple and free because e-mail doesn't have postage charges. In doing that, you're building a community. If they've asked you to put them on this list because they're interested in your site, there will be no bad will generated by the fact that you're sending them unsolicited mail—because it's not unsolicited. And if it has value, and it's not just a sales flyer, or if you're announcing a sale they might be interested in, you're bringing back the same customers, and you're keeping yourself fresh in their minds, so you're getting word of mouth. And word of mouth is a great thing on the Internet, like it is anywhere else.

"All these things can be accomplished in three hours a week with no money spent, with a modem and a 486 [i.e., an obsolete computer]. And if you're diligent, and you have a product that has value, you can be quite successful, I think.

"The fourth great way to promote requires more *chutzpah* [guts or nerve] than time or money, and that is to promote yourself to the media. Right now, any time someone talks about a site they've launched, if it's got something even slightly interesting, it may be of interest to the big media, the medium media, or the small media, but trust me, someone in the media is interested.

"There's always a radio show that needs a guest. There's always a newspaper that needs a little article. It may not be the big newspapers, it may be a community newspaper. Again, if you're doing something that's of benefit to cats and dogs, maybe there's a publication on cats and dogs that has two or three column inches that need something in there. And your press release or your phone call to the editor that does the on-line section of the cats and dogs magazine, gets you a piece of coverage. Internet is sexy right now, no matter what you're doing, and if you're brave enough and personable enough, you can get attention.

"The fifth great way is always make sure that you put your Web address or your e-mail address on every printed piece of material that goes out anywhere.

"There are two other thoughts that come to mind that pertain to doing this right. Number one, invest in actually getting that domain name for yourself because if you use a free hosting service like geocities.com, and your address is "geocities.com/~abc123," instead of "dogsandcats.com," then obviously it's going to be harder to find and harder to remember. But more importantly, when geocities.com starts to suck speedwise, or they tell you that you've overrun your allotted number of free hits and you've got to move somewhere else, you've got to change your address. A domain name is portable, so you must invest that $100 with InterNIC and buy a domain name."

Getting paid, as described earlier, can also be a problem, so Epstein had a suggestion on that, too, if you aren't set up to accept credit cards: "If you can't pay by credit card over the Web, you can go to companies that have a 1-900 [phone] number and they'll give you a proprietary overdial number. So your clients call the 900 number, and punch in site number 13579, and it says 'This is Hope's Metaphysical Mindscape. If you want to have $10 put on your phone bill, and get an access number to have your fortune told, please press 1 now.' And it gets invoiced by phone bill instead of by credit card. So there are a number of ways to collect the money without having to be a bank yourself, or whatever."

P itfalls

"No matter how small your venture is," says Epstein, "in terms of its technical complexity or how much you're spending on advertising, or whatever, one of the things users are most sensitive to is how long it takes for them to download your site. If they've used a search engine, and they're checking 10 sites to find the one that appeals most, if your site takes too long to load, they're gone! Even at the simplest level of doing business on the Internet, that is still a critical, critical factor. I mean, who wants to wait at a restaurant that they've never eaten in before, that has no reputation, if there's a line-up at the door, and they don't take reservations? Stupid. Human nature says they won't do it, not if there's another one right next door with no line-up, which is what it's like to be listed on a search engine. The site addresses returned by a search engine are all in a row, so the first time you hit a line-up at one, you backpedal and go on to the next one.

"So anyone, including the baby-talk, baby-steps Web sites, must pick a Web hosting place that has the delivery speeds. And the minute that their friends start to tell them that their Web site takes too long to happen, they have to ask themselves two questions: Is their design inadequate? This means, you know, their graphics are too big or their code is bad, which then may be worth investing even just a little bit of money, like $100 bucks, to get a graphic artist to shrink down their graphics so they're very quick to deliver. Or is it your access provider? Did you go with the guy who's $50 a year for Web hosting instead of the guy who's $150, but you're slow instead of fast? Big, big, big decision-making influence.

"The next big mistake is SPAM [junk e-mail messages]. It is very, very tempting if you're a small guy to be seduced by one of these companies on the Internet that says, 'I will e-mail your site address and information about what you do to a million Internet users for $100.' This is one of the biggest scams on the Internet. Not only is it terribly destructive to the Internet [because it clogs up messaging capacity], but it doesn't even deliver the value that they say they offer. What invariably happens when they take your $100 and mail your e-mail out to however many people they actually mail it to, the response is so overwhelmingly negative that two things happen. Number one, you lose your Internet access when your provider shuts you down because of all the angry, hostile, and sometimes damaging mail that comes back. Number two, your company instantly gets a reputation as being a non-Internet friendly company. And forget about getting on newsgroups, or exchanging links with anybody—you just blew that, too. But it's so tempting: $100 and we'll send you to a million e-mail addresses, and that is guaranteed failure. It's also illegal in many places, but first off, it's just a bad business decision."

So, should you be aiming at the Internet? Well, as with other businesses, you need to do your homework. What kind of product or service will you offer? Will you be able to offer it in an Internet-friendly kind of way or will you be fighting against the medium? Do you know how you'll get paid? How much competition is there for your kind of product? Do you have a reliable guru to help you? Are you using the Internet just because it's sexy, or is this truly the right medium?

Earl's right: this is a gold rush, and most of the people who made money during gold rushes were the people who sold things to the miners—not the miners themselves.

There is enormous opportunity here. But I guarantee that it won't come easily.

F ranchising

A franchise is a relationship defined by contract where a local representative follows a business plan and uses resources developed by the franchisor to market the franchisor's products or services in a local market. Probably the most famous example of a franchise is McDonald's, where franchisees pay for the right to use the name, fame, advertising, marketing expertise, and business management knowledge of the McDonald's Corporation.

Each side of the relationship brings something to the party. In theory, the franchisee (who is the individual that operates the local outlet) provides capital to expand the market reach of the franchise beyond what the company might be able to do on its own (although there are other ways of raising capital for good companies), and, more importantly, the energy, initiative, local management, and hard work to make the location or locations work. The franchise company (or franchisor) provides a detailed business plan, a brand name, management training, marketing expertise, advice on location selection (or even a pre-selected site), plus business relationships for financing and supply of necessary materials and equipment. Hopefully, the franchisor also supplies a market position in the mind of potential customers that will draw them to the franchise location.

In simple terms, the individual supplies the money and work, and the company supplies the brains and experience. In theory, if you're looking at a franchise, then you're looking at buying a do-it-yourself business kit. Each step is laid out. You don't have to find a winning formula, devise a business plan, invent a product or service, nor convince a bank that it is a sound idea. In a good franchise, all of this is already done; all you have to do is add cash, initiative, and hard work.

That's the theory. The practice is different for several reasons. First, there is no "just add water" success. Even in a proven franchise formula you must learn the local market; adapt your franchise to local needs; stretch the business formula provided by the franchisor to make the most of your resources; provide solid, disciplined effort; and manage your employees, which is emotionally just as hard as managing employees in any other situation. In fact, the major advantage of a good franchise is that it's all been done before, so you know it's possible.

The most important thing to be aware of is that a franchise is governed almost exclusively by the contract you sign with the company providing the franchise. That means if you sign a contract that allows the company to tie you up and rob you blind, then you're stuck with it. You have very little recourse if you sign a bad agreement, other than to go bankrupt (which will probably cost you everything you own) or wind up on the wrong end of a lawsuit. Consumer protection laws don't apply and won't protect you unless the company has actually committed fraud, in which case you may be able to sue them (or not, depending on how hard they are to catch, and how much money you can spend on lawyers). So the same advice applies to buying a franchise as starting your own business from scratch: do your homework.

T he crucial part of a franchise relationship

A good franchise works because both parties benefit. Indeed, sound franchise agreements are clearly arranged to ensure that one party benefits only if both do.

Buying a franchise usually means paying an upfront franchise fee, buying supplies and equipment from standardized suppliers, and paying a royalty to the company, usually based on the volume of sales. In a good franchise arrangement, the company will make all of its profit from the last of these three elements, because then the company and the individual both benefit at the same time. However, all three elements carry risks, and need to be examined carefully.

If the company makes too much money from the franchise fee, then it may not really care whether you succeed or fail. In fact, if you fail, it may be able to resell your franchise and take another franchise fee from another sucker. Or, if you don't have a protected territory, it may be tempted to sell another franchise close to yours, causing both to fail. What you really want to pay for in a franchise fee basically just covers the company's cost of helping you establish yourself in business. Of course, this can be hard to determine as you probably won't have access to the company's accounts.

If the supplier relationships mandated under the contract allow the company to make too much of a profit on supplies or equipment sold to you, or too much rent on the location you are required to take, then you may wind up working your heart out just to stay alive, and find that all the profit is being scooped up by the company, its designated suppliers, or the landlord. And since you'll be locked into a multi-year contract, you'll be stuck with it—with bankruptcy or a lawsuit as your only alternatives.

Finally, if the royalty rate is too high, you may work hard to make a profit—and then wind up giving it all to the company in royalties.

So, how do you protect against these things? By thoroughly researching possible franchises, and by hiring a top-notch franchise lawyer.

"I TELL PEOPLE TO INVESTIGATE before they invest," says Paul Jones, a franchise lawyer with the law firm of Miller Thomson in Toronto, "just as they should for stock market investments. In fact, this is even more important as the franchise will probably become their livelihood. This is not a passive investment, it's as active as a job.

"A good place to start is to buy books and publications about franchises. Here in Canada, I'd recommend that people buy *The Canadian Business Franchise Handbook*, published by CGB Publishing, and *The CBF Directory* by the same people. They should also call the Canadian Franchise Association (905-625-2896), who can give them a lot of material to guide them. In fact, if they don't contact the Association, they really haven't done the work they need to do. They should also get the *1999 Franchise Annual*, or whatever the current edition is, published by *Info Franchise News*. It doesn't have articles about franchising in them, but it does have a huge list of different franchises so they can figure out what their options are, and who to contact about each on. As well, there are a couple of books on the subject that are okay, like *Franchising in Canada*, by the Self-Counsel Series, and *The Complete Canadian Franchise Guide* by Douglas Gray and Norman Friend. I don't use either one a lot, but they're not bad.

"Another one I'm keen on is an American book called *Franchising 101: The Complete Guide to Evaluating, Buying & Growing Your Franchise Business*, edited by Ann Dugan, a business school professor who once owned a pizza franchise. Each chapter is by a different person and deals with a different subject. Some of the chapters are written by business school professors, who may not have as much hands-on experience, but then again, how shall I say it, they may be more objective than most of the other people in the game.

"You want to look through lots of different kinds of franchises, looking for those that might suit you, and those where the franchise is gaining in popularity rather than those that are on the decline. Remember that you're buying an asset here— the right to operate that franchise for a defined period of time. Many franchisees buy a franchise, build it up, then sell it at a profit to someone else. So if your franchise becomes more valuable as the franchisor's name becomes better known and their products or services more popular, then you can benefit from that improvement as well as from your own efforts."

T he major pitfalls in picking a franchise

I asked Jones what the major dangers were in selecting a franchise.

"The greatest danger is either the franchisor or the industry chosen, because it's not always the franchisor's fault that it doesn't pan out. I mean, you're tying yourself into a system and if buggy-whips aren't selling any more, then the buggy-whip franchise really isn't worth very much.

"Next, the Internet is changing everything, so watch out. Franchisors and non-franchisors alike are just wondering where the hell it's going, and the answer is that nobody really knows at this stage.

"People aren't going to order that many hamburgers over the Internet, I don't think. Pizza, maybe, but that's not that much different from ordering through a central telephone line. There are other products that might be affected more. You know, a bunch of pills in a bottle, for example, the company might cut out the middle man and try to get customers to order from the manufacturer by mail and the Internet. If that happens, what's going to happen to your store? That works for commodities; it doesn't work as well for anything with a requirement for service. Selling is a little bit more intricate than just ordering.

"In fact, that's another danger. If you've got no experience in retail, then, well you've got a lot to learn. The franchisor can't supply street smarts. There's no joke about it; you're an independent contractor, and there are some things the franchise just can't do for you.

"The next danger," says Jones, "is that the franchise just doesn't go anywhere, and you've bought in depending on the fact that this is going to become some sort of chain expanding into your region, and without the chain you're stuck because there's no brand recognition in your area.

"If you're buying a greenfield [new] location instead of buying an established one, it can be dangerous. Is that the right place? If so, how do you know that it's the right place? How do you know that there's going to be enough traffic to support your business?

"Personal suitability is a major danger. For example, if you pick up a beauty salon franchise, you're likely to be working with a distinctive type of people. Do you really want to deal with the staffing problems you'll have with those kinds of people? Is that your culture? If it isn't, then stay out.

"And the same goes with the classic hamburger franchise—do you fit the mould? Are you a Rotarian, community-service, keep-the-teenagers-happy sort of guy? Or are you really a sort of an intellectual that wants to run things your own way and not follow the crowd? Do you want to do the things that go with running a hamburger stand for the kind of people who come into hamburger stands?"

And once you've considered the possibilities, I asked, how do you then choose a franchise?

"You shouldn't just pick one franchise, but you should go through a lot of possibilities, coming down to something like four or five that you're willing to get serious about. Then you start doing to the real research.

"When you have narrowed your search, forget about the paper and legal stuff. Get on a plane, fly down to L.A., or wherever the franchise head office is located, and meet the people behind the franchise. Get to know them personally. Decide if you'd like to be married to them, because that's what a franchise is really like. It's a partnership, in a non-legal sense, that works (when it works well) like a good marriage.

"If you don't think the same way, get on well together, have similar values, and like each other, then the odds are the relationship won't work any better after you're committed. Don't just think about money; think about how the relationship is going to work.

"Ask yourself:'Do I like this industry? Can I see myself wearing that uniform, and doing this kind of work for, say, the next

20 years?' Where is this franchisor in this industry? If they're the first into the market for this kind of product or service, they may be too expensive, or they may be peaking and on the decline. If they're fourth or fifth in the industry, they may have such a small share of the market that it will be impossible to make a living.

"How about the people? Are they committed to making the franchise system work? Are they going to be there for the long haul? I remember one start-up franchise system where the owner was a 65-year-old man. I couldn't see him putting his heart and soul into it for the next 20 years—and there wasn't anybody else to pick it up after him. Are the head office people good team players who will support you, advise you, accommodate your differences to some extent? I mean, if you're the franchisee in Yellowknife, or Chinatown, you don't necessarily run by the same rules as you do in, I don't know, suburban Edmonton or Toronto. So ask yourself: Would you like to be on their team?

"Talk to the franchisees, but be careful about it. Not many people will give you the unvarnished truth, because to do so might be to admit that they've made a mistake. Listen to the meaning behind their words, ask about problems they hadn't anticipated when they started. They may be smiling, but are they happy, or are they just putting on a brave face? Divining the truth isn't easy, so dig.

"There's a trend emerging where one of the leading franchisees are asked to evaluate potential new franchisees for the company. The company may ask you to work for no wages in a store for a week so that they can evaluate whether you'd make a good franchisee. And that's a good opportunity for you to decide if you like the lifestyle, as well."

Clearly, just because you've decided to buy a franchise, it doesn't mean that there isn't going to be any hard work. Quite the contrary; you're going to have to do almost as much homework as you would if you started your own business from the ground up. It will just be more focused, with more specific questions than you would have if you were on your own.

B e prepared to pay for your research

"I tell people that they had better be prepared to pay for up to four sets of negotiations with four sets of legal fees. And I don't just say that because I want to collect more than one fee. You need to know what's in your franchise agreement, because it's going to rule your life if you sign it. If you find, in the process of investigation and negotiation, that a particular franchise is not right for you, or that the franchise agreement is not going to work for you, or that the location is wrong, then don't feel that you're trapped and have to go ahead with that one just because you've got some sunk costs in the legal work, and haven't budgeted for a review of another franchise."

Echoing something I said earlier about starting your own business, it will be cheaper to pay the legal fees on a franchise you don't sign on with than to go into a bad franchise and fail. Failure is expensive.

"I've seen agreements, such as one for a beauty salon, where the agreement specified that the company decided how much inventory you were going to carry. That's potentially an invitation to disaster, because if they [the franchisor] decided they needed some more money for some reason, they could force you to buy inventory from them, whether you can sell it or not, just to fill their pockets.

"You may also notice something about the location that requires a local variation to the franchise agreement. Now franchisors don't like to change agreements. Not only does it mean legal costs, but it also means that they may wind up having to explain to other franchisees why you got an exception and they didn't. Again, it's like a marriage; parents can't treat their children differently, because it's an invitation to disaster. But if they're good, and you really do need an exception or a change, they'll understand and accept it.

"Of course, someone like McDonald's, that's been around the block and seen just about everything, and that has such a large system—well, you can forget about getting them to change their agreement. You either accept it or you don't get one of their franchises."

W hat to do once you've made the commitment

"Once you've bought a franchise, and made the commitment, then assuming that you're right about it being the right company, and the right team, then implementation becomes key. If you're selling food, then food costs and labour costs are crucial. If you get lots of traffic at lunch and supper, but you've got your restaurant fully staffed in the middle of the afternoon when the place is empty, it's going to eat up your profits.

"It's about being organized, learning the key cost and profit variables and managing them; watching for trends in your local market and adapting to them; and keeping your accounts straight so you know how you're doing.

"But at the end of the day, it's up to you to make the franchise work. And an extraordinary franchisee can make spectacular sales.

"It was a dead-end hamburger location in a four-unit strip-mall in Scarborough [Ontario] that taught me that. This guy bought in to an existing location. He just looked at the mall; the landlord wasn't paying attention: paper flying around, weeds, stuff like that. So this guy said, 'It's not just about me, it's about this mall. What do I do?' You can't sell food in a place like that; nobody wants to eat food in a place like that. So he started to clean up first, then went and negotiated a deal with the landlord where he would be the property manager for the mall. And he went out there and ran around and policed the area in the sense of picking up paper, and a bunch of other things to just make the mall work. He also did other things inside the store with labour, and food, and put all the pieces together and got sales way up. Then he sold it, and got his money out.

"The next manager who came in had 18 stores, and woof! sales dropped because it didn't get the management attention. But the guy was at least a wheeler-dealer in assets, and he sold to a couple of immigrant investors who looked at the sales and thought they could do it. Of course, sales dropped further.

"But the two immigrant guys really hung in and went through a big fight with the landlord because they didn't understand what had happened to the mall. It took a long, hard fight, but they did eventually get the sales up to where they could justify what they paid for it.

"That's just one store. The store didn't move, and competition wasn't the big issue. I think what really happened was different managers. And it's about cleanliness, staffing, cost control, fliers, local marketing initiatives, and so on."

This story is important, so think about it. This one franchise had three operators each with very different results.

What it all really comes down to is you, how well you manage, how hard you work, how innovative you are about attracting sales—and making sure you've done your homework and are buying the right franchise. Even though you're buying a formula, that doesn't mean you can cruise to success. Nothing will let you to do that.

There is no such thing as a secure job, even if you buy one as a franchise. As with everything else, you create your own security.

Ⓝ etwork marketing

Network marketing (also called multi-level marketing, relationship marketing, and various other things) is a brilliant idea that should enjoy more success than it does. Unfortunately, it has been dogged by so much controversy, because of unprofessional conduct and poor execution by its practitioners, that many people tend to reject it without ever thinking about it seriously.

In a successful network marketing system, such as Amway Corporation's, you can make profits of almost $34,000 annually while personally selling less than $4500 worth of products. Moreover, you can do this with an initial investment of less than $200—and just walk away if you don't like the experience. I'll work through this example in detail later on.

A network system works by having distributors both sell products and recruit additional distributors. The recruiting distributor then makes a profit on both her own sales and receives what amounts to an override commission on the sales of any distributor she recruits. If the second distributor recruits additional distributors, then the original distributor makes a small profit on the total sales volume of the second distributor's entire group. If you sponsor enough distributors, and build a big enough group, this network can turn into serious money.

All of this is perfectly legal and very simple in concept, but it is not easy and it is not a get-rich-quick scheme.

Network marketing has become very popular for certain kinds of products, and is particularly successful with immigrant groups and in developing countries. Among the more successful and better-known companies in North America are Amway (which I will use as a case study in the discussion below), Mary Kay (cosmetics and skin care), Shaklee (nutritional supplements), NuSkin (cosmetics and skin care), and Excel Communications (long-distance telephone service). Although statistics for network marketers are not broken out specifically from other, non-network direct sales organizations by the Direct Sellers Association of Canada, direct sales organizations as a group had about 650,000 sales agents who sold about $1.5 billion in products and services in 1997.

Let's first discuss the common misconceptions, advantages, and pitfalls of network systems, and then we'll consider the key factors in weighing them as an alternative.

P opular misconceptions

Let's start by saying that it is crucial to deal with a reputable company, such as those I've mentioned above. If you have any question about whether a particular distributor system is reputable, contact the Direct Sellers Association in Etobicoke, Ontario (416-679-9555). Various scam artists package themselves as bona fide network marketers, but their intention is fraud rather than sales.

Now to the misconceptions:

1 It's a pyramid swindle

The diagram of a network marketing system often resembles a pyramid (as does a traditional corporate organization chart), and to those who don't understand how it works, a description of a network may sound like a pyramid. However, pyramids are illegal, whereas networks are as legal as ice cream. The major difference is that distributors in a network only make money if products or services are sold to an end user, whereas a pyramid scheme purports to pay you for recruiting people, requires you to buy expensive training sessions and materials, or sells you at "wholesale cost" a lot of inventory that you may never be able to sell and cannot return. When a pyramid runs out of suckers, nobody makes any money, but a successful network can make profits without ever recruiting another individual through the continued sales of products or services.

An easy way to tell the difference between the two is that if you are sponsored into a network, you can make more money than the person who sponsors you if you sell more products than they do. You can also make money without ever recruiting anyone else. So networks are *not* pyramids.

2   This is an easy way to get rich

Well, network marketing is certainly a simple formula, but that doesn't mean it's easy. And it may make you rich, but if so, it will only come after a lot of disciplined, hard work over a period of years—not days or weeks. In fact, one of the biggest criticisms of network distributor groups is that they tend to oversell the potential of their system in order to attract new recruits, to the point where people start imagining flying around in their own 747 jets and owning mansions in the south of France before they've even started working. Raising expectations to such unrealistic heights is a major mistake, and one of the areas where I believe that network marketing systems do fall down through unprofessional conduct. Granted, many people have made quite a lot of money from network marketing systems, but they are in the very small minority, as I'll discuss in a moment.

3   This is nickel-and-dime stuff; there's no serious money in it

This is a half-truth. Amway of Canada commissioned a study of their distributors in their fiscal 1995-96 year, and found that the average compensation for a participant in the Amway sales and marketing plan was $66 a month. However, that doesn't tell you much since a large percentage (there are no statistics on this, but I suspect it might be 50% or more) of people who hold Amway distributorships are either inactive or merely buy the products for their own use at wholesale and don't try to sell them to others. On the other hand, the largest annual bonus ever paid by Amway of Canada was $1,069,701, and the largest monthly performance bonus paid was

$55,899. Moreover, while Microsoft Corporation is responsible for creating more millionaires than any other corporation in history, Amway Corporation is reported to be in second place. That doesn't mean that everyone will make that kind of money. Most of the potential of a network marketing system has to do with how seriously and professionally you execute the marketing plan.

4 Networks exploit people

Absolutely true. However, it's true in exactly the same way that corporations profit from (or exploit) the efforts of their employees. And in case you didn't know it, if your employer isn't making a profit on your efforts (i.e., getting more from your efforts than they pay you), your job will quickly disappear.

The override commissions paid by network marketing systems are no different from the override commissions that a sales manager in a computer store or a stock brokerage firm makes on the sales of the people that work for him.

5 Network organizations are cults

Network distributors are independent contractors, and have a formal, but arm's-length, relationship with the company that manufactures or supplies their products or services. The manufacturer has little control over distributor behaviour beyond that—nor should they. Some distributor organizations hold sales or recruiting meetings that can resemble Bible-belt revival meetings, complete with personal testimonies, stories of Damascus-like conversions, chanting, singing, and sloganeering. Some people find this tacky, shocking, and distasteful. However, if you've ever attended the annual sales meeting of a major computer, car, or golf-ball manufacturer, you'll find much of the same hoopla, although such companies usually spend more money on glamour and sizzle than distributor organizations do. This type of activity has more to do with motivating salespeople than it does with cult activity.

6   Their products are grossly overpriced

Maybe, maybe not. Again, take Amway Corporation. Their literature says they pay out an average of 55% of each dollar of sales in commission to their distributor network. Some people think this means that the retail prices of their products have to be highly inflated to accommodate such high commissions. However, in retail sales, a mark-up of more than 100%—sometimes much more—is not unusual, so in this regard network commissions are not overly rich.

The real test involves valid price comparisons. (Note, though, that it's important to compare apples to apples. For example, Amway markets many products that are highly concentrated. When diluted to usable strength they are often cheaper than off-the-shelf products that have a lower sticker price.) However, there's nothing that says a company has to price its products competitively. If you're considering buying a distributorship, then you certainly don't want to choose one where you must sell overpriced goods. So look carefully at the product line you are thinking about representing, much as you would for a franchise.

7   I don't like selling

There's no question about it, selling is difficult. It's especially hard until you figure out that people are not rejecting you personally, but are instead rejecting what you're offering. Until you understand this distinction it can feel like personal rejection when it's not, and it can lacerate your ego.

Anyone going into business for themselves will have to sell something, whether to investors, the bank, their employees, or their customers. In fact, I'll go further: to be successful in today's world, everyone in business will have to sell to someone as part of their career management. But direct sales is the sharp end of the stick— sales in its purest form—and it may not suit you. However, sales technique can be learned, and if you plan to succeed, it must be learned. There are lots of resources in this field—books, tapes, seminars, personal trainers—and only one excuse: cowardice. But if you are willing to try, you can become an accomplished sales-person, no matter what your background is.

8   I might as well sell life insurance

This is true, up to a point, because in both systems you can pro-duce residual income streams. Moreover, selling life insurance does offer one advantage: most insurance companies provide profes-sional sales training, which many distributor organizations do not. However, if you're selling life insurance (or mutual funds, or what-ever), you are working for someone else, and your destiny is not ultimately under your control. In a network marketing system, as long as you live up to the terms of the agreement, no one can take it away from you.

9   It's not my cup of tea

This is a valid concern, and a sound reason not to own a network distributorship. But before you discard network marketing as an alternative, consider the advantages.

The advantages of network marketing

Let me again use the marketing system of Amway Corporation as my example. Amway is one of the oldest and most successful net-work marketing systems, and is widely imitated by other compa-nies, largely because it works so well.

The classic presentation of the Amway marketing system resembles Figure 6.1 on the following page.

All the figures are approximate, and this is a simplistic example for illustration purposes, although the approach is based on the actual bonus system. To keep the explanation as simple as possible while giving adequate detail, I've made the following two assumptions:

Figure 6-1 **An Amway Network Example**

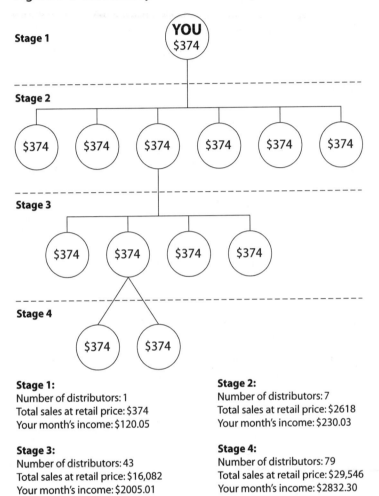

Stage 1:
Number of distributors: 1
Total sales at retail price: $374
Your month's income: $120.05

Stage 2:
Number of distributors: 7
Total sales at retail price: $2618
Your month's income: $230.03

Stage 3:
Number of distributors: 43
Total sales at retail price: $16,082
Your month's income: $2005.01

Stage 4:
Number of distributors: 79
Total sales at retail price: $29,546
Your month's income: $2832.30

1 Saving money is equivalent to making money. Most distributors use their own products, which they obviously buy at the wholesale price (which Amway calls "distributor cost" or "business value"). Hence, instead of *making* a profit of 30%, which is the difference between the wholesale and retail price, they are *saving* this 30% by not paying it to someone else on the products they buy.

2 The performance bonuses are calculated based on the Amway business value (BV). In this example, I've assumed that BV is 30% less than the suggested retail price. However, products or services from other companies distributed by Amway carry a much lower direct profit.

Stage 1

Throughout this example, you are the first distributor at the top of this diagram, and you start by selling or using $374 of products per month, valued at the suggested retail price. On this, you make a 30% profit, or $112.20, plus a performance bonus on total group sales, which at this level is 3% of distributor cost, as shown in the bonus schedule in Table 6-1 (below). This produces the following profit: $374 retail price × 70% to convert retail price to distributor cost = $261.80 × 3% bonus = $7.85 plus $112.20 direct profit, for a total of $120.05.

Table 6-1 **Amway Performance Bonus Schedule**

Monthly group sales volume	% Performance Bonus at suggested retail price
$28,071 and up	25%
22,457	23%
14,971	21%
9,357	18%
5,614	15%
3,743	12%
2,246	9%
1,123	6%
374	3%

Stage 2

Suppose you recruit ("sponsor") six people (so that you have seven people in your group, including you), and each person sells or uses the equivalent of $374 worth of products a month at retail value. Your personal profit is still $112.20, but now your group volume is $2618 (i.e., 7 distributors × $374 each), which qualifies for a 9% bonus, or $164.93 (calculated as: $2618 at retail × 70% to convert to distributor cost = $1832.60 × 9% bonus = $164.93). From this, you pay six bonuses at 3%, or $7.85, to each of the distributors you've sponsored, totalling $47.10. This leaves you with a net bonus of $117.83, plus your $112.20 direct profit for a total income of $230.03.

Stage 3

Now suppose the six people you sponsored each sponsor four people (meaning your group now consists of 43 people, including you), and that everyone sells or uses the equivalent of $374 at retail. Then your total profit is $2005.01. (Your total group volume at retail is now 43 distributors × $374 retail each = $16,082. You receive a performance bonus calculated as $16,082 at retail × 70% to convert to cost = $11,257.40 × 21% bonus rate = $2364.05. Each of the six distributors you sponsored has a group volume of: 5 distributors × $374 each = $1870. This means you pay six sets of performance bonuses calculated as: $1870 at retail × 70% to convert to distributor cost = $1309 × 6% bonus rate = $78.54 per group × 6 groups = $471.24 in total. This leaves you with a bonus of $1892.81, plus your own direct profit of $112.20 for a total of $2005.01.)

Stage 4

Finally, suppose each of these four distributors sponsors two people (by which time you have 79 people in your group), each of whom sells or uses $374 a month at retail value. Then your total income is $2832.30. (Total group volume is 79 distributors × $374 each at retail = $29,546, on which you receive a group performance bonus calculated as $29,546 retail × 70% to convert to distributor cost = $20,682.20 × 25% bonus rate = $5170.55. From this, you pay your six distributors a total of: 13 people per group × $374/distributor = $4862 at retail × 70% to convert to distributor cost = $3403.40 × 12% bonus rate = $408.41 bonus per group × 6 groups = $2450.45 total payout. This leaves you with a bonus of $2720.10, plus your own personal profit of $112.20, for a total monthly income of $2832.30.)

If you were to have a group that produced this result consistently over the course of a year, then you would be making an annual income of $33,987.62 while selling or using only $4488 worth of products yourself at retail. Where else can you make that kind of return?

How realistic is this model? I'm sure reality is much messier; I doubt if there are any groups that precisely fit this structure. However, Amway reports that of the approximately 75,000 distributors who renew their distributorships at the end of each year, just over 1000 of them reach the 25% bonus bracket consistently. This is a ratio of one distributor at the highest bonus level for 74 others, which fits almost exactly with the plan outlined above, which shows one distributor at the highest bonus level with a group of 78 others. Accordingly, the marketing plan seems to be quite realistic, and you should gauge your expectations accordingly.

There are other bonuses on top of the ones outlined above as your group expands in numbers and sales volume, but this sets the tone: you are paid bonuses on the total group volume, plus profits on what you sell yourself. Now let's look at the advantages and disadvantages of this approach.

A dvantages of network marketing

The first, and perhaps most important, advantage is that the idea is simple, and you have a comprehensive blueprint how to create a business. Remember all the brainstorming and market research we went through in earlier chapters in an effort to help you find a business that was right for you? None of that is necessary here, because it's all been done already. That doesn't mean you will necessarily like this business, but at least it's clear and straightforward.

Moreover, the kinds of products that are sold are widely or universally used: soaps and cleaning agents; non-perishable foods; food supplements, vitamins, and nutritional products; long-distance telephone service; cosmetics and skin care products, and so forth. Amway Corporation sells about 500 products they manufacture themselves, plus another 6000 products and services supplied by other companies which have lower profit margins than the Amway products, including AT&T long-distance service, Cantel cellular service, clothing, food, and electronic equipment. Almost all of the products sold through networks have two major characteristics: they are widely used (and hence, are relatively easy to sell), and they are used up and have to be repurchased, leading to repeat sales once a customer relationship has been established.

The next most important advantage—and it's a huge one—is the size of investment required: there virtually isn't any. The cost of buying an Amway distributorship, for example, is currently around $150. Since all reputable network marketing organizations make their money from the sale of products, rather than from recruiting fees or dumping inventory on their distributors, the cost of securing a distributorship is almost always less than $1000. You could easily spend many times that just on legal fees or market research in establishing your own business or researching a franchise before ever even starting. You might also risk almost all of your savings, your house, and all of your assets in a start-from-scratch business, depending on the kind of business you start. If it fails, then you may well lose everything you own.

The same is true with franchising: you will pay tens or hundreds of thousands of dollars to secure a franchise. You'll probably go in hock for everything you own to a bank to secure a line of credit.

If you decide you don't like it once you're committed, it may well cost you everything.

In contrast, suppose you buy an Amway distributorship and work at it for six months, then decide that it's not for you, and give up. Your income drops to zero, but that's all (unless your group carries on without you, in which case you will continue to receive performance bonuses as long as you continue to renew your distributorship, even though you're not doing anything). Your risk is non-existent by normal business standards.

Next, you will have help. Just as your performance bonus is calculated on the total volume of everyone in your group, so your group's bonus is included in the total volume of the person who sponsored you, and their volume is included in the volume of the person who sponsored them, and so on up the lines of sponsorship. Accordingly, your sponsor has a powerful incentive to help you succeed, as does their sponsor, and their sponsor, and so on.

Of course, this help is only useful to the extent that the people involved are skilled. Indeed, when I said earlier that unprofessional conduct and poor execution were the worst flaws of network marketing, I was also referring to the low level of professionalism that too often passes for "help" in many network marketing organizations. This means that you want to choose your sponsor carefully if you decide to go into network marketing.

ⓣ he pitfalls of network marketing

Picking up on that last point, the key pitfall in network marketing is people. If you are sponsored by someone who is unprofessional and you can't find anyone above you in the organization with whom you want to work, then you're on your own. Moreover, if you sponsor people who are unprofessional, then you are pretty much saddled with them. You can't even fire them, as they aren't your employees. (I suppose you could refuse to deal with them, although I'm not sure how distributorship agreements deal with that.)

The next pitfall is that it's easy to treat a network distributorship as a toy or a hobby, which means that people often fail to take it seriously. I mean, how much status does a business that costs $150 and sells cleaning products or cosmetics have? How impressive is it? But if you don't treat it seriously, conduct yourself professionally, and expect respect from people, then you will find yourself desperate to recruit anybody at all and you'll be ashamed to talk about it to people whom you do respect. The result is that you will sponsor people whom you would never consider going into partnership with, and they will be difficult to work with, unprofessional in their own conduct, and sponsor more just like them. In network terms, this is called "sponsoring down," and it leads to a poorly structured organization populated with people who aren't interested in or capable of working hard, but want to get rich quick. This is one of the main reasons why networks have such a bad reputation and why they disintegrate when reality sets in.

Accordingly, remember that the people you work with, both above and below you, will define the nature of your business. You should be just as cautious about selecting the people whom you recruit and are recruited by as you would be in selecting a partner for a partnership. You may not have much money at stake, but you will certainly devote a lot of personal time and energy to it—and while you can replace money, you can never replace time.

Another pitfall is that you have to accept that you are in the business of selling—just as anyone in business today has to sell to someone. I've seen distributors in network systems who almost wriggle with embarrassment when you ask them what they sell, and go into verbal contortions to avoid admitting that they are, in fact, selling a product or service.

If you are going into direct sales, then you should learn how to sell. This means you read books, listen to taped lectures by sales trainers, and attend sales training seminars. All of these things cost money, but they are all a small price to pay to learn how to look someone in the eye and feel proud about what you do, and be able to do so successfully and with confidence.

Some distributor organizations teach sales technique and bring in professional sales trainers to work with their people. Many, however, shy away from the whole concept of selling, and concentrate on creating large organizations of consumers, who buy the products for their own use, but sell very little of it to anyone else. As an outsider, I don't think this is a sustainable model for a serious, full-time business, and suspect that such organizations tend to fall apart over time, but then again, there are successful organizations that have been created that way.

Accordingly, if you are considering joining a network marketing organization, ask to examine the sales training materials that they use. Look for tools that will be useful in helping you learn how to sell professionally and successfully, not just motivational, rah-rah noise with very little content.

Finally, not enough organizations teach their distributors how to be profitable—focusing instead on the glamorous prospect of big money. That's why the turnover rate in network marketing is so high. Amway Corporation has the lowest rate of turnover of any direct sales marketing organization in North America, whether network or otherwise, yet it still loses about 40% of its distributors each year (most of them new distributors who try it and wash out, I suspect). This can be hard on you if you've worked hard to build an organization, only to see it collapse as people become discouraged and quit.

If, instead, new distributors were taught how to make a few hundred dollars in direct profit each month through their own sales, and how to establish a reliable group of customers, then they would be much more patient about waiting for the long-term prospects to materialize. This would also make them more confident that the distributorship they were offering to other people was valuable, and hence make them more choosy about whom they were willing to sponsor.

So the risks in network marketing are very different from almost any other kind of business. They are not primarily financial, as you aren't betting your life savings on your business. Instead the risks relate more to the emotional experience of being a distributor in an apparently low-status business, and dealing with the rejection that is an everyday part of selling products and recruiting new distributors.

Network marketing may not be for you. You need to do what I suggested when I discussed franchising: imagine yourself doing this for the next 20 years or so. Is this a lifestyle you would enjoy? Are these people you would like working with? Do you like where it might take you? If so, then research the company, its products, and its marketing system. Do they make sense, will they fit with who you are and who you want to become, and will they take you where you want to go?

Set a time limit and a realistic objective to gauge whether this system will produce the results you want. In doing so, remember that the classic pattern for a successful business is that it will lose money—potentially a lot of money—in its start-up year. It may break even in its second or third year. And it will only start to produce a decent living in the fifth year. Accordingly, if you've set your sights on owning your own yacht at the end of the first or second year, you'll almost certainly be disappointed. Not many businesses can offer that, so it's not a realistic goal.

And if you decide that this is a path you want to pursue, then do it wholeheartedly, and treat it like a serious business, not a hobby.

N etwork marketing and the Internet

Recall that in talking about franchising, Paul Jones discussed the possible effects of the Internet, which might allow companies to sell directly to the end-customer, bypassing the franchisees, and leaving them high and dry. The same may apply to network marketing. If the Amway Corporation, for instance, can develop enough of a Web presence to start building its volume of sales that it could bypass its distributor network, might they do it?

Well, as it turns out, the most devoted Amway customers are Amway distributors, as is usually the case with network marketing systems, so if the company bypassed their distributors, they'd also lose their best customers. Yet they can't afford to just ignore the Internet phenomenon either. So how are they handling it?

Amway and most other network marketing systems are still evolving their strategy in this area. As I understand it, the basic idea behind Amway's approach is that whenever someone buys an Amway product over the Internet and does not identify a distributor as being the sales agent, the company will use the customer's shipping address to identify the nearest distributor, and then give the distributor credit for the sale, even though they may have had no involvement with it. In other words, distributors will wind up making money for sales that they didn't even know happened.

It's an interesting concept, because what it does is make the distributor network more devoted than ever. It might preserve the network (and hence, the company's most devoted customers) while putting company resources behind the Internet, so that if the Internet becomes a major source of sales, the company participates in that growth.

Whether it's the right approach or whether any network marketing company has the right approach, remains to be seen. Moreover, the Internet is evolving so quickly, and has such enormous potential, that it's important to consider its effects in making any decision.

7 How Long Until You Can Order the Ferrari?

Most people don't have the patience or skills to fully scout their market, plan and test their marketing approach, then develop a complete business plan. If you've read this far without preparing to do these things, and don't intend to go back and do them before you start your business, then your odds of ever affording a Ferrari—or whatever else is important to you—are poor.

But if you are willing to force yourself to do these things, and do them properly, then you can give yourself similar odds to those I quoted earlier for proven franchises. If you know what steps to take and in which order, and you are certain that each step can be done successfully, then your plan will serve as a path to take you where you want to be. Now ask yourself: is the lifestyle you want worth the effort necessary to do this? If you can answer "yes," and follow it up with action, then the next question will seem slightly foolish: do you actually know what you want?

Lots of would-be entrepreneurs have only a hazy feeling that they'd like their life to be easier and simpler. They'd like a job to replace one they lost or one they can't find. They'd like a large enough income to pay the bills, put the kids through school, find a nursing home for their mother, and stop worrying about money. To many, this would be heaven. Others have grand fantasies of driving a fancy car, taking exotic vacations, and living a life of lazy affluence. I'll say more about lives of lazy affluence in the last chapter. For now, I want to zero in on the clarity you must have to turn your dreams into reality.

Y ou've got to be *driven!*

Motivation has become an overused word in business, but motivation is what pulls people through the tough spots. And there are two major kinds of motivation: dreams and dread. Let's start with dread, because I want to spend some time on dreams.

You can be haunted into success. I recall very clearly one time when a client explained to me what had motivated him to work as long and as hard as he had. He had built one of Canada's leading communications companies from scratch, and then sold it for hundreds of millions of dollars. I asked him what drove him to accomplish these things.

"It's very simple, Richard: fear," he explained. "We grew up poor, and my father died when I was in my teens. I just couldn't stand the thought of ever being poor again. It was fear that pulled me out of the ghetto I grew up in, and fear that forced me to smile at clients I wanted to strangle, and fear that made me push to get the things I needed to build the things I had to have."

And, I might add, it's that same fear that continues to drive him today, even though he's well into his fifties and has more than enough to retire and never work again. He reacted to his fear in a constructive way—and built a great business out of it.

But you don't have to be driven by fear. You can also succeed by following dreams.

MYRA AND HER FRIEND Carol Rosenfeld started a business in Carol's kitchen, preparing family recipes for items such as antipasto and mustard. This humble beginning launched Sable & Rosenfeld Foods into an international success story in premium gourmet foods.

In 1982, 10 years after they started the business together, Carol Rosenfeld asked Myra to buy her out because she couldn't keep up and didn't want to hold Myra back. They remained friends, but Myra was driven whereas Carol was merely interested. Myra wasn't driven by fear—but by her dreams.

"I want **BIG!**" Myra told me in 1988. "I want to be as big as General Foods. There's a terrific sense of power and achievement of being my own boss, so that even if I failed, I couldn't work for someone else.

"I'm a creative type and I love selling. I've never had any problem selling Sable & Rosenfeld products. But along the way, with all our enormous growth, the structure got left out. I hated doing that kind of thing—but I'm the boss! No one else is going to put the structures in place, so it's *got* to be me."

If Myra hadn't had the dream, she would never have bothered doing the things she hated. She would have let the business muddle along without structure, and accepted whatever results she got, but she was driven by wanting to be **BIG**.

W here did all the dreams go?

When you talk to people like Myra Sable, the excitement generated by their sense of purpose crackles around them. But when you talk to a "normal" person with a "normal" job, there's no excitement at all—everything's just going along, there's nothing to get excited about. Ho-hum, more bills to pay. Oh well, another day at work. Gosh, I wonder where I'll go for vacation this year. How many more years to retirement? Thank God it's Friday.

Dr. Rollo May is a psychotherapist and psychologist who has spent years trying to fathom the toughest mysteries of the human spirit. He has much to say on apathy and dreams, not all of it comforting:

> Apathy, operating like Freud's 'death instinct,' is a gradual letting-go of involvement until one finds that life itself has gone by.... To cease wishing is to be dead, or at least to inhabit a land of the dead ... [Yet] emptiness and vacuity and futility are greatest where all wishes are met. For this means that one stops wishing.... Life comes from physical survival, but the *good life* comes from what we care about.[1]

"To cease wishing is to be dead," says the good doctor, and he reminds me of a comment by Benjamin Franklin, one of my heroes: "Many men die at the age of 25, but aren't buried until they're 65."

Dreams fade. When we're kids, we dream big dreams, and aren't concerned if they're fantastic or outrageous. When we grow up, we've been disappointed too often, and hurt when we don't get what we dream about. To compensate, we scale down our dreams, get "realistic," and learn to "keep our feet on the ground." Too often this means that we don't have any dreams at all.

Try this experiment: the next time you're at a cocktail party or some other relatively relaxed gathering, ask your friends what they dream of achieving over the next 10 years. I predict that most of the answers will fall into three categories: vague, tame, or angry. The vague people will fumble for an answer—they haven't had any dreams for years. The tame ones know they're supposed to have dreams, but want to make sure that their dreams are easily attainable so they won't be disappointed. And the angry ones get upset with you because they don't want someone bringing up a subject they'd rather forget. They believe they won't get what they want out of life, but haven't yet accepted the blame for it.

But aren't dreams childish? Don't we mock people who are "dreamers"? After all, why wish for the moon when you know you can't have it? The answer is that without the wish, the reality never happens.

"A man will never do everything he dreams," said William James, the American psychologist and philosopher, "but he will never do *anything* he *doesn't* dream!"

 reams come first

For you to get excited about something, two elements must be present: there must be something you really want, and you must believe that there's a clear path that will lead you to it. If there's nothing you want, then you won't get excited—and why should you? This is the apathy that Dr. May discussed. And if you really want something, but don't believe you'll get it, you won't get excited because it's just a fantasy.

If you're like most people, nothing springs immediately to mind when someone asks: "What do you want out of life?" Your fondest wish may be something vague like "I just wish all these problems would go away." That's not very specific, and it won't get you excited enough to get out there and bust your butt making it happen. If you have a particular dream that motivates you, terrific; you're way ahead of the game.

If not, then you must *decide* what you want, and do it in very specific terms. That's actually an unusual thing to do: you're going to make a conscious choice as to what you desire. And most people have a problem doing something like that. It's too off-beat— too out of their normal experience for them to feel comfortable doing it. After all, why would you work at trying to be dissatisfied with the way things are?

"THE BIGGEST PROBLEM MOST PEOPLE FACE," explains Michael Levy, co-founder and CEO of the Sports Clubs of Canada, "is that they trap themselves by saying 'I'll wait' and never even get started. They should put whatever they want in front of them—a Ferrari, if that's what they want—and then go after it. I tell my people that if there's something they want, they should get a picture of it and put it up on their office wall where they'll see it all the time. But don't wait—time isn't going to make things any easier.

"Do it or don't do it! The problem with most people is that they live in fantasy and nothing ever happens for them. Set yourself a goal, and *go do it!* If you do that and you're prepared to sacrifice for what you want, you'll succeed 95% of the time.

"The greatest danger to an entrepreneurial business is for the head of the company to lose purpose. You've got to have something to strive for.

"For me it was a boat. About a year after I started the business, I was confident that things were going well enough that I could afford to take out a loan and buy it. Of course the people around me told me I should wait, that the business was too young, that it would be more prudent to wait, and for a while I believed perhaps they were right. But then I thought, 'What am I, crazy? There'll always be a reason not to buy it. I've always wanted a boat, I've worked hard to get to this point, and I deserve it.' So I went out and bought it.

"Don't forget why you went into business for yourself. Don't let someone else run your dream!

"Or take a friend of mine. He started what is now a major company, and works like a dog. But now he's starting to take time off, spend more time with his family. And when he travels, he always travels first class, and stays at first-class hotels. I asked him why he spent so much on travel expenses, and he said, 'If I was going to travel like I would if I worked for the Bay, I might as well work for the Bay.' So rather than me convincing him, he convinced me. There's a recognition of what I've accomplished now when I travel."

So you need to know what you want, and then go after it. And make sure the dreams are your own—you can't borrow someone else's, and you can't let someone else control yours.

F inding your dreams

If you don't have much experience in creating a dream for yourself, let me give you an exercise that may help. It's called "If I Won the Lottery," and it's a fantasy game you may have played before. Whether you have or not, play it now, but this time keep a pen and paper handy, and jot down your thoughts.

Suppose someone gave you a lottery ticket for your birthday, and you won $25 million, tax-free. Also assume that somehow there was no publicity, and no one even knew you had the money so that, if you chose to, you could continue living exactly the life you've got now. What would be the first thing you would do? Jot down whatever comes to mind. Don't try to censor or critique your ideas—for now, just relax and let your imagination run wild.

What would you do next? Travel? Buy a new house? Pay off debts? Do something wonderful for someone you love? Help a particular charity? Have a summer home and a winter home? Drive a different car? What colour would it be? What model? What kind of lifestyle would you like? What would you do on a perfect day? How late would you sleep? What would you do when you got up?

In what part of the world would you be? Who would be with you if you could choose anyone you wanted? Don't worry about being realistic right now. Just assume you could have it all your own way, with no strings attached.

Once you'd spent some money, and got some of the initial thrill out of your system, what kind of work would you do, if any? Would you be president of your own company? What would that company do? How would you dress? Where would you buy clothes? Would it be a big company, or just you alone? Give yourself permission to imagine anything you like. Remember to jot down brief notes as ideas come to you.

Who would you spend your time with? What would you do and where would you do it? Would you pick up some new skills, learn to play a musical instrument, or fly a plane? Would you fly to Europe to shop? Where would you spend your vacations when you weren't working (if you did work)? How often would you go on vacation, and where? At what times of the year? How would you travel?

Keep going until you feel pretty good about the kind of life you'd be living. Enjoy it—this game is absolutely free, so have fun with it.

N ow tally up the score

Now take your notes and rewrite them, this time in more detail. Don't leave anything out—don't chicken out—right now you're trying to think big. Then, review your list, this time in the clear light of the here-and-now. Now comes the hard part: I'm going to tell you something you may not believe, but for the moment, just pretend you believe it and act accordingly:

You can have anything you want on that list. In fact, you can have all of it, if you want. But you'll have to pay for it yourself— nobody's going to give you that winning lottery ticket. And you'll pay for it in blood, sweat, and tears—plus pain, stress, and triumph thrown in for good measure.

With that in mind, go back over your list, and see how many of these things you want enough to pay for them. Don't worry if the things you choose are far-fetched or very expensive. You're simply narrowing your focus to answer the key question: *do I really want it?*

(By the way, if you chicken out at this stage, and start hoping that someone will give you that lottery ticket, then you are what is known as a "prisoner of hope." You'll stay where you are until you accept that you have the most control over your life—not luck.)

Highlight the things on your list that you want enough to be willing to pay for them. Take some time. Think it through carefully. Replay "If I Won the Lottery" as many times as necessary until you think you've got a list of things you want badly enough to work for them.

Now to check your results, ask yourself: if I were on my death bed, looking back over a long and full life, and I had achieved all of the things on my list, would I have any regrets about anything I didn't achieve? If so, add those things to your list. If not, then you've done a pretty good job.

H ere's a secret of your success

Earlier I explained that you didn't have to believe that you could have anything and everything on that list, but you should pretend that you could. Now I'll let you in on a secret: you don't have to believe you can do something in order to do it. If you *act as if* you can do it, then you can do everything you need to do, get everything you want, and you still don't have to believe it's possible.

This "act as if" principle comes from William James, whom I quoted earlier. The belief that you can do something, such as successfully running a company, comes from having successfully done it or something like it in the past. But if you've never run a company before, then you have no basis to believe or disbelieve in your ability. In such cases, your belief may have no relationship to your actual ability—or at least, in your ability to learn the new skill you want.

In these situations, if you use the "act as if" principle and work at and learn the new skill, then you turn the principle into a self-fulfilling prophesy. You do it successfully because you try it and learn how. However, if you take your lack of belief as being correct, you won't even try—and, again, it becomes a self-fulfilling prophesy.

"If you think you can, or you think you can't, you're right either way" said Henry Ford. It's not necessary for you to believe you can do something to do it. So act as if you can do the things necessary to make your dreams come true—but do it within the framework of your business plan to increase your odds of success.

W hat's the difference between a dream and a goal?

Turning a dream into a goal requires three things: a means of achieving your dream, a timetable, and a set of steps. Let's suppose you really do want a Ferrari. Find out how much it would cost to buy one. Once you know how much you need, ask yourself if the business idea you've chosen can produce enough to buy your car. If it can't, then you've chosen the wrong idea. Don't break your heart building a business that can't deliver what you're working for. Look for another idea instead.

If your idea can produce enough to buy the Ferrari, the next question is: when do you want it? Balance this "when" with the knowledge that you can have it as soon as you earn it. In any case, set a specific date.

Once you've set the date, then you can transform the dream into a goal by dividing your progress into steps. You know what your business has to produce to give you the car, and you know when you want it. Now assume that the business will reach the payoff point by the payoff date. For illustration purposes, let's assume you've chosen a date four years from now.

For your business to pay you enough to be able to buy a Ferrari four years from now, what must it have accomplished? Where will it be in the market? What mileposts will it have passed? What will it look like? Write down all of this information. To reach that stage four years from now, what stage will it have to be at three years from now? Again, figure out the mileposts and write them down.

And to reach that stage three years from now, what must your business have accomplished two years from now? One year from now? Six months from now?

Finally we move into the realms of planning. For your company to reach the mileposts that you've just noted for six months from today, what things will you have to do between now and then? Write these out in as much detail as possible. It helps if you write them down in any order first, and then worry about putting them in the right order later.

I won't go though the whole planning process again at this point—we did that in Chapter 5. But the main point here is to take your dream, put a date on it, then work *backwards* from the future until you've close enough that you can reasonably plan steps for it, then turn around and execute those steps, one by one.

If you do that, you will *know* when you can order the Ferrari because you can see the path that will take you there.

And that's when you'll get excited.

8 | Where Can You Get the Financing You Need?

"YOU SHOULD WRITE THE WHOLE BOOK about how to find financing," the tall, portly entrepreneur told me. "For sure, that's the hardest part of being an entrepreneur."

Sam Stauber should know. He started a business in the paging industry with nothing—no money, no previous business experience, and no expertise in the field he was entering. He was in his forties, married, had six kids, and degrees in psychology and administration, and had spent 20 years working in the helping professions—a far cry from the business he was entering. Yet he managed, through sheer perseverance, salesmanship, and force of personality to parlay his situation into one of the dominant radio-paging companies in his market, which was then sold. But financing was the bane of his existence.

When I asked him how he thought entrepreneurs should go about raising money, he told me some things that surprised me.

"Finding investors is a 'eureka' process." he said. "You find that major piece all of a sudden, and the rest falls into place after that. But you've got to find that major piece first. And that can take a lot of presentations to a lot of skeptical people.

"I remember when I was trying to put my company together. I'd been travelling all over North America, looking for investors, and had come up dry.

"I reached my low ebb in New York City. I'd been working on this business for months and getting nowhere. I was running out of cash, I owed money 16 ways from Sunday, and I was paying for my airfare and hotels on credit cards, hoping that something clicked before the bills came in. I had no job, and no prospects of one, and I still had to support my wife and kids. And nobody wanted what I had.

"I was ready to quit. The only room I could find in all of New York was in a seedy, third-rate hotel.... I called a good friend and confidante, as I often did, to let her know what was happening, and told her I was going to give up.... She gave me a pep talk, and got me up off the floor. It wasn't any ideas or information she gave me—it was just that she believed in me. That's what I needed most; that's what kept me going.

"A couple of days later I found my lead investor. Everything fell into place very quickly after that."

Before we look at this "eureka process," let's step back a moment, and find out what kind of financing you need. This will depend largely on how much you need, and what you need it for.

 he five types of financing

There are five primary sources of money: your own pocket, blood money, bank financing, unsophisticated investors, and professional investors. Let's examine each of these sources.

1 Your own money

My favourite form of financing is your own money, for the simple reason that there's no time limit on it and nobody's waiting for you to pay it back. In Chapter 4, entrepreneur Konrad Tittler noted, "Banks or outside investors have expectations that put constraints on what and how you do things. If you don't take in that kind of money, then the only interest you have to pay is your living expenses. You can spin that out for as long as you're prepared to put up with the discomfort." But if you're using your own money, then you call all the shots. If you start using other people's money, then you must satisfy them before you satisfy yourself.

The other advantage of using your own money is that you know it's a scarce resource. One of the classic mistakes that entrepreneurs make is to accept money from an outside investor, and then use it to buy a fancy office or a snazzy car. But in order to survive, you must recognize that that's your money you're spending—and spending it before you've got it significantly increases your chances of failure. This demonstrates the point that when you work with your own money, you're less likely to make big mistakes. It's guaranteed that you will make mistakes; they're unavoidable. However, you're better off making small mistakes that don't cost much rather than big mistakes that cost a bundle.

Although using your own money is the easiest form of financing, rather than just putting money into the company on an informal basis, make the relationship formal, and document it. In particular, if you are lending significant amounts of money to your company, have the company's officers (that's probably you) sign promissory notes acknowledging the debt. Then, periodically have your lawyer register the debt so it's formally recognized. Otherwise, if your company fails, and there is no formal acknowledgment of the money owing to you, you'll stand at the end of the line of creditors and may wind up with nothing. With formal acknowledgment, however, you stand in front of most of your creditors (but always after the bank).

2 Blood money

The next easiest form of financing is blood money. This is also called family money, but I think blood money describes it better, because you pay for the cash in blood—especially if things go wrong.

Many people are squeamish about approaching their relatives for money. They're afraid that the risk of doing so is greater than approaching a complete stranger. After all, if the money is lost, at least you don't have to live with a stranger, whereas losing a relative's money could mess up your family life.

I know of one instance where an aggressive young businessman put up his own life savings, and borrowed the rest of the money he needed from his parents. Then, despite his best efforts, the business failed, losing everything that both he and his parents had invested. His parents wrote off the loss, chalking it up to experience, and acknowledging that he had taken his best shot. The entrepreneur, though, couldn't shake off the guilt of losing his parents' money. He dragged his sense of failure around with him for years, and never tried to run his own business again, even though he had a natural aptitude and would probably have succeeded if he had tried again with the wisdom he had gained from his first failure.

But while it's true that there are other risks aside from financial risks in blood money, two elements make it important to consider seriously. The first is that your relatives know you pretty well. They may be able to see qualities in you that an outsider might miss. Professional investors consider the quality of management to be the most important factor in determining a new venture's success. Your relatives may have a better understanding of what you are capable of achieving than any stranger could.

This familial insight, however, cuts both ways. Your relatives may be able to see that you are getting into a situation that you won't be able to handle. They may avoid investing in your business *because* they know you. So if you find that your relatives will not invest, you should at least examine the possibility that they might know something about you that you haven't admitted to yourself.

But my second reason for considering blood money is a blunt one: if you don't have enough confidence to risk your relatives' money, ask yourself how sure are you that you're going to make it? And remember: the odds of getting any other kind of money are much worse than your chances of getting blood money.

3 Your banker is not your friend

The third type of money is bank financing. First, I'll give you the bottom line on bank financing, then circle back and explain about managing a relationship with a bank.

The big Canadian chartered banks talk a good game, especially in front of Parliamentary committees, but the truth is the banks are not interested in lending your new business any money. I'll go further: the banks won't lend your new business a dime. (Exception: if you're buying an existing business with a good credit record and proven profitability, they *might* lend you money.)

They may, however, lend it to *you* while pretending to lend it to your company—if you're a good credit risk. By that I mean that they will lend it to your company, but they will make you guarantee it personally, and force you to put up collateral—say, by taking a mortgage on your house—that gives them more than ample coverage, so they're not really risking anything. Then, if the business fails, they'll get their money back and you'll go broke.

Now let's talk about your relationship with bankers. It's often described as a love-hate relationship: entrepreneurs love the money and hate the banks. In fact, many entrepreneurs don't want to be quoted talking about their bankers, largely for fear that their banker will pull the plug on them. Here are some of the more reasonable things said about banks.

DANIEL IS AN ENTREPRENEUR IN HIS mid-fifties who built a solid business from the ground up. He has very strong opinions about bankers, mostly springing from the problems he's had with them. When his company reached the size where it was a respectable account, but was still being treated like a shaky, fly-by-night operation, Daniel knew it was time for a change and found another banker. From this at times painful experience, Daniel has evolved a rather pointed philosophy about dealing with banks.

"Never let your banker know you're scared," he says with a wry smile, "but kiss his ass a lot to keep him happy.

"Seriously, though, working with your banker can be rough. You've got to find out what he needs to keep him happy and then make sure he gets it. The secret in dealing with your bank is that you *have* to play by their rules, but you *can't* let your fear of what the bank might say dictate how you run the business. If you do, then you're dead, because you make all the wrong decisions. You get scared about what the bank's going to think, and you play it too conservative, you pass up opportunities, you just don't run the business for the business' sake.

"You have to work with the bank, but you still have to do what's best for the business. It's a balancing act. And the truth is, that's what they really want you to do anyway! The best thing you can do for your banker is to be successful. And that means you *can't* let the bank dictate how you run your business."

Sandy Spicer of NICs Garage says that dealing with banks was one of the most unexpected—and unwelcome— aspects of running her own business. "When you're working for someone else, you don't think about dealing with the bank, but it's a really difficult part of being in business.

"I don't think that banks really understand small business, no matter what they say. When we were planning NICs, we spent a whole year planning the business. But most of this— maybe eight months of it—was putting the pieces together that we needed to get the support of the bank."

Sherry Orr owns a successful trucking company in Alberta, and is a high-profile executive on the provincial industry association. She says flatly, "I'm very anti-bank. We had a bank manager for five years, and everything was fine for most of that time. Then they brought in a new guy, and we just didn't see eye to eye. For one thing, he said he didn't think a woman should be running a trucking company—and this is in the 90s, right?—and that I should get a real job.

"I walked out of that meeting and said to myself, 'We've got to get out of here.' So I refinanced my home, refinanced all our equipment, factored our receivables, and paid off the bank. And you know what? Even though, financially, it was very expensive to do things this way, I figure I'm ahead of the game. I used to spend 80% of my time dealing with financing issues and trying to keep the bank happy. Now I spend my time running the business instead.

"The banks aren't listening, they're just not listening, no matter what the head honchos say in public. They aren't there to lend money, they're there to collect fees and make profits off of you. And it isn't just me or my industry. I was asked by the Calgary Chamber of Commerce to sit on a committee dealing with banking issues, and I can tell you that the bank management and the front-line people are so far apart in what they're saying that management obviously doesn't have a clue what's going on.

"I told the bank executives on the Chamber of Commerce committee exactly what had happened to me, and they all swore that it was a mistake, and they promised they'd get back to me with something more reasonable. They never did. And when I saw them again at committee meetings, they just looked embarrassed.

"So don't rely on your bank, because the money just won't be there."

Many entrepreneurs view bankers as villains. They think of bank managers as people who don't have to produce anything themselves—but sit in an ivory tower and make life difficult for people who do. But if you're going to approach a bank for financing, it's important to understand how things look from the banker's perspective. To maximize your chances of getting the money you need on terms you can live with, you've got to know what pressures your banker is feeling, and why he responds the way he does.

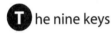 **he nine keys**

There are nine keys to dealing with bankers. Let's go through them one at a time.

1 Finding the right bank and the right banker
Banks pay lip-service to lending to small business, but they really consider it a necessary evil. They do it mostly for public relations, not because they want to.

The big banks—like the one on the corner—would prefer to lend to a big corporation or make a well-secured consumer loan than lend to a small business. And this is a perfectly reasonable approach if you think about it. After all, would you want to lend to a group of people, 80% of whom will fail in the first three years? And if you did, wouldn't you want to make sure that you got the first pick if there was anything left to salvage? That's what bankers do, and that's what they must do to stay in business: lend money and get it back.

So how do you find a bank? Well, if you're effectively going to borrow the money personally anyway (i.e., provide your personal guarantee and personal collateral), then you might be best off going to the bank that knows you. However, that's not automatic. What you want is a banker who is at least sympathetic to what you're trying to accomplish, and you'll have to convince them that you've got a shot at doing it successfully. You see, the loan officers at the big banks cannot say "yes," but they can certainly say "no." Accordingly, find one that's prepared to believe in you.

Individual banks, and individual bankers, go through phases, just like kids. If they've recently had a bad experience with another company in a business similar to yours, then you probably won't even get the time of day. If that happens, try another bank. It's worth searching for someone who's willing and interested in listening.

At time of writing, two banks might be high on your list to try: the Hongkong Bank of Canada and the Bank of Montreal's new small business unit. The Bank of Montreal is, in truth, no more interested in being in small business lending than any of the other major banks, but they've apparently decided that they need to show the flag by making a public commitment to small business. Their ability to back up their public fanfare remains to be seen.

There are other banks active in Canada as well, such as Citibank and Deutschebank, but they are really only interested in commercial loans in the tens of millions of dollars. Finally, if you can justify borrowing in excess of $1 million, and can back it up with receivables and inventory, then there are branches of two American near-banks located in Toronto that are distinctly more aggressive than the Canadian banks: Congress Financial Corp. and the Finova Group. They really prefer to lend in amounts of $5 million and up, but will go down as low as $1 million. And remember that situations change. Things may be different now than when I wrote about this.

The next step is to find a banker with whom you have good personal chemistry. It won't make any difference to the computer formulas that the banks will run your loan application through for approval, but it will make a difference as to whether you even get that far. Bankers don't have much leeway these days, but they always have the power to say "no."

2 Understanding the banking business

Once you've found a banker you get along with, she's still going to make you jump through hoops. She has to make sure you live up to all sorts of those awful covenants the bank wants, and she's still going to demand all the security and collateral she can squeeze out of you. And no matter how chummy you get, you must always remember that she's neither your friend nor your partner; her interests are not the same as yours.

Unlike the investor, who profits only when the company profits, a banker profits as long as you can pay interest and repay the loan, even if the company falls apart. And also unlike the investor, the banker has no upside: if you're wildly successful, the bank still only gets the agreed-upon interest and fees. Hence, they are taking a risk on the downside, and not getting any of the upside. So it's your banker's responsibility to make sure that the bank gets paid, even if it pushes you into bankruptcy. If she doesn't, it's her neck on the line—and her career as a banker will be short.

3 How to approach your banker

Start by asking your banker what she would like to see in a business plan to help her get it approved. Don't give her what you've prepared just yet, because it's probably not all that she needs. But find out what she does want, then go away and make sure that what you give her is complete, makes sense, can be independently verified, and is convincing.

You may need to take some time doing this. Sandy Spicer of NICs Garage spent months getting all the details together for her bank. But do it right or don't bother.

4 Is all the necessary financing in place?

Next, do the projections in your business plan show that the bank's financing is the last piece needed to make the venture work? If there's a gap in the cash flow that shows you're going to need more financing down the road, your banker will spot it and ask how it's going to be filled. If you can't provide a believable answer, you won't get the loan.

Of course, part of the answer may be that once you've met with the specified degree of success, you'll need more money to finance growth, and that you expect to come back to the banker for more working capital. That's an acceptable answer—especially if your projections show that your cash flow, receivables, and inventories can secure and justify additional money from the bank.

The point is, though, that you'd better be ready with answers to questions like: "Where's the rest of your financing going to come from?" Bankers know how tough it is to raise outside financing, and don't want to jump into a situation where the financing is not assured.

5 Give your banker something to go on other than your say-so

Your projections are based on your estimates and expectations of sales and profit margins. Support these assumptions with any research on the marketplace, your competitors, profit margins, or anything else that might lend credibility to your numbers.

Include any relevant credentials of you and your management team in the business you're entering. Include information such as your established track record with one of the major companies in the industry. Or, if you've taken over an existing operation, include the goodwill that has been established, and how that will affect results. And, if you've used a financial professional to assist in preparing your projections, include that information—or better yet, take that professional with you to explain how you arrived at the figures on the paper.

"Most entrepreneurs are not good financial people," says Rick, a banker of my acquaintance. "They're usually concept people or marketing pros, good at selling themselves. It makes a lot of sense for them to have someone who's good at finance working with them."

Daniel echoes this thought: "I'm a firm believer in taking in a strong financial partner—not so much for his money, but for his expertise in dealing with money people and problems."

6 Identify your contingency plans

Bankers know that businesses never go as expected, so they'll want to know about your contingency plans. Build a cash reserve into your working capital, so that your plans don't show that you're down to your last penny before your cash flow turns positive.

Also account for your plans for additional outside financing in case such financing is necessary. For example, if you think you can keep your personal assets out of the security pledged for the loan, then you might note that if additional outside financing is required, you'll borrow the money personally and include it as equity.

7 Know what kind of loan you want, and for how long

Bankers make different kinds of loans for different purposes. For instance, if you're buying an existing operation and need a bank loan to complete financing for the purchase, and your plans show you'll be able to pay the loan back within three years, then you should probably ask for a fixed-rate, fixed-term loan with principal repayments deferred for the first six months while you get things revved up. The same may apply to the purchase of equipment or fixed assets.

If you're financing inventory or operations, then you'll probably want a revolving credit, secured with inventory or receivables, drawn down and paid back as money is required or produced by customer demand. So during your exploratory interview, review what kind of loan you'll need, and what kinds of restrictions such loans have.

There's one kind of financing your banker won't do, though: "We're not here to finance [unplanned] losses," says Rick the banker. "Entrepreneurs have to cover losses from their personal resources."

So be prepared to tell your banker how much you want, how long you want it, how you plan to secure it, and when you expect to be able to pay it back.

8 Be prepared to discuss your personal financial position

The bank will also want to know about things that you will consider private. This will include a listing of everything you own: house, cars, cottage, personal possessions, investments, life insurance—the works. They'll also want to know about your liabilities: car payments, mortgage on your house, credit card balances, and so on. If you own a house, they'll want to know in whose name it's registered.

And they'll want to know something you probably haven't even thought of: what outstanding tax liability do you have, if any. "Lots of people come in, say in October or November, and, if they think about it, they know they're going to have some tax to pay in April of the next year," says Rick the banker. "If a guy does, that's not going to disqualify him from getting a loan, but we sure want to know about it before it happens."

They'll also want to know about any contingent liabilities you may have. Have you guaranteed a loan for a friend or for another business?

Then they'll want to see your credit cards and your social insurance number. Why? So they can run a credit check on you and see how you've handled money in the past.

However, don't volunteer this information. Have it ready if asked—especially if you know you're going to be on the hook for the company's loans personally. But don't offer it until they ask.

9 Sex appeal counts, so look good

As with any investment presentation, use eye-catching graphics, illustrations, and photographs whenever possible and appropriate. Even though bankers must stick to their dreary lending guidelines, a sexy business presentation is more likely to win their hearts than a dull one. Make your presentation sizzle as well as make sense.

Dress the part. As Adrian, a successful marketer, put it: "It's important that you look like you're worth putting money into. That includes how you look, and how you present your case. Remember that you're selling to this guy, so treat him like a customer."

And Rick replies, "If an entrepreneur comes in with the package of information already prepared, it shows us he's organized, serious, and has given some thought to what the banker is going to need to make a quick but educated assessment. People who come in with ideas scratched on a piece of paper and without enough financing usually fail."

The care and feeding of bankers

Now that you've got the loan, how do you keep the banker from making your life miserable?

Obviously, the first and best thing you can do is to succeed. Remember that bankers need to be on lots of winning teams to look good to their management. If you're doing well, you'll receive a warm welcome when you visit the bank. And make sure you build on that welcome—things won't always be good, and there may be a time when you need a bunch of money in a hurry. So nurture the friendship. Go in with a smile and a good word, even when you don't need to. Having a solid relationship never hurts.

Next, be prepared to fill the obvious mechanical reporting requirements. Your banker will expect a monthly statement of inventories and receivables. He's going to want quarterly financial statements, showing income, cash flow, and balance sheets. These probably don't need to be audited—your internal staff can prepare them. But they should be timely, so the banker can see what's happening in your business now.

Last, and perhaps most important, get bad news to him early. This doesn't mean that he has to know of every stumble or missed sale. But if problems are on the horizon, let him know early—and absolutely before the cheque that puts you over your loan limit hits the bank.

"If things don't go according to plan," says Rick, "tell your banker about it early. He's going to find out about it eventually anyway."

Some entrepreneurs caution, "Don't tell your banker anything"

Not everyone agrees with me that you should keep your banker informed. Adrian, the successful marketer, explains it this way:

"You really don't want the sharpest banker around. The sharper the banker, the less likely he is to want to let you do as you think necessary. When you come right down to it, you're going to con your banker, and paint the rosiest picture possible, not so you can steal his money—he's going to have you all tied up anyway—but so that he doesn't interfere with how you run your business."

Then there's the stories of bankers as villains to contend with. A friend of mine had his company pulled out from under him by his bank. He described his experience like this:

"Business wasn't going quite as I'd planned, but cash was coming in, and I was pretty sure I could make it work. Unbeknownst to me, though, the bank had gotten cold feet and decided that the business was going down the tubes. They wanted to close it up and sell off everything they could before it was too late to get their money out.

"The first I heard of it was when I went to the plant one day, found a padlock on the fence, and a sheriff's order allowing the bank to seize the assets.

"They did such a lousy job of selling them off that they wound up having to go after my house and personal assets as well. A lot of the receivables never came in because the bank notified everyone that payments should come to them, not me, and so lots of my customers started claiming incomplete shipments, quality defects, and so on. It was a real horror show.

"I did manage to keep the house—mostly because my wife hadn't signed a guarantee, as the bank had wanted. Everything else was gone, though. It was a horrible experience, and the bank not only precipitated it, they made everything 10 times worse than it otherwise would have been."

A banker replies

Asked about these kinds of comments, Rick shakes his head and replies: "Don't surprise us. We have very little time for entrepreneurs who do things they shouldn't be doing and keep us in the dark. And when they don't succeed, we have very little sympathy.

"We don't want to take some guy's house. Our objective in a crash-and-burn situation is to get the money back from the sale of the company's assets rather than personal assets, even though seizing such assets may be much easier. I mean, we have feelings, too.

"But when all the assets that can be realized are gone, and we end up with a residual debt, we have to look to the guarantor to pay the balance. And remember that interest is ticking all the time. We don't do anyone any favours by delaying collection in a hopeless situation, including the guy we're moving against.

"A large majority of people we finance succeed. That's why we screen loans so carefully. But if there's going to be a cash-flow problem, tell your banker about it in advance. We're flexible because we're interested in seeing your business succeed, and the loan paid back."

Sandy Spicer of NICs Garage is another good example of this. About six months after they opened, they made some mistakes and ran into trouble. "We owed every supplier we had, and didn't even have enough money to cover the payroll. We hadn't been talking to our suppliers, we hadn't been talking to the bank, we hadn't even been doing a cash-flow statement so that we'd know how much was coming in and how much was going out. Then the government froze our bank account because my partner didn't know the PST [provincial sales tax] had to be paid. I truly thought that January [1998] was going to be the end of the business. It was an incredibly emotional time.

"The bank called us in for a meeting. Before we went, we got to work. We talked to all our suppliers and worked out payment schedules so they'd keep supplying us. We reworked our business plan, had new projections, and were prepared to talk about what we'd done wrong, how we had corrected it, and why the business would work now.

"When we walked in, our banker did not look happy. He told us afterwards that the purpose of the meeting had been to call the loan and shut us down. But the work we had done, and the plan we'd come up with persuaded him that they'd have more luck getting their money back if they kept us alive than if they shut us down. So we got an extension, dug in, and made it."

NICs Garage had just about as close to a near-death experience as it is possible to have and still survive. And they were awfully lucky that their banker believed them—you might not be as lucky. So learn from their mistakes rather than your own by:

- keeping to plan;
- dealing with problems as they arise;
- making sure you know the financial position of your business (that's the cash-flow statement). You may need to know your cash position on a daily basis, depending on your business.
- keeping your banker in the picture.

Don't wait until you're over your head to talk to her. If she starts making threatening noises, that's a warning, not something to be avoided. Nothing makes a banker more nervous than not knowing what's going on.

But entrepreneurs have to know how bankers can and cannot operate. It's part of the game, and a part you'd better learn to play well. So learn your banker's rules—and then work with her within those boundaries. Scream and shout at her, by all means. But do it in private—and speak nicely to the banker while she's got your heart in a jar. Remember: she wants you to be a winner so *she* can look good. So help her do it.

4 Unsophisticated investors

If you're looking for private investors, the natural tendency is to approach people with a lot of money. And sometimes that works. Sam Stauber's lead investor, for example, was a wealthy man.

But wealthy people are approached all the time, and they're more than slightly skeptical about any presentation. If you know and are liked by the individual, or share the same social and economic strata, you may have a shot at convincing them. Otherwise, you'll have a tough time explaining why you can do something with their money that they can't. (We'll discuss wealthy investors later.)

On the other hand, people of more moderate means, as a group, offer you a lot of advantages. First, they haven't heard it all before. They don't get dozens of presentations every month, and they aren't always being hit up for investment capital. So they'll come in with a fresher outlook, and be less cynical and more willing to believe. And they don't have lots of alternatives available for making a fortune (or at least, they don't think they do).

Next, they have to work for a living. If they're interested at all, then they're looking for a way off the treadmill. They want to believe that they can invest a modest amount of money, and have it produce enough of a fortune that they can quit work in a short period. This is the great appeal of lotteries: they offer a big step up in lifestyle—and fast.

Working for a living also means that they can't devote as much time to checking you out, or harassing you once they've made their investment. For the most part, they'll be silent—or at least quieter—investors. But do such people have the money to invest? Surprisingly, yes, they do. If they really believe it's important to their future, if they think it's going to make a major difference to the way they can live, they'll find the money somewhere. It may be that no one investor will have enough, but putting 10 middling-sized investors together may eventually be better than trying to find one big one.

Making the small investor feel important

If you do finance your operation with several small investors, then the "eureka process" comes with the first one to commit. Once you've got one, then you can say to all the others, "Look, Smith believes this is going to work. Don't take my word for it—ask Smith!" Someone who's sold on an idea will be enthusiastic about it. Let them do some of the talking for you.

Getting your first small investor to commit can be a problem. They see that you need a lot of money, and they only have a little and conclude that there's no reason for them to consider being involved, and that their piece wouldn't be important anyway. You must overcome these two obstacles for them to become enthusiastic about investing.

To do so, you must come up with a reason why their piece is important. And here's the reason:

"Look, Mary, I know you've only got $50,000 and we need a million, but you're missing the point. The way I'm raising the money is to find 10 investors with $50,000, and then I'll go to the bank for the rest. So here's how we'll do it." (Note the change from "you" to "we.") "We'll put the money in an escrow account where it can't be touched unless we successfully get the half a million. If we can't do it in 30 days, then we're quits, and you've lost nothing. If we raise the money, then you're in on the ground floor of a well-financed operation. So, do you want the shares registered in your own name, or your company's?"

By taking this approach, you reassure the individual investor that his or her piece is important—forming, as it does, the cornerstone of the whole enterprise. And investors can see how, even with their small piece, the whole enterprise will get the financing it needs.

This is not to suggest that middle-income earners are suckers. If you don't believe in what you're doing, then you have no right asking other people to bet their savings on you. But if you truly believe that what you're doing makes sense, I see no reason not to persuade others to join you. And one more piece of advice: talk to your lawyer to make sure you're not infringing upon any securities laws. Otherwise, if things go sour, it could mean jail rather than just bankruptcy.

Looking for Daddy Warbucks

Let's suppose, though, that you decide to pursue wealthy investors. There are, after all, some real advantages. They have money and connections so they may be able to complete your financing needs. But even better, they have credibility, so when you're talking to people of more moderate means, you can point to your lead investor and say, "What does he know that you don't?" But how do you go about getting skeptical old Daddy Warbucks?

You find wealthy individuals in much the same way as you find middle-income earners: through friends and acquaintances. Perhaps you know some wealthy people yourself, but have been intimidated about approaching them. If that's the case, then you must decide which is more important: your feelings of discomfort or your business. Go and talk to them. They will probably say "no" (but then, most of the people you talk to will). But they may say "yes"—or they may know someone whom you should ask. Once you start asking, then you may well find that you can work your way through an entire network of people. Most of them won't be people who can help you directly, but one of them may know the people who can.

Sam Stauber found his lead investor through the son-in-law of a friend, who put him in touch with someone in finance, who knew a wealthy man in the communications business—who became Sam's lead investor. So just keep climbing up the ladder of contacts until you find the people you need.

Finding people who know people

If you don't know anyone who's even vaguely in the right area, go talk to your lawyer or accountant, or a lawyer or accountant you know. They probably have clients who have extra money. And if you can convince the lawyer or accountant that you've got your head screwed on right, then you'll start out with an advantage— you'll have been introduced by someone the potential investor knows. The prospect then knows that the idea has at least been screened for reasonableness.

There are also people who hover around the fringes of the financial industries who make money by putting deals together, usually in the form of a finder's fee. Such fees may either be a percentage of the money you raise (say, six percent) or a piece of the action. Don't hesitate to use such people—as long as they only get paid if they get results.

Some people will tell you they can raise the money for a fee— payable in advance. In general, I wouldn't use them unless you have an excellent reason for believing that they can deliver. If they're so confident of their abilities, what difference does it make to them if they get the money as a flat fee up front or as a percentage of what they find? The difference is only important if they can't deliver.

Now let's look at the process of converting a suspicious, skeptical prospect into an eager, enthusiastic investor:

1 **You only get one shot.** You only get one shot at a potential investor. If you blow it, you don't get a second chance. This means you've got to hit the right chord, and do it quickly. To do so, you must know the person you're presenting to. You must know what appeals to them, what they want, and how they want it. This means

that you have to either know the person, or be introduced to them by someone who does.

Remember earlier when we discussed blood money? The issue there was if you didn't have enough confidence to risk your relatives' money, how would you have the guts to run the business in tough times? Well, the same applies here. To a large extent, you'll be leaning on your network of friends and acquaintances to find potential investors.

If you don't have the guts to ask friends for money, or for the names of people they know who have money, you're unlikely to get very far. You must believe in your own project—or you're not going to have much luck convincing others.

The first answer to where you should find potential investors is: look around you. The people you know and see every day are your first best source. This is not to say that you can approach them casually. In fact, you must do a lot of preparation before even mentioning your idea to them. There's no such thing as an *initial* presentation. Don't try to find out whether they're interested before you start selling to them. All you'll succeed in doing is scaring them off—and eliminating them as prospects.

But to approach people you know—or people who are referred to you by friends—you should have answers to all the standard questions: who you should approach, what they want, what you should ask for, when and where you should talk to them, and when you should try to clinch an agreement. Without an understanding of these elements, you're fighting an uphill battle on a slippery slope.

2 **Know your prospective investor.** Knowing the people you're presenting to doesn't mean you need to know how they like their spaghetti cooked, or whether they prefer skiing to surfing. It means: what would they find interesting about your investment?

With small investors, the major motivation is simple: will this make me rich? Or, will this improve my lifestyle significantly? There may be other reasons as well, but usually these are the keys.

With big investors, the focus switches. Since they have lots of opportunities to make money, making money is usually not the key, although your enterprises must also promise to make money. Instead, often it has to do with: do I want to be involved in this business, and is this the best way of going about it? Or do I want an excuse to travel to this location on "business"?

Some people only invest in their own industries. Others only invest in things that they find interesting or glamorous. Some just want investments with muscular rates of return. Find out what your prospect looks for in an investment.

But one of the major things they'll all look at is: do I want to spend time with this crazy person who's trying to get me to invest? For, whatever other reasons they may have, people rarely invest only in a business. They usually invest in a person. You've got to be the person they want to invest in, and part of that picture is they have to like you enough to want to spend time with you.

3 **Nobody will invest in your hobbies.** Make no mistake: nobody wants to invest in your hobbies. Unless they see that you're going to sink or swim with your business, they're not going to gamble on it. This is a ticklish business. You've got to convince investors that their piece of the puzzle is important, and that you personally are either going to lead them to the Promised Land or die trying. Yet, you also can't let them think you're desperate (even if you are) or else they'll run and hide. Almost as bad, if they think they can squeeze the last ounce of blood from you, they'll probably do just that. But then, you won't find it exciting, and won't work as hard as you would if you could win big. Net result? You'll both lose.

4 **It ain't what you say...** it's the way that you say it. Actually, it's both. Investors have to like the message—but they have to hear it first. That means they have to consent to hear it, either directly or indirectly. Which brings us to set and setting. It's important to understand *how* people think, and also *when* they think. For instance,

if you approach a friend to make a presentation, and you do it at his office, you're working at a disadvantage. Different settings cause people to act and think in different ways.

In a business-like surrounding, people will act and think in a business-like way. They'll be skeptical, ask tough questions, and demand more than you might want to give. A business lunch may seem better, but it's worse because in between thinking about what he's eating, your prospect is wondering how soon he has to get back to the office. Not only is your time restricted, but your prospect's attention is divided in the time you have.

On the other hand, if you catch them in a relaxed setting, and approach things in a casual manner, they won't be functioning at the same level of efficiency. With their guard down, they'll be more open to new ideas and possibilities.

Selling by the swimming pool

The best time to make a presentation is when someone's on vacation, away from the office, with their mind switched to neutral. They'll be less likely to be skeptical, because to do so means they'll have to drag themselves, mentally, back to the office, which is just what they're trying to escape. Failing this, find a way to see them outside of working hours, in a relaxed setting.

If necessary, invent such a setting. For instance, invite your prospect and his wife for drinks at a nearby international airport. The unusual setting will pique their curiosity, and the jet-set image will set the stage for glamour and excitement.

How important is setting? Let's go back to Sam Stauber.

"I LINED UP ONE OF MY investors when he was on vacation in Florida. I called him long distance, and said I was going to be in the neighbourhood, could I stop by to see him? He naturally said yes.

"I then went out to the airport, hopped on the next plane, and flew down to sit by the pool with him. We chatted about the family, the fishing, mutual friends, and that kind of thing for some time. When the opportunity came up for me to talk about what I was doing in a casual way, I took it. I gradually built up a picture that he found exciting—all without suggesting anything about his participating. When I saw that he was wishing he had a piece of the action, I asked if he knew of anyone who might be a logical investor, who could help us achieve the goals we'd set out.

"He laughed and said, 'You've been doing a sales job on me, haven't you?' I laughed with him and said, 'Sure—how big a piece do you want?'"

And that was Sam's third biggest investor. After they concluded their conversation, Sam put his shirt back on, and hopped on the next plane home. But the best part of the story is that the guy only lived two kilometres from Sam's home, and was returning the following week.

So wasn't it crazy, spending all that money and travelling a couple of thousand miles to spend two or three hours by the pool?

"It worked. If I'd approached him at his office, he would have squeezed me in between three other appointments, the phone would have rung continuously, and it would have been impossible to get him into the right frame of mind.

"As it was, he had the time to listen, to absorb what I was saying, and to decide that it was something he wanted to do. I didn't do a snow job on him—I just gave him the opportunity to discover it was something he liked."

5 **Don't close until your investor has mentally bought.** Sam's story also illustrates several of the other pieces involved in finding your investors. Set and setting we've talked about—he seized the opportunity to talk to his investor when he was relaxed and had his

guard down. Sam was able to take his time, and to choose the right moment to close the deal.

And timing is crucial. If Sam had tried to close in on this investor before he had decided to invest, Sam would have come across as pushy. As it was, they were able to laugh together about what Stauber had done.

Too often salespeople try to close the sale *before* the prospect has decided he or she wants to buy. All this accomplishes is to push the prospect into a corner and increase resistance. Notice that there's a subtle, but significant, difference here. A buyer does not buy once he's decided he wants something. In fact, he may still say "no" for some time after he knows he wants it.

That's where knowing how to close a sale is important. *Closing a sale is the process of helping a buyer figure out how to overcome the obstacles that prevent him from buying what he wants.* If the buyer hasn't decided he wants what you've got, you're not closing a sale, you're creating resistance and hostility. Closing is a *cooperative* effort, with the seller and buyer working together, usually *after* the buyer has said "no" at least once.

If you push someone into disliking you or your methods, if they feel hostile towards you, then they'll say "no," even if they look like fools doing so, just to get even. You can only clinch an agreement when you and a potential investor are working together to find a way to overcome the obstacles that are stopping him from making the investment *he's already decided he wants to make.*

So what do you look for? How do you know when to try and close the deal?

6   **Knowing when to close.** Don't listen to what your prospective investor says. He'll *say* "no." What you're looking for is what he *means*, not what he says. In particular, you're looking for signs that he'd like to invest, but he has this problem, and if you can just help him overcome it—he's with you.

Now that's not the way it will *sound*. It'll sound like "Well, gosh, I think it's a great idea, but right now I've got all my money tied up in real estate. I just haven't got the money to do it. But it's a great idea."

You need to listen past the surface meaning of the words to hear whether your investor wants to do it. Never mind that he says he can't. Investors will always say that. First you must find out whether they want to. If they want to, you can both probably find a way to let him. If he doesn't want to, he won't try.

The signs you're looking for are in his body language. Is he leaning towards you? Is he looking you straight in the eye? Is he smiling sincerely? Does say things that include the two of you together, like "We'd be great in this, wouldn't we?" Does he talk about how it might be, or say things that show he's putting himself in the picture? Is he flushed with excitement? Are the pupils of his eyes dilated?

Not all of these things will happen, but you need to look for any of these signs, or any other body language signals that indicate that he's "leaning in your direction." Moreover, this will represent a *change* in body language from when you started. When you began to paint your picture of success, he didn't know what you were going to say. He was probably leaning back in his chair, just taking it all in. Not involved. Not excited. Cool, detached, distant. When he's mentally bought—when he'd like to say "yes"—that will change. The change may be more noticeable than any specific sign of emotional acceptance.

Until you get these signs, you shouldn't move in too close. You keep painting your glorious picture, and showing how it's going to work.

Once you get signs that he's bought the idea in his mind, you *immediately* try to close by asking a question that requires a partial commitment on his part. For example, you might just stop, look him in the eye and say, "So tell me, Larry, how does it sound so far?"

That's a pretty innocent-sounding question. After all, you're explaining the idea to him to get his reaction. What could be more natural than to ask for it? And the nice part about it is that if he says "Terrible," or something equally encouraging, you can always say, "Right, because I haven't told you about our expansion plans yet. Now, it works like this. . . . " And then you continue with your presentation.

If you get a positive answer, even if it sounds negative, like "Well, it sounds OK, but hasn't this been tried before?" then he's with you so far, and has moved partly into your camp. So you ask for a slightly bigger commitment, like "Well, let me ask you something. If you can convince yourself that this will work where other projects that sound similar haven't, would you find it interesting?"

From here, the process of give-and-take can become complex, and is really just an extension of classic sales technology, particularly dealing with objections. You should read up on such technology if you're not already familiar with it.

But the key points to remember in this process of closing are: 1) don't move in on him until you believe he would like to invest, and 2) the objections he throws up that prevent him from investing are nothing more than the paving stones on the road you have to take to get him involved. If you can work with him to figure out how to overcome them, he's with you.

7   **Sell what your investor wants to buy.** If your prospect starts focusing on the glamorous setting where you'll be holding the annual meeting, don't spend your time emphasizing the rate of return on invested capital. Sell what he wants to buy—and at the pace he wants to buy it.

You see, you're going into this with your presentation all scripted out, with a game plan, and all kinds of expectations about how things will go. But your prospect hasn't read the script and doesn't know his lines. So, if you're not paying attention, you may carry on with your script while your investor has already told you he's interested in buying if you'll just tell him some more about something you consider trivial.

And there's an ego issue here as well. Most of us want people to agree with our ideas. Too often, you'll find yourself almost dragging somebody into studying an aspect of your business that *you* think is important, when *they* think something else is of greater interest. You want them not only to invest, but to invest for the *right reasons!* Don't. You shouldn't care if they invest because they like the tie you wore, or because they think it'll be sexy to be associated with one of the other shareholders. So *listen carefully to the kinds of questions they ask and then sell them what they want to buy!* Who knows? Maybe what they think is important *is* important. Maybe you're wrong. Don't push it.

As for pace, different people like to do things at different speeds. Some like to get down to the bottom line, right away, and will stop listening if you dilly-dally. Others want to discuss their wife and kids, whether you've still got the boat up at the lake, and how's your old Granny before they can consider talking business.

The trouble is, you've got your own preferences regarding speed, too. So the rule is: try to move the presentation at the speed your prospect wants, always remembering that you've still got to close the deal before your time's up. Make sure you ask "How much time do we have?" before you start, so you know what you have to do, and how much time you have to do it in. This will force you to compromise on questions of pace, but do it out of necessity, not out of your desire to do it at *your* speed instead of *their* speed.

8 **Watch for the pitfalls.** There are several kinds of pitfalls to watch for, not all of which I can predict. But here are some of the ones I know about:

> **Time wasters.** Some people get a sense of power out of controlling others. Unfortunately, when you're looking for money, you can sometimes find yourself feeling like you're begging. That feeling can be unintentionally communicated to other people,

and you can wind up feeding someone's ego by mentally kissing their feet when they have no intention to buy.

Keep asking yourself about what's happening behind the words you're both saying. If your prospect isn't serious about what you're saying, pack up and leave.

People with veto powers. Typically when you're dealing with someone who's married, they're going to ask their spouse for their opinion. Spouses and other "second-opinion" people rarely have the ability to say "yes," but almost always have the ability to say "no." You may have to invest some time winning their good opinion, just to ensure they don't torpedo you.

Lawyers and accountants. Of all the people whose opinions you *don't* want, your prospect's lawyer or accountant tops the list. They know their client can't lose money if they say "no," but *they* can lose a lot of credibility if they say "yes" and you blow it.

If your prospect insists on asking his lawyer or accountant, smile and say, "Great. So what you want from your lawyer [accountant] is just her legal [accounting] opinion on this, is that right? And if she sees no legal [accounting] problems with it, you're set to go? OK, then let's call her right now and set up an appointment for me to go see her. I'll go make the presentation to her and answer any questions she may have. That way she'll get all the informations she needs to give an informed opinion, and I won't have to wait to hear from her. Now, can I use your phone?"

Incidentally, if your prospect *is* a lawyer or accountant, don't worry. Treat them like anyone else. What you want to avoid is having your prospect give a sketchy, secondhand outline of your idea, with none of the sizzle or pizzazz, to a third party who has a vested interest in saying no.

"Let me think about this for a few days and get back to you." If you're willing to wait those few days, you might as well quit now. First, they're not going to phone you. Second, if you phone them and ask, "Have you thought it over?" they're going to say, "Yes. NO!"

Worse, they're *not* going to think about it for the next few days. They'll spend maybe 20 minutes thinking about it—if you're lucky. And if this 20 minutes is spread out over two weeks, they'll forget most of the important points. You need them to focus on the decision quickly and complete it soon. Otherwise, the answer's sure to be "no."

If you can, conclude an agreement immediately—at the first sitting. If you can't, define specifically what must happen before you can go any further, and *make sure you are physically present for any future steps that must be taken*. If your prospect is going to consult someone, be there with them. If they need to think about it before giving you an answer, meet them face to face when the time comes, and give them a reason why it has to be soon.

If you're not there in the flesh, then sales studies show that your odds deteriorate to something like three to one against successfully completing an agreement with them. It's much easier to say no at a distance than it is in person.

And when you do get back together, plan to make the whole presentation all over again, focusing on those things the prospect has shown interest in, under the guise of reviewing the proposal. Again, this approach should be covered in any good book on sales technique. Study up.

9   **Know how much to ask for and what to offer**   Ask for more than you think they can afford. If they don't like what you've got, they won't invest a nickel, so it's useless saying, "But it's only a small amount!" And if they want what you've got, they'll stretch—hard—to come up with what you ask for.

They'll let you know if they just plain can't make it by trying to negotiate for a smaller piece and a smaller amount. So don't hesitate to ask for a bunch if you can see that they want a piece of the action.

The second half of this point is: know what you're offering. Decide whether you're offering common stock, convertible debentures, debt with warrants, or something else. If you sound definite about what you're offering, you're more likely to inspire confidence.

"Enthus*iasm*" ends with "I Am Sold Myself."

If you are sold yourself, then finding investors won't be hard. Tedious, yes. You'll have to knock on 100 doors to find the one or two that will open for you. But that's effort, not difficulty.

Be willing to take the pains to prepare properly. Use your network of friends and acquaintances. Listen for the messages behind what people seem to be saying. And believe in what you're doing with all your heart.

5 Professional money

The odds are against you getting professional money unless you are (a) buying an existing business, and have a solid track record of previous success; or (b) happen to be in a business that is so hot and so sexy that even the professionals lose their grip on reality.

The first thing to know about professional investors is that, as a rule, they have a minimum deal size. If you fall below their deal size, they won't even consider investing, no matter how attractive the deal is otherwise. Second, the smallest minimum deal size for professional investors in Canada is almost always $1 million, and relatively few investors will go that low. This means that if you need $250,000, you won't be able to attract professional money; you'll need to go back to one of the other four forms of capital. Third, the Canadian venture-capital market is very shallow, and limited in the kinds of deals that can be done. The three primary types of venture-capital investments are seed capital, start-up capital, and expansion capital. Seed capital is money used to test an idea that sounds like it should work, where everything looks great, and while no one has a working model, and nothing's been sold, everyone involved agrees that it's a sure-fire winner.

With start-up capital, the prototype product or service already exists, it works as advertised, everything is set to go—all you need are customers and capital to make a fortune, but the company's either not in the marketplace yet or isn't profitable yet.

Finally, with expansion capital, the company is a going concern, has several clients, a proven, successful product, is already turning a profit, and just needs money to expand its production and marketing base.

Venture-capital companies in Canada won't give you a penny for seed capital (although a few of them will pay lip-service to it). They will sometimes invest in start-up investments—but only if they think it's an absolutely slam-dunk idea that can't possibly go wrong, and the people involved have impeccable credentials. This happens about as frequently as an ice age.

So the vast majority of venture-capital money goes into expansion capital because the risks are lower, management has proven its concept and its ability to sell, and there is a track record from which the venture capitalist can make some kind of meaningful projections.

If you can't justify needing in excess of $1 million (and note that I said "justify," not "want"), if you don't already have a going concern that's turning a profit, and if you're not looking for expansion capital to make a good thing better, don't waste your time looking for professional investment capital.

If you are in the small minority of people who can justify that kind of investment, then you can get a lot of information about venture capital firms from the Profile List published by the Canadian Association of Venture Capital Companies. Phone or write for a copy:

The Canadian Association of Venture Capital Companies
234 Eglinton Avenue East
Suite 600
Toronto, Ontario M5S 1Y6
(416) 487-0519

Your provincial government also probably has a department (or even a ministry) of small business. Staff members there may be able to tell you who's active in your industry and who's active right now. The federal government also may be of some help through the Business Development Bank of Canada (BDBC), which runs seminars on how to prepare a business plan, and how to approach venture capitalists. The BDBC has offices in most major cities across Canada. However, when dealing with governments, remember that you're dealing with bureaucrats, not people who necessarily have small business experience themselves.

Raising financing is undoubtedly the most soul-destroying thing a new businessperson can do, which is why I started with my favourite form of financing: your own pocket. If you can possibly manage it, you want to avoid taking money from anyone else, at least in the initial stages of your company's business.

Outline for a Written Investor Presentation

Executive Summary Should provide the big picture of your business, why it will work, how much investors can expect to make over what period of time, your corporate strategy, and a general description of the background and experience of your management team. The first sentence is absolutely key, and must be immediately seductive; if you don't hook them right away, they'll never read any further.

The Business A description of the industry, the target market, your marketing strategy, pricing, and especially the competition. It should also detail the recent pattern of growth and new developments in this industry, as well as your projections of future growth for the industry as a whole, as well as your particular niche, if appropriate.

Management The experience, character, and ability of your management group. Your financial backing to date. The commitments—financial and otherwise—made by you, your management group, and your employees to the success of the business. Anything else that would constitute an edge or advantage.

The Investment How much is required, what you are offering in exchange, what rate of return an investor can expect in a specified period of time, and how you believe the investor will be able to get his investment back at the end of that period.

Appendices
- Financial Projections—Three- or five-year projections of sales, cash flow, income statement, and balance sheet, plus the calculations leading to the rate of return expected on investment.
- Market research to support your claims.
- Resumes of your management team, their qualifications, and experience.

Text should be double-spaced. Great attention should be paid to attractive presentation, type face, and clear, concise writing. Graphs, charts, illustrations, and simple tables should be used in preference to unadorned text. Relevant photographs may be included as additional pages. A professional-looking corporate logo is a plus. The projections *must* be exciting (but remember that you're making a commitment to them).

The object is to make the report short, interesting, authoritative, factual—and seductive.

9) How Much Will It Hurt if You Fail?

This will be a short chapter. People contemplating success don't like to think about failure, and I certainly don't want to dwell on it.

But the fear of failure, and the fear of what other people will think and say if you fail may be holding you back. So let me spell out for you just how bad it could be. Then you can decide whether to cope with the fear and proceed, or give in to the fear and stay where you are.

You may fail—it happens. And if you do, it will hurt in many different ways. You might lose everything you own—your house, your car, all your savings. A business collapse can strengthen your marriage—or destroy it. The stress may affect your health. You may have creditors screaming at you for their money, and hounding you day and night when they don't get it. You can stand helplessly and watch as everything you've slaved, sacrificed, and struggled for crashes down around your ears. I've seen all of this. And I've heard the agony of self-doubt and anger crackle in the voices of people who've tried—and didn't make it.

And worst of all is having to bear the opinions of the people around you: friends, neighbours, even family. Maybe especially family. All the people who were secretly hoping you'd fail will line up to tell you that they told you so, you were a fool to try, you should have kept your old job making shoelaces down at the factory, next to them. "What a dope!" they'll crow. "I knew you'd never make it!"

TAKE MY FRIEND MARC, for example. He had a very successful business that kept him running flat out, just to stay up with new demand. Then he reached just a little bit too far, extending himself just before a recession—and lost everything.

In Marc's own words: "Howie, my next-door neighbour, married a girl whose father has a lot of money and who set him up as an executive in the family business. When I was running my company, he was always very respectful of my opinions, coming over when I was out in front unloading groceries or washing the car to ask my opinion on something, or just to talk.

"When I lost the company, I didn't see him for several months but didn't think anything of it. Then one day I saw him just in passing and said hi. He looked at me as if I was a panhandler—and it dawned on me that he was afraid I was going to ask him for money.

"Then I found out he'd been telling his wife and friends that he'd always known I'd self-destruct, that I didn't know anything about business, that my earlier successes had all been luck.

"I would have strangled him, except he didn't seem worth the effort. Why waste your time worrying about someone whose opinion you don't care about anyway?"

This is a crucial turning point for you

There's a sign in Virginia City in Nevada, put there by some of the pioneers who settled the American West. It reads:

> "The cowards turned back.
> The weak died along the way.
> We made it."

Failure is every bit as painful and haunting as you imagine it might be. All your worst fears are justified. So what? There's defeat in every life. Some people just fail gradually, so that by their life's end they can look back and say, "I never had to face any crises." But they're also forced to say, "I never tried to live the life I wanted." And, of course, by then it's too late.

So whether you decide to go ahead and create your own business, or delay, postpone, and avoid doing so has a lot to do with how much you will appreciate your life when you look back on it.

"If you don't try, you've already failed."

ALAN SOBEL WAS VICE-PRESIDENT of Lucitron, a hi-tech company that didn't make it. He lost many years of work and most of his life's savings when the company failed. His reaction?

"Aw hell, Richard, if people are going to worry about whether they might fail, tell 'em to stay in their jobs. Sure I regret seeing all our work and all that money go down the tubes, and sure, I'd do things differently if I had it to do over again. But it's only money. I'm still healthy, I've still got my family, and now I'm one of the leading men in my field, which won't hurt my employment prospects at all.

"Lucitron operated for nine years and spent about $6 million. It provided gainful employment for as many as 23 people, most of whom not only earned money but learned a good deal in the process. We advanced the technology, although that was clearly not an economic success. My greatest regret is that various people lost money as the result of our failure.... That our failure hurt other people is a hard burden for me to carry.

"But if you don't try, you've *already* failed."

Or, going back to Marc's story: "At first, when my lender pulled the plug on me, it felt like I was in free fall, that I'd just fallen over the edge of a cliff, and I was scared shitless. I was just waiting to go 'SPLAT!' on the pavement when I hit.

"But I just kept falling without ever going 'splat,' and finally realized that life goes on. You only imagine that you're falling, so you get up off the floor, try to find some pieces you can salvage from the wreckage, and keep going. My heart didn't stop because I failed. My wife and kids still love me. I'm still the man I was before my business failed.

"I can remember when I was at my lowest ebb, being invited up to some friends' cottage for a weekend. This was when I didn't even have enough money to buy food for my kids, and was really depressed. The cottage was still under construction, and I recall being surprised that the lady seemed to be just as depressed as I was. In her case, though, it was because the custom Italian cupboards she'd ordered were late in arriving, so they couldn't finish the kitchen on time.

"That taught me a lot about our reactions to problems. Everybody has problems, and people get just as depressed with things you consider trivial as you do with things you consider vital. It put things into perspective, and helped me get back on my feet. It also taught me not to expect a lot of help or support from most of the people around me. They're too occupied with their own problems.

"It's more like the weather than falling off a cliff; sure, some days it's going to rain on you. But you don't sit down in a puddle and cry just because you've gotten soaked.

"I'll be back. And I can't wait until Howie comes over to ask for my advice again—as I know he will. My only question is whether I kill him then—or carry on as if nothing's happened. In some ways, carrying on would probably be crueller."

W hat is fear, anyway?

The two classic fears that hold people back from trying are the fear of failure and the fear of people. But let's start by looking at the nature of fear itself.

If you're walking through the woods with a friend, and your friend suddenly cried out "Rattlesnake! Look out!" certain physiological responses happen within your body. Adrenaline is secreted into your blood, your heartbeat increases, and your blood pressure rises, blood is drawn away from your digestive tract and pours into your brain and your skeletal muscles, and large amounts of sugar are dumped into your bloodstream. All this prepares your body to defend itself in a "flight-or-fight" reaction.

We're all familiar with this feeling. We get it when we've had a close call in a car, or had an argument with a relative or spouse, or been dumped on by the boss. In fact, almost the only time we get that feeling is when something unpleasant happens, so it's natural that we associate it with bad situations. Moreover, this is the body's built-in reaction to a threat, so, again, it's natural to associate the feeling with threats and unpleasant things.

Now, if your friend turns out to be a trickster, and there really wasn't a rattlesnake, your body still reacts as if there were because you believed it was true. The adrenaline flows and triggers all those unpleasant feelings based on what you believe.

Your body does not react to what's real. It reacts to what you believe is real.

Consequently, if you believe, consciously or unconsciously, that taking the plunge in your own business is a dangerous step, then that's how your body will react, *even if it's not as dangerous as you think!*

Now most people don't like unpleasant feelings and situations. And if your body is going to give you signals that going into your own business is unpleasant, you're going to avoid even thinking about it. And you may not even be aware that it's happening.

Now let's turn back to the two common fears mentioned earlier. First, the fear of failure—which we think of as the fear of losing everything—is closely tied to our fear of death. It strikes at the most basic foundation of our psychological needs—the need for survival. In modern terms, this need is often expressed as the need to "make a living." What happens if our business fails and we *don't* "make a living"? The answer, we may subconsciously assume, is that we die. So the fear of failure is wrapped up in the fear of death, despite the fact that failure almost never means death—only a lower standard of living.

Second, the fear of people is actually the fear of what people will think about us, and this too relates to one of humanity's basic needs: the acceptance of peers. Human beings evolved as tribal animals because separation from the tribe often meant death—the individual caveman wasn't strong enough to survive on his own. So even though each of us needs space and solitude in varying amounts, it is the impossibly rare individual who can bear permanent isolation or ostracism. The need to belong is strong, almost overpowering, and, again, wired into us by evolution.

So if getting into your own business is something that shakes you, either consciously or subconsciously, you'll find it tough to get started.

C oping with fear

Make no mistake; dealing with your fears isn't easy, especially if the fear is rooted in your subconscious where you can't get at it. So how do you cope with fears that hold you back?

Well, you've already taken the first step: you're aware of the fear. If you can step outside yourself long enough to say, "Yes, that scares me," you've gone a long way toward dealing with it. There's nothing wrong with being scared. The only shame comes if you let the fear stop you when you know you should proceed.

Next, understand that there's a big difference between what you feel and what you think. It may be that, intellectually, you can see that the chances of success are pretty good, and well worth the risk. But your fears may be telling you to back away from the brink and not take the risk.

And part of your subconscious mind's tasks are to keep you from doing dangerous things. But that doesn't mean you shouldn't do them. It does mean you should look before you leap. But the leap may make sense, *even if it scares the pants off of you!* There's no relationship between the way you feel and your chances of success. Don't let your emotions dictate your actions.

So carefully consider what you may be about to do. Weigh up all the factors, including your own fear. Then decide if it makes sense, if the odds are in your favour, and the rewards are worth the risk. If so, accept the unpleasant fear sensation that may run through your body, and jump anyway. It may well be the hardest part of the price you have to pay to have the life you want—so pay it.

"But what if I fail?"

The chances of success or failure are only affected by your fears if you allow your actions to be guided by your emotions. But, ironically, your emotions are affected by your success or failure. Walt Whitman said, "Face the thing you fear and the death of fear is certain." If you succeed at doing something that scares you, it won't scare you as much next time you do it—and eventually the fear will disappear.

But even if you successfully cope with the fear of people and the fear of failure, or any other fears you have, you may still fail. Then what? Back to my friend Marc:

"You know, it's funny. Before my business failed, I was scared to death of failing. I had never failed at anything. My friends, my wife, my parents—everybody—expected me to succeed.

"Now that my business has failed, I've had a lot of comments that really hurt and a lot of bad things have happened to me. But failure doesn't scare me anymore. Having been through it, I know what it's like—and while it's bad, it's not so bad that it's going to stop me from trying again. I know now that every problem has a solution.

"I think that the fear of failing was worse than actually failing."

Let me highlight one thing: Notice that Marc said his *business* failed. He didn't say—nor does he think—that *he* failed. And, as Henry Ford said, "The great thing about failure is that it allows you to try again with more intelligence."

After the fear

"HOW DO YOU LIVE WITH FEAR?" I asked several different entrepreneurs.

"If you're worried about failure, don't go into business," said Michael Levy of the Sports Clubs of Canada. "You have to believe you'll do *anything* to prevent yourself from failing. But as for living with the fear—look it right in the mouth, and say 'What's the worst that can happen?' It's not usually so bad."

"The time to worry about failing is before you start," says Sam Stauber. "Once you're on your way, don't even think about failing. It never enters my mind that I could fail. It's not even a possibility. If it was, I'd be paralyzed and couldn't function. So once you've made the decision, don't look back."

"Being in business is a never-ending chain of failures," says Konrad Tittler. "I don't mean this in a destructive way. It's just that every setback is not a failure, it's an opportunity to learn something useful. Every day you will face the possibility of some small failure, but I view it like yesterday's cold. It's bad while you have it, and you know you may have another cold sometime in the future, but it's really not important anymore.

"I was the only guy in the world who went bankrupt every day," Tittler concludes, "but I was also the only one who didn't accept it. You don't fail until you accept that you've failed."

"Go for it anyway," said Myra Sable, "even if you might fail. Even if I failed, I couldn't work for someone else. I'd have to try again. There's a terrific sense of power and accomplishment in running your own business. I like being my own boss. It's worth it."

And Sandy Spicer recalls her feelings when they were in trouble with the bank. "It would have been so easy to just give up. Everything looked like it was stacked against us, and we were doomed to fail. But something deep inside me said, 'No! Don't let go!'"

A final thought

Before we finish with the subject of failure, let me leave you with this thought from Teddy Roosevelt, 26th President of the United States:

"Far better it is to dare mighty things to win glorious triumphs, even though checkered with failure, than to rank with those poor spirits who neither enjoy nor suffer much because they live in that gray twilight that knows neither victory nor defeat."

10 Your Only Guarantee of Success

"A man is not successful because he hasn't failed. A man is successful because he doesn't let failure stop him."

—attributed to the *Analects* of K'ung Ch'iu, c. 500 B.C.

"I THINK THAT ONE OF THE strongest traits you have to have to succeed is persistence. There are so many times when things don't go exactly how you have them planned out," says Sandy Spicer of NICs Garage. "You have to be able to be persistent and look at other ways to get at your end goal.

"When we were setting up, we found a site that we liked, and a building that we really liked. After we'd signed the lease, we found that city hall wouldn't give us our business licence because you're not allowed to back tow trucks into a garage, and you're not allowed to back a vehicle into a place of business anymore. We had to come up with some way of solving this, or we were dead before we started."

With the lease already signed, they were contractually

committed to that site. With the clock ticking, with money running out and nothing coming in, yet without a licence to operate because of the building, it looked like they were sunk.

No matter how carefully you sift through different ideas, craft your business plan, arrange your financing, and size up your market, you're still betting on the unpredictable turn of future events. There's always the possibility of failure in every venture, no matter how carefully thought out.

But you can guarantee your own success by overcoming all of the obstacles that come up. Just about every entrepreneur I've known has lived by the motto "In crisis lies opportunity." So sooner or later you're going to run into an impossible obstacle. You won't be able to get over it, under it, around it, or through it. You'll be dead, with no hope of making it. What do you do then? You get by it anyway. You turn the impossible back into the possible. How? Any way you can.

"If you fall flat on your face," says one entrepreneur, "you just get up, regroup, and start again."

And what keeps you going when there's no possible hope? How do you face the impossible challenge? That's the subject of this section.

The name usually given to continuing to fight when a reasonable person would quit is persistence. But putting a name on it doesn't help—it hurts. No sooner do you start to discuss persistence than people tune out. They've already decided how much persistence they have; don't confuse them with the facts.

I'm a perfect example of this. For years I'd heard some very smart people talk about where persistence comes from, how you get it, what you have to do to have it, and I still didn't know. Why? Because when I heard them tell me, I discounted what they said. "Yeah, I already know that," I thought, "but tell me what you *really* have to do."

It wasn't until I met an extraordinary man by the name of Martin Rutte that I really understood where persistence comes from. Martin helps companies get the most out of their executives, and the executives get the most out of their lives. And the important point is, he didn't tell me this secret; he led me to discover it myself.

It was like a light bulb coming on when I finally saw it. It was so clear—and it had been right in front of my nose for years.

So, as Martin did for me, I'm not going to tell you where you get persistence. I will try to point it out to you and let you find it yourself. But you have to keep thinking about it until you figure it out. I don't believe you can understand it any other way, not because it's so difficult, but because it's so obvious.

W hat's the difference?

Think for a moment about something simple that you do on a regular basis. It could be making coffee in the morning, tying your shoes, or straightening up your files. Now think about a time when you set out to do something simple, and you didn't complete it. Why didn't you finish this simple task?

Now think of something very difficult that you successfully accomplished at any time in your past. It could be turning in a good term paper in your most difficult subject in school. It could be completing a project at work when there wasn't enough time, or you didn't have the right resources. Or perhaps you were playing tennis, and managed to rise above yourself and beat someone who habitually beat you.

Now think about what was the difference between the simple task you didn't complete and the difficult task you did complete. If it's not clear what caused the difference, then think of two other tasks that you did and did not complete. And if you still don't get it, think about it for a few days, then come back to this exercise.

What made the difference between the success and the failure?

I'm not talking about luck. Luck comes and goes in waves, and at most we surf atop the good waves and try to survive the bad ones. What I will say about luck is that we each get our share—good and bad. Maybe it evens out, probably it doesn't. But with luck you have two choices: either you accept the luck that comes your way and carry on, or you use bad luck as your excuse for giving up. Thomas Jefferson said, "I'm a great believer in luck, and the harder I work, the luckier I seem to get."

So it's not luck I'm talking about.

If you haven't got it yet, try to think of, or imagine if you must, two times when you faced the same situation, either easy or difficult. One time you succeeded. The other you failed. What could make the difference? Where would this difference lie? What would it come from?

Ⓛ ife's more than a lottery

Let me draw an analogy. Suppose we decided to buy lottery tickets in order to make our fortune. Let's concentrate on the Big One—call it $20 million, after tax, in each draw.

One way to win the lottery would be to keep buying tickets for separate draws until we won. If we lived long enough, sooner or later we would draw the winning ticket—we'd be rich.

Another way would be to buy all the tickets for a single draw. Then we'd be certain to win. The only problem with these ideas is that the price of each ticket is $5, and they sell 10 million tickets for each draw. That means that if we buy one ticket per lottery, then unless we get lucky early on, we're going to lose a lot of money over the years. Or, if we bought all the tickets in one lottery, we'd pay $5 × 10 million tickets for a total of $50 million, and would win $20 million. That's a net loss of $30 million.

That's very much like running your own business. On any given draw, the odds may be against you. And to keep on taking chances will eventually clean you out—you only have so much money, time, and energy to invest.

But the analogy breaks down at this point for two reasons. First, you get to choose which lottery you play (which business you run), and each lottery has a different chance of success. Naturally, you want to choose the one with the odds that are most heavily in your favour. That's what the earlier chapters of this book dealt with.

But the other important difference, and the one this chapter is about, is that in business you can change the odds *after* you've bought the ticket. How? By running the business well. Choosing good people to work with you. Doing all the right management and marketing and financial things.

But most important, by making *this* chance succeed. You see, the game isn't over until you say it is.

IN THE LAST CHAPTER I TALKED about Marc, whose business failed during a recession. After the collapse, he analyzed what he'd done wrong.

"More than anything else, I failed because I stopped. When my lender called the loan on my business, I packed up because there was no way I could repay him.

"If I were going to do it again, I'd just keep right on running the business. If they'd taken away the bank account and all our assets, I would have run it without them. If they'd sold all the furniture, I would have worked on the floor. If they'd shut off the phones and locked me out of the offices, I'd work from home or a pay phone or the library. And I could have pointed out to them that their only hope of recovering their money was if I made it back for them.

"I mean, what could they do to me? They already had everything in their hands. There was nothing more they could take from me. I'd already been hurt as badly as I could be hurt.

"But what beat me was that I stopped. That's when I failed."

"We have a terrible problem."

What was your "darkest hour," Myra Sable?

"There've been so many it's hard to tell.

"But I remember the time when we first managed to interest a major food distributor in carrying our line. We'd just delivered our first batch of antipasto to them—and discovered the batch was bad, spoiled.

"We had to tell them. If we hadn't, people might have gotten sick, we could have had lawsuits—it was unthinkable. So we had to tell them. But we were so afraid that it would kill their interest in carrying our products.

"Fortunately they were very understanding. These things happen in the food industry, and as long as you do your homework, nobody gets hurt.

"So now we had to replace the antipasto right away. Sooner, even. So I called our food chemist, who was in charge of production, to get him started on a new batch right now while I called my customers to try and stall for time.

"Only it turned out our chemist wasn't there. Apparently he didn't like the new packaging we were using, and so had locked up the plant, taken the keys, and left the country with his family."

What do they know that you don't?

What would you have done if you were Myra Sable or Sandy Spicer? Think about their situations, and try to figure out what you would have done if faced with their problems, because rest assured you'll face situations just as tough or tougher in your own business.

But as you put yourself in their shoes, remember that you have an unfair advantage over them: you know that their problems were eventually solved. When they were facing them, there was no such assurance.

Or was there? Remember what Sam Stauber said about fear: "Once you're on your way, don't even think about failing. It never enters my mind that I could fail. It's not even a possibility. If it was, I'd be paralyzed and couldn't function. So once you've made the decision, don't look back."

"Lots of people fail," said one young entrepreneur, "because when they hit a brick wall they think 'Well, I guess the Good Lord didn't mean for me to make it,' and they go home and cry. If you do that, you've failed. You can't stop. You keep going anyway."

Think about it. The power that guarantees your success is right in front of you.

B e—Do—Have

One of the most interesting—and useful—success formulas I've ever heard consists of three short words: Be—Do—Have. If you think about it, people who have carved out the kind of lifestyle you'd like have done so by the things they've accomplished. The fruit of their actions is luxury.

But their actions stem from the kind of people they are. You wouldn't expect an ordinary person to do extraordinary things—except in extraordinary circumstances—would you?

So to have good things, you must do things well, and to do things well, you must be good at doing them, right? Be—Do—Have.

And certainly I've noticed that the successful people I've worked with are good at what they do, and it shows in what they have. The three are linked in fact, not just in theory.

But here's the kicker: with the exception of the rare genius who is born with overwhelming talent, like a Mozart, nobody is born great. Heroes don't spring, fully armoured, from the forehead of Zeus, chief of the gods. They *become* experts, shaped by the pressure of their desire to do and have good things. And that means, though you may or may not believe it, you can do great things in order to have fine things. And you can do it by reshaping yourself.

"Luck has nothing to do with success"

"I don't think luck has anything to do with success," says Sandy Spicer of NICs, echoing a thought I heard repeatedly from entrepreneurs. "Little things that happen may be purely luck, but I think for anything to come of it, you have to put work into it."

Your habits will determine your success—they will make or break you. Yet, even though much of what you do during any given day is habitual, you're probably not even aware of most of your habits. Consider the routine you follow when you wake up in the morning. How you dress. Which shoe you put on first. What you eat. How you act towards other people. What you say to yourself. How you drive. What you do first at the office. What you do last.

Even such intangible things as how you feel, and whether you're courageous, whether you're happy or sad are largely a matter of habit. And if you develop great habits, they'll help you achieve great things.

Of course, if you leave your habits to develop themselves, you'll get random results, or laziness congealing into bad habits. So you must learn to control and shape your habits if you are to succeed. And doing so is within your grasp.

H abits save your sanity

Why do we depend so much on habits? What purpose do they serve in the functioning of the human animal? Well, habits serve two major purposes. First, they keep your senses from being overloaded. There's a technical term for this: *habituation*. Habituation means that after you've seen or heard or experienced something often enough, your mind tunes it out so that you can focus your attention on the things that change. We discussed this concept earlier in the example of visiting your friend who has a grandfather clock. For the first day it drives you crazy with its ticking and bonging every hour. But after you've been there for a couple of days, you wonder why the clock has stopped making any noise.

This adaptation is part of what saves your sanity. There's just too much going on around you for you to take it all in, all of the time. If you did, you wouldn't be able to handle it all. So your mind filters stuff out as soon as it becomes familiar with it. (By the way, this is the reason advertising places such a heavy emphasis on the word "new." Advertisers know that you've stopped seeing or hearing the "old," and they want you to notice their message, so they make it pop up as "new" to get past your mental filters.)

Habits also save you from having to make too many decisions. For example, you'd wear yourself out if every time someone offered you a cup of coffee you had to stop and think, "Gee, let's see. What would it taste like with cream? What would a little sugar do to the taste? How about a lot of sugar? Would I like it real sweet? And what would it be like with cream *and* sugar?" Of course, you don't do that. Instead, you decide *once* how you like your coffee, then you don't even think, but just answer, "Cream and a little sugar please," without having to stop to ponder the subtleties of taste.

I never realized how important this concept was until I spent a year working as a technician on an oceanographic research ship.

As you might expect, our mission was to spend as much time out in open ocean as possible. But because we were in an isolated, controlled environment, very few decisions were required of us, and it was incredibly relaxing. Coming back to land was like being plucked from a nice warm bed and dropped into a traffic jam in a snowstorm: instant frazzle.

Every time you make a decision, big or small, you use up some energy. If you make lots of decisions in a day, you're bound to come home absolutely bushed, even if the decisions have been such trivial things as "Do I want a hamburger or a hot dog for lunch?"

So having habits saves you effort, keeps your energy up, and keeps you from sensory overload. But woe betide you if you let your habits tend themselves. You'll "fall into bad habits," and habits, my friend, are easier to make than break.

How habits are formed

Most people harbour two misconceptions. First, they tend to think of habits as bad things. I mean, how often do people talk about their "good habits"? Second, people believe that they're held captive by their habits—that habits cannot be changed. Both of these perceptions are wrong, but since the first one is obvious, let me focus on the second.

What is a habit? A habit is a pattern of behaviour that you've practised long enough that you do it without thinking. There are two key points here: "practice" and "without thinking."

When you create a habit through laziness, that is, just by falling into it, you start doing something without even thinking about whether you want the results. For instance, you may start by leaving papers on your desk when you go home rather than putting them away, and you end up by having a habitually messy desk. You never *planned* to have a messy desk, but just by doing the same thing over and over, you build up the habit of having a messy desk anywhere you go. And, because of habituation, you even stop seeing that it's messy. When you see something too frequently, you stop seeing it at all. So you are probably not even aware, except in a subconscious, background kind of way, that you *have* a messy desk. It got that way purely because you practised something—leaving papers out when you went home—on a regular basis.

To "break" this bad habit would involve changing the whole pattern of your behaviour around the events that surround going home at night. First you'd have to decide you wanted a different result—specifically, you wanted a tidy desk instead of a messy one. From past experience you know that breaking a bad habit is tough, so you have to *really* want a tidy desk to make the change. This is true of reshaping any habit: because of the effort involved, the payoff has to be *much* more important than the price, or else you won't follow through with your intentions.

And making the decision is draining—decisions cost energy. So, it's much easier just to slide back and say, "Well, I've always had a messy desk—that's just the way I am" and leave the habit unchanged. And that's how habits are made, not invented.

⒣ ow to invent a new habit

But suppose you wanted to invent a habit. To illustrate, let's talk about something harmless and simple: let's create a habit of touching the door frame every time you walk through a door. How do you do it?

Well, mostly you just need to remind yourself that you want to do it until your subconscious starts doing it for you automatically. You see, most of the time you walk around in a bit of a trance, on auto-pilot. You let the back of your mind run your body and do the routine things, while you think about the things you want to do that *aren't* routine. So you need some way of breaking into your auto-pilot's program to remind it to reach out and touch the door frame as you walk through.

The first way of doing this is just to keep reminding yourself: "Oops! I just walked through a door and forgot to touch the frame. I'll go back and touch it, just to remind myself." Every time you do that, you reinforce the message your auto-pilot gets about what you want done.

Next, put up little notes saying "TOUCH THE FRAME!" Because they're new, your auto-pilot won't filter them out, so you'll notice them, read them, remember, and touch the frame. Again, each time you do that, you reinforce your auto-pilot's programming.

Of course, after a while—a surprisingly short while—your auto-pilot will start filtering out the little notes. Try putting them higher up, or lower down, or upside down, or in a different colour. Make them new again so they get through your auto-pilot's filter and smack into your awareness.

If you keep this up for several days, you won't have to remind yourself. Your auto-pilot will have received the message and will incorporate door-frame touching into its programming. Then, unless you make a conscious choice to break out of door-frame touching, you'll spend the rest of your life touching door frames. Your friends will comment on it, and you'll wake up and either deny that you do it, because you're never aware of doing it, or you'll smile sheepishly and say it's a silly habit you picked up somewhere. Then you'll go back on auto-pilot and keep doing it without thinking.

T he great thing about inventing habits

Do you want to know the best thing about inventing good habits? You can set up the habits to do all the things you know have to get done, but that you hate doing. Once the habits are established, habituation sets in and the things get done without bothering you—you never think about doing them. When you've reached that state, just slide back, don't let anything interfere with this great habit that's doing the work, and watch the work get done.

However, the price of carving out new habits is being painfully aware of having to do these distasteful things until they become habits. Worse, the process of creating the habit can feel forced and phony. The first 15 or 30 times you do something, you'll think, "Who am I kidding? I know I'm just trying to force myself to do this stuff 'cause I hate it. I'll never make this into a habit." Despite this, if you keep doing it, it'll become a habit. But you must ignore the phony feeling, and just do it as automatically and habitually as possible.

And make it easy to continue and hard to stop. For instance, let's go back to our messy desk habit. First ask yourself what gets in the way of having a tidy desk. Possibly it's that you don't have enough file storage space. Or perhaps you need a better filing system so you can decide where to put stuff quickly, without a lot of pondering. Or maybe you let mail pile up on your desk rather than dealing with it immediately.

Once you've identified specific problems that make it tough for you to keep your desk tidy, find ways of making it easy to overcome them. If you need more file space, take a whole day to weed out old files, find somewhere to store archival files, and see if you can get some more space for stuff you don't need to handle on a day-to-day basis.

If you need your files organized better, get some help from a colleague who is particularly well organized (people always love to give advice). Then set aside a special day devoted solely to organizing files. If incoming mail is a problem, deal with it as soon as it touches your desk: decide whether it should be filed, placed in your "to-do" list, or trashed. Or, set aside the first half-hour of every day for dealing with mail so it gets off your desk. But make it a systematic thing that you can do automatically, with as little thought as possible.

Notice that it's generally easier to set up a "special" time to do rearranging than to cope with tough stuff on a daily basis—especially if the tough stuff involves many decisions. Make as many decisions as possible in advance, so material flows smoothly to the proper places without a lot of attention from you.

Then, once you've got things set up to run smoothly, start reminding yourself, both mentally and physically (by writing yourself notes, tying string around your finger, or any other kind of reminder you can think of). After a few days your reaction will be "All right, ALL RIGHT! I'm doing it!" It doesn't matter. Just as long as it gets done. Force yourself to practise your new habit—and finally, you'll do it without thinking, and never even notice that it got done.

D on't try to do too much at once

When people start out on a self-improvement kick, which usually revolves around some kind of habit pattern (smoking, weight loss, saving money, and so on), they will often try to do everything in one big, virtuous burst. They commit to lose 15 pounds *and* quit smoking *and* keep their desk neat *and* save $200 a month *and* play with their kids more *and*... Of course, they wind up not doing any of it. Why? Because they're trying to change several habits at the same time. That means they're forcing themselves to rub their noses in *lots* of the things that they hate doing all at once. The result is that they rebel against all this horrible stuff that's hitting them, and throw everything out the window at the same time.

The trick is to choose one habit, get it right, and lock it in before going on to the next one. In fact, if you do it that way, you're also *creating the habit of successfully building new habits!* Once you've got a track record at changing and building habits, you will come to expect yourself to be able to successfully tackle any habit—old or new. And that's when you'll really move into high gear.

G etting rid of bad habits

Now let's turn to the dark side of the force of habit: bad habits. How do you get rid of them?

The first thing to remember is something you learned in grade school science class: nature abhors a vacuum. In this case, *your* nature abhors a vacuum. It's really tough to stop doing something. It's much simpler to replace it with something else instead. For example, if you're the kind of person who is persistently late for appointments, don't try to *stop* being late. Instead, *start* being five minutes early. The new, good habit automatically cancels out the old, bad one.

Going back to our messy-desk example, don't *stop* leaving papers on your desk. Instead, *start* trying to get rid of paper as soon as it touches your desk. The habit of avoiding a single, unsightly piece of paper marring the beautiful perfection of your desk will ensure that your desk stays tidy.

And reward yourself for your successes. If you keep your desk clear for five consecutive days, buy yourself a new pen set or go see a movie. Again, with rewards, they have to be suited to the task, they have to be something you want, and you only award them to yourself if you cross the finish line that you've set for yourself.

Conversely, don't beat yourself up for failing. If you fall flat on your face in working on your habits, pick yourself up, dust yourself off, and start again. Changing habits requires persistence (see the discussion above) because habits are formed and re-formed through practice. The problem that most people face when forming habits is they blow it two or three times and then throw their hands up in disgust, almost as punishment. "Well, I'm so stupid at this, I guess I don't deserve to have a clean desk," they seem to say to themselves. "I'll show me! I'll give up—that'll teach me to be so stupid!" Where I come from, this is called "You can't win for losing."

The trick in forming habits is to be willing to blow it as many times as necessary in order to get the habit locked into place. If you get up one more time than you fall down, you win. If you stay down on the 547th time you fall down, you lose. It's that simple.

W hat habits are you going to need

Obviously a whole book could be written about habits. In fact, a whole industry has grown up around habit formation in the form of diet books, books on personal finances, "how to stop smoking" courses, and so on. I can't go into much more detail in the space available, nor is it really necessary.

Let's turn, instead, to the question of which habits you're going to need to succeed in your own business. I'm now going to give you a checklist of habits to consider. Some of these habits may not strike you as habits at all, but they are. Even though we don't normally label them as habits, they still represent patterns of behaviour that we've practised long enough that we do them without thinking. Here, then, are habits you might like to pick up:

1 Practise positive self-talk

When you speak to yourself, say nice things. Most of us aren't aware of it, but we spend more time talking to ourselves than to anyone else. If your comments to yourself are always negative, you'll erode your self-esteem. Practise self-praise as well as self-criticism—and do it often.

2 Keep an optimistic attitude

If reality is an opinion, what does that make a "realist"? Never mind; the point I'm trying to make is that you'll try more, and *achieve* more with a positive attitude than a negative one. This doesn't mean a positive attitude will overcome all problems. For example, I can have the most positive attitude around and I'll still never be the heavyweight champion of the world. But optimistic people achieve more than pessimistic ones.

That doesn't mean not making contingency plans for disaster or problems. Plan for the worst, but expect the best.

3 Put business before pleasure

Do the unpleasant things first. Get the tough stuff done, then enjoy the easy stuff. People who eat dessert first may die of malnutrition—or obesity. You need to be a lean, mean, fighting machine, so do the hard parts early and make life easy for yourself.

4 Attract people to you

This doesn't mean you have to win a popularity contest. In fact, there are times when you'll have to be a whirling, chrome-plated bastard to get things done.

But people won't work their guts out for you if that's the way you are all the time. Just like investors, people must *want* to be around you and to follow your leadership in order for you to get the most out of them.

One of the key reasons that Lloyd Segal gives for the dramatic success of Advanced Biotech is the people they were able to attract: "We created an environment, a sense of trust, a sense of sharing that a lot of small companies talk about, but that we really have. And it's a big part of what makes us love this business, because we all love coming in here and being with the people with whom we've surrounded ourselves. We invest in these people a lot, we give them a lot of latitude, and we've hired the kind of people who thrive on minimum direction and maximum achievement."

Clarissa Desjardins echoes this sentiment: "We've given a lot of thought to the psychology of our people; we treat them the way we'd like to be treated.

But attracting people to you is too broad to really classify as a habit, so let me break it down into four subsections:

1 **Smile.** People like people who smile much more than people who frown. Practise smiling. I know it sounds dumb, but do it anyway.

2 **Give loyalty to get loyalty.** Stand up for your people. Read the riot act to them privately for their mistakes, but defend them in public, even if they've done something really boneheaded. Be aware of what they need from you as much as what you need from them.

3 **Lift people up.** If you greet somebody when they're at an emotional level of 6 (out of 10), and you leave them at a setting of 8, they'll look forward to seeing you again. But if you greet them at 6 and leave them at 3, they won't want to see you again. Look for opportunities to lift people up, anybody, anywhere, anytime—but especially the people you work with. Praise them often. Admire them frequently—and only when you honestly mean it.

4 **Think about what they feel.** If you're going to treat people the way you want to be treated, you need to know how they're feeling and what's going on in their heads. This means taking the time to think about the situation from *their* perspective. This is called empathy, and it allows to you stay in tune with the people around you—and helps them stay in tune with you.

5 Be courageous

"When courage fails, all fails," said James Barrie, the Scottish playwright. There will be times when you'll need to do things that scare you or continue to do the right things when you're scared everything's going to fail. Courage is not the absence of such fear. Courage is carrying on despite such fear.

We discussed fear in Chapter 7. Notice your physical reaction to fear. Acknowledge that you're afraid. Then decide what's the right thing to do, and do it. The time to take counsel of your fears is before you start, not when you're committed to a course of action.

6 Be ingenious

There are times when you'll have to invent your way out of problems. Now, the human animal has far more ingenuity than most of us ever practise. And practise is the key word since the more we do it, the more comfortable we feel doing it. So decide that you are ingenious, then set out to invent solutions to problems you encounter, rather than running away from them or hiring someone to solve them for you.

And the list of good habits goes on. It's as long as you want to make it. So try this experiment: imagine that you're interviewing someone whose accomplishments you admire. Examine their lives, examine what they do and have done. What habit patterns do they have, or must they have? Then, if those are habits you're likely to need, carve them out to be your own.

And may the force of habit be with you!

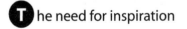he need for inspiration

There are gonna be days, just like your mother told you, when you shudda stayed in bed. Sooner or later, you'll find yourself up against an impossible situation, or beset with an unbelievable run of bad luck, or faced with unbeatable odds. You'll go through months of work with hardly any sign that the light at the end of the tunnel is anything but a freight train coming in your direction. Your employees won't solve problems; they'll create them. Your creditors will get nasty, and your suppliers will ask for cash on delivery instead of offering 30 days net. Potential clients will lead you on and then tell you they don't want what you've got. Your family and friends will complain they never see you any more. Your doctor will say you should be taking it easier—you're working yourself into a heart attack. Your financing will unravel when your sales fall behind projection.

How do you cope with the pressure? How do you find the solutions? *Where do you get the inner resources you have to have to get through the tough times?* In answer, I offer not a specific solution, but a general purpose tool that you *must* use to succeed. It won't solve any of your problems directly, but will enable you to invent solutions when you need them, and then to apply these solutions. This tool is called *inspiration*.

D on't let the bastards grind you down!

When you start out on a venture, it's new and exciting. The prospects are great and your success seems inevitable. As your business unfolds, however, you stumble, run into brick walls you never knew existed, and get slammed in the face by disappointments and tragedies. Your enthusiasm and energy seep out like a slow leak in a balloon, until finally you feel flat, stale, discouraged, and helpless.

In that frame of mind, you're finished—it's game over. The *only* thing that will keep your business running through the bad times and the disasters is your own energy and conviction. You've got to marshal that energy carefully, and keep your batteries charged, even if times seem to be good, in preparation for the problems that lurk ahead.

I REMEMBER WHEN the hi-tech company owned by one of my clients had gone through some battering, punishing times. As a result, the president and founder had to raise some additional financing, and lost his majority position. He was forced to dilute his control so that his company could survive. It was a bitter blow.

Now the bank was on his back, plaguing him about continuing losses from one of his divisions that was eating the profits made by the other operations.

As we were talking, I noticed that he was speaking in a much more subdued fashion than normal. He almost seemed like he didn't care, that he'd given up, and had accepted that he was going to go back to being a cog in a company he didn't control.

Specifically, he talked about selling more shares, and named a price I thought was way too low—it gave no credit to the tremendous advances that his most promising division was making.

"Why don't you go on vacation for a week?" I suggested. "Take your wife and go down to the Caribbean and lie in the sun. Relax. Stop thinking about the company and it's problems for a while. Read some good, trashy novels. Enjoy yourself for a bit. You need it."

"Well, Richard, I'd love to, but I can't. I can't leave the company at this time, and I can't afford to spend a week down south. All my money's tied up in the company," he replied.

"You can't afford *not* to go," I replied. "You're talking like a beaten man. The price you've set for your stock is way too low—you're giving the company away. And you should be telling the bank to go to hell, not mousing around, begging for crumbs. You *have* to go."

He eventually went, whether on my advice or just because he felt the need himself. When he returned, he was the cocky, boisterous man who had started the company. He did raise additional financing, but much less than he'd been talking about, and so gave up less of his own position.

What I could see, not feeling all the pressure that he was experiencing, was that the company had turned the corner and, barring a disaster, was going to make it, and make it big. All he saw was the everyday disaster, the perpetual emergency, the constant, grinding pressure that had worn him down to the point where he doubted his own ability.

T his state of mind can kill your business

You can't allow yourself to reach that state. Nothing will kill a venture faster than lack of confidence or enthusiasm on the part of the CEO. And to avoid this from happening means that you must take care of your state of mind.

This is where inspiration comes in. Inspiration has two meanings that are particularly relevant here: to exalt or enliven, and to pluck ideas out of thin air. And both meanings are related—you often get the ideas you need when you're getting some life and spirit pumped back into you. And, ironically, inspiration also means to breathe in. This also fits, for there are times when you just need to catch your breath.

And catching your breath can mean just that. One entrepreneur I know recommends going for long walks: "It's important to have some quiet time because there are enough heavy, intensive times in running a company." For others, their source of inspiration can be music. One of my clients has season tickets for two symphony performance series. Others collect or study art, or become involved in charitable work, or go out on their sailboats on breezy afternoons or weekends. Exercise is a great way of both working off frustrations and getting out of your problems for a while.

The activity itself is not important. It has to be a change of pace—something completely divorced from your daily grind, and something that can give you a sense of perspective and, well, breathing space about what you're doing. Here's how best-selling author

Robert Pirsig wrote about this process: "The gumption-filling process [of inspiration] occurs when one is quiet long enough to see and hear and feel the real universe, not just one's own stale opinions about it. But it's nothing exotic... You see it often in people who return from long, quiet fishing trips."

And that's what you need—the distance to see and hear and feel the real universe, to get away from your own stale opinions, to get some distance, and recover your sense, not only of task, but of self, of who you are, and why you've got what it takes to make your business successful.

"What has worked for me," says Sherry Orr of Trans-Mutual Truck Lines, "has been going someplace quiet with no outside distractions—no books, no TV, no radio, nothing. I just try to get myself back into perspective. Then, once I've got myself back together, I can start to deal with the problems again.

"Living in Calgary is great because I can just take a couple of hours and go up into the mountains. Somehow, being up there helps me turn the business off and get everything back in focus."

But don't wait until you're flat and stale to seek such inspiration. Cultivate the habit of seeking breathing space while you're in the thick of the action. Make the time, even though you don't have the time. Otherwise, you won't know what works for you or where to go to get what you need to recover yourself.

And ideas will come when you're looking the other way. Even as you put distance between yourself and your problems, your subconscious will be working away at your problems. You may come back from a night at the opera with an answer to a problem that had been threatening everything you've worked for.

C ultivating ingenuity

The brain is divided into two halves, or hemispheres, and the tasks the brain performs are divided between them. Generally speaking, logical, rational thought and planning, as well as speech, reside in the left hemisphere. Artistic, creative, intuitive and pattern-matching activities generally reside in the right hemisphere, which also tends to be the centre for the physical coordination of things like sports and dance.

Inspired ideas tend to come from the pattern-matching right hemisphere. Since this is the non-verbal half of the brain, such ideas seem to burst into your head suddenly, and are not fully verbalized. But too much activity in one hemisphere dampens activity in the other. This is why spending time on non-verbal, non-linear activities, such as sports or music, can allow your right hemisphere to put pieces together and come up with a good idea. So there's a direct connection between the "catching your breath" kind of inspiration, and the "plucking ideas out of thin air" sort.

You can also improve on the natural process of ingenuity by accepting it as a real mental force, and being supportive of what it's doing. Since it takes place in the non-verbal half of your brain, it can seem mysterious. We tend to understand things more easily if they're pinned down with words. But it's really just a mental activity like any other.

But if attracting the thunderbolts of inspiration is an unfamiliar process to you, here's how you can encourage them:

1 Have a guiding theme

You should know what you're trying to accomplish, provide a target for your ingenuity to aim at. It should be clearly defined and in concrete terms, such as "What can we do to get customers to buy our old product instead of our competitor's new product?"

2 Write down all of your thoughts as they occur to you

Sit and gaze off into space. Don't try to direct your thoughts, just let them flow. Remember that the process is one of fitting pieces of a puzzle together, and this is not always a systematic, logical process. Then, as these random thoughts come, jot them down so you can recall what went through your head. You may eventually discard many of these ideas, but some of them may bring solutions from surprising directions.

3 Learn to frame your questions properly

A well-phrased question is almost half the answer. You can tell if you've chosen the proper question because a good one suggests ideas; a bad one leaves you facing a blank wall. My earlier question was "What can we do to get customers to buy our old product instead of our competitor's new product?" which begins to suggest a focus on what customers want, which customers we should pursue, what prompts consumer responses, and so on. A bad question would be something like "How do I get out of this mess?" as it suggests nothing except surrender.

4 Try to organize your random thoughts into a logical framework

Once you've listed several haphazard thoughts on paper, see if you can fit them into some semblance of order. The process of playing around with different thoughts can prompt the "Ah-ha!" reaction of an inspired idea.

5 Do any part of the problem you already understand

If some part of the solution is already clear to you, work on that one first and lay it out in clear form. Then go back to the whole problem and look at it again. It may be that you will find another part that has become clear in the meantime, or you might have a new perspective on the whole thing. Remember, much of your creative thought takes place outside of your awareness and away from the verbal focus of your left hemisphere.

6 Talk over your ideas with a sympathetic listener

Bringing the verbal left hemisphere directly into play sometimes engages both parts of the brain at the same time. Explaining your ideas to someone else will also clarify them to you. You'll be forced to take the hazy, unverbalized concepts that your right hemisphere has produced and strain them into the verbal containers (words) that such an explanation requires. This will also reveal many of the hidden, and often incorrect, assumptions that these ideas are based on. Note, however, that you want someone who will *listen*, not comment. You may not want their comments (depending on who they are). But you certainly want them to listen without criticizing. Explain that in advance.

These steps will not guarantee an ingenious idea that will save your company. That may come as much with persistent slogging as frothy genius. But you are certain to have more luck finding a good idea if you are looking for one than if you dismiss the possibility that one exists. So exercise your ingenuity—it's good practise. And, as with most things, good practise will improve ingenuity.

D on't be afraid to feel discouraged

There's nothing wrong with feeling discouraged. Problems are going to occur, and it's only natural that you will have an emotional reaction to them. The mistake lies in staying that way. So when discouragement sets in (and it will) seek inspiration to rest; seek encouragement to recover; and be open to new ideas that appear out of thin air. Then get back in the fight.

That's the way—the only way—you'll win.

For at the end of it all, you are the best thing you've got going for yourself. You are the best guarantee that you will succeed.

11 Are You the Kind of Person Who Can Make It?

A while back, I was in Cambridge, England to negotiate a contract for a client. It was one of the strangest business trips I've ever taken. I spent four days and several thousand dollars travelling 8000 miles back and forth across the Atlantic, all for a one-hour meeting. It was worth it, however, as the negotiations were concluded successfully—and might well have ended in failure had I done things any other way.

Once I was sure that the negotiations had been successful, I grabbed a cab to Heathrow airport in an effort to return home a day earlier than originally scheduled. There was a delay in getting out of Cambridge, however, caused by a man in a powered wheelchair bumping slowly along the rather narrow street we needed to get through. This took some time, as the street wound around quite a bit and nowhere would it have been safe to pass.

At first I thought my cab driver was simply being polite to a poor unfortunate. But when the driver told me who this man was, it was clear that his patience was more out of respect than pity.

The man in the wheelchair was Stephen Hawking.

Stephen Hawking is the victim of Lou Gehrig's disease (amyotrophic lateral sclerosis), which he contracted when he was eight years old. When I saw him, his body was completely paralyzed except for three fingers, which he used to operate his wheelchair. He couldn't write, and could no longer speak since his trachea was removed to enable him to breathe.

Despite all this, Professor Stephen Hawking is believed to be the most brilliant astrophysicist of our time—our generation's Einstein—and the author of the best-selling book, *A Brief History of Time*. Seeing him in person was proof to me that someone can be a giant without having the outward appearance of one.

C an anybody make it?

One argument that I've never been able to win—yet have never lost—is on the question of whether anybody—anybody at all—can become a successful entrepreneur.

I once had this debate with an industrial psychologist who worked for the government. She proposed that not everyone has the ability or psychological resources required to become a successful entrepreneur. I asked her about the unusual successes: the high school dropouts, the bums who had gone on to build fortunes, the people who were too old or too young, of the wrong background or didn't speak the language, or had some deformity or disability or inferiority complex that should have prevented them from making it.

"Exceptions to the rule," was her reply. Then she countered, "Do you think that everybody can become successful entrepreneurs? If so, then why don't more people do it?" And to this question, I would reluctantly have to say that no, I don't think everybody can become successful entrepreneurs—but I also cannot determine in advance who can and who can't. Their eventual success or failure separates them.

In fact, I believe that anybody *could* make it—but most people *won't*. Few people would agree with such a rash statement. But I'm not alone in believing that people are capable of much more than they give themselves credit for.

AND WHEN I ASKED ENTREPRENEURS what they thought the necessary qualities of a successful entrepreneur were, the list of things they came up with generally said nothing about age, sex, background, talent, education, or ability. Instead, they discussed qualities that come from within, rather than those that are evident from outside.

"I believe that everyone has what it takes," says 46-year-old Sherry Orr, owner of Trans-Mutual Trucking, "but succeeding depends on what you want. You've got to believe in yourself, to believe in what you can do and accomplish. You've also got to be a little bit of everything, be able to do a little bit of everything.

"That didn't just happen for me. It took me a long, long time to grow into the person I needed to be. You've got to have a little bit of guts, and be a bit of a risk-taker, though. So finally, it's a question of whether someone wants to do it or not."

Nineteen-year-old Jonathan Strauss likes to quote Wayne Gretzky on trying: "'One hundred percent of shots not taken are missed.'

"I don't believe anybody can make it. It takes a willingness to take risks, which not everyone is prepared to do, and the foresight to see opportunity where others may miss it. There's no secret to success. It means having a product or a service that your clients need, then working hard and not becoming complacent.

"Complacency really bothers me, and it's one of the major reasons why businesses fail in the first year. People will try something, and it'll work, so they think, 'Hey, this is easy!' Then they stop doing the things that created their early success, and fail.

"I don't think that luck has anything to do with anything, but I think that timing is absolutely everything. You need a bit of luck in anything you do, but at the end of it, I don't think luck matters. I look at how hard we work around the office, and I know that luck has nothing to do with what we've been able to do."

"What do you need to be successful?" muses 65-year-old Konrad Tittler. "Persistence. If you don't have it, stay employed.

"It's important to recognize when you've been lucky, and don't let it blow your ego out of size. If you can do that, then you can deal with bad luck when it comes, then you can say, 'It has nothing to do with me.'"

"For sure, work for yourself," says Marci Lipman, "Maybe in the beginning, sure, go to work for someone else to get experience in business. There's a lot to be learned, and you might as well get someone else to pay you to learn. But then get out there on your own.

"The fun part of working for yourself is to bring something from your imagination into reality. I don't think it would be as much fun working for somebody else. You have a lot of freedom to create if you're creative. You don't have to go to someone else for approval: if you bomb, you bomb!

"I have friends who work for big corporations, and they keep saying they envy me and my lifestyle. So I tell them they should try, they should quit their jobs and just try it. But they never do; they're afraid to give up their job security.

"I don't think there is any job security working for big corporations, or anybody else for that matter. So I suppose you've got to have a small element of being able to take a risk—even though I don't think you're any more at risk working for yourself than working for someone else. But you have to be willing to try, and many people just aren't.

"It's not a matter of intelligence or talent. I think there are a lot of unintelligent and untalented entrepreneurs who make buckets of money. But the passion has to be there. Finding out what the market needs is only half the equation."

"I don't think that just anyone can do it," says 28-year-old Greg, one of three partners of Snug Industries. "You gotta have drive and motivation. You have to have an understanding of business, and be willing to learn what you don't know. And you have to know your market, not just research your market."

"I don't think that everybody can be a successful entrepreneur," says Sandy Spicer, founder of NICs Garage. "People who don't follow through, people who don't see that time is important and let things slip, can't make it. These things can hurt you quite quickly.

"But most people, if they were determined enough, and had the goals, and worked very hard at it, then they could succeed."

Y ou can't tell from the outside whether someone will succeed

It's impossible to look at someone and tell whether they could become a successful entrepreneur. And it's even harder for the person him- or herself to know if he or she has the capacity to succeed.

SANDY SPICER'S STORY—told in detail in Chapter 2—confirms this. Remember, she started out broke, a single parent with a two-year-old daughter, and an old car. She was a high school dropout who hadn't finished her grade 12. But she had the three things an entrepreneur must have: the desire, the courage to try, and—most importantly—the willingness to change from what she was into what she had to be.

While working at a clothing store, she went to night school and finished her high school equivalence. Then she went to university and earned a degree in commerce, taking five years to finish a four-year degree program. She worked in business as a financial analyst for BC Transit, then she and her partner spent a year preparing a business plan. And then jumped. The result? "I love being an entrepreneur," says Spicer. "I've always been a hard worker, but before I worked hard without questioning why I was working hard. Now I know why I'm working hard, because when you work for yourself, if you put more in, you get more out. That wasn't always true when I worked for someone else.

"I've changed a lot working at NICs. I can see a bigger picture now, my focus has broadened quite a bit. It's good."

So, you tell me, which woman is more likely to succeed: a young, broke, uneducated single mom; or a university graduate with lots of business experience and a well-thought-out, well-planned business? And the answer is that they are the same person. But the university graduate emerged only because the broke young mom had the desire and the courage, and was willing to change. And in my professional opinion, that's what makes the difference.

C an only certain special kinds of people make it?

But, if you can't tell by someone's background, by their previous experience or training, and if they themselves can't tell if they've got what it takes, then how can you tell if you've got it? Well, perhaps it's true that only certain kinds of people can make it. Or maybe there's a profile that we could develop that would tell people whether they should try—or go home and abandon the whole idea.

The temptation is to say yes, there is a certain type of person who will become successful. However, anyone who would say that would probably quickly amend it. They'd likely say that there are certain kinds of people who are *more likely* to succeed than others, and there are certain kinds of people who are *more likely* to fail. And I would agree—but I'm not entirely sure I could tell one group from the other.

In fact, one entrepreneur put it to me this way: "People who have grown up with disadvantages find it easier to become successful. The ones that grew up in a comfortable surrounding and never faced any real adversity, won't be able to cope as well with the problems of building a business."

A FEW YEARS AGO I WAS coordinating the production of a television documentary for a group of clients, and got into a conversation with a producer who was filming profiles of successful entrepreneurs. She explained how frustrating it was working on the series. Why?

"These people have nothing in common," she complained. "Some are old, some are young. They're from rich backgrounds and poor, they're highly educated and illiterate; they're male and female and from minorities or established WASP families. I can't point to one set of rules and say, 'Here's what all these people have that makes them successful.'"

I thought for a moment, and then said, "No, I can tell you two things they *all* have in common: the desire to be successful and the courage to do something about it."

A case in point is Natalie MacLean, a Cape Breton woman who moved to Calgary, and eventually started a business called The Advisory Group with three friends. The Advisory Group consulted to entrepreneurs, and consequently dealt with them all the time. MacLean had a list of three things that all entrepreneurs have in common: the desire to control their own destinies; the desire to seek out challenges and stretch themselves; and the desire for greater rewards than conventional opportunities offer.

"We looked at ourselves and our creation of The Advisory Group as good examples of these three qualities," she says. "And yet, when we reviewed our own goals, we found that although we all want the rewards—the cars, the houses, the vacations, and so forth—it's the control and the challenges that really turn our crank and push us to work all kinds of crazy hours. We do it because we love it."

Does this mean that anyone can decide they want to have control, challenges, and rewards, and become successful entrepreneurs?

"No. To succeed you need a few other characteristics as well. You need to be able to recognize your own personal weaknesses so you can build in systems or hire people to fill in where you're weak. Most people don't do this; they hire people who are very much like themselves—and have the same weaknesses.

"Next, you have to be interested in and willing to work with other people. That especially includes being willing to communicate with and delegate to the people around you, recognizing their strengths and weaknesses, too.

"You have to know when to ask for help. You have to believe that all problems are solvable. Oddly, most people can cope with some kinds of problems, but are totally stymied by others. You almost have to be an eternal optimist and believe that every problem has a solution. You may not solve it in a way you like, or the way you originally planned, but you can certainly find a solution."

Note, however, that all of these qualities are very difficult to measure. They're even difficult for you to discern in yourself. And also notice that what we're talking about are things that come from inside—not from your background or accomplishments.

"The mechanics of business you can go to school and learn, like I did," says Natalie. "You may not have the money you need, but you can get that from other people. Any outward thing you lack, you can go out and get. But you have to have the desire and the guts to go out and get them, and not just fold up and say, 'I guess it wasn't intended for me to make it.'"

So let's talk about what goes on inside people that may make them *more likely* to succeed.

T he ideal entrepreneur

Let's assume for the moment that there is an ideal entrepreneur—a "person most likely to succeed." What would he or she look like? Well, the ideal entrepreneur would be likely be self-confident, aggressive, meticulous, self-disciplined, intelligent, determined, inventive, capable, experienced, careful but willing to take calculated risks, goal-oriented, well-organized, persuasive, capable of motivating and inspiring others, charming and personable, yet capable of being ruthless when necessary, and possessed of great self-honesty, clear personal goals, a good sense of humour, a successful track record, and strong financial backing. Moreover, I'm sure that the longer I think about the virtues such an ideal person should have, the more I could add to the list. So let's start with these.

This is such an impressive list of virtues that it would be fair to ask if *any* successful entrepreneurs have them all. I certainly don't know of any, although such an animal may exist.

But let's turn the question around: can someone become a successful entrepreneur if they're missing most of these wonderful virtues? The answer is: yes and no. Successful entrepreneurs may not have these qualities when they start, but if they manage to struggle through to success, they'll have many of them when they finish. The process of becoming a successful entrepreneur will force them to develop these qualities. Someone who achieves extraordinary things is not likely to remain an ordinary person.

But if none of these great traits are vital to success, what qualities *must* you have to become successful? If the process will instill many of these virtues in you, what must you have in order to start?

W ho are you, anyway?

When I reached this point in considering this whole question of what entrepreneurs must have, I got the sneaking suspicion that there's something more central to the successful entrepreneur—indeed, to the successful human being—than all these wonderful qualities. I recognized that all these virtues were like clothes that we put on and take off, and that we may have more control over which qualities we choose to wear than we think we do.

This led me to wonder just who we are under all these identification badges we wear. I mean, if you play it like a game of "Who am I?" and forbid the use of identifiers such as name, address, race, nationality, height, looks, or hair colour, and then go further and forbid descriptions like "hard worker," "self-confident leader," or "meticulous planner," what's left? Who are you underneath all that stuff, anyway? Is there anything left if we remove all of that?

Of course there is, but it's so uncommon for us to deal with this area of our humanity that we really don't have any good labels for it. In religious traditions it might be called the "soul," but as this word carries so much emotional baggage, let's talk instead about the "spirit" of the individual.

W here does the will to win come from?

If patterns of behaviour like perseverance, careful planning, optimism, and so on are merely surface reflections of someone's underlying spirit, then where does this spirit come from? Where does the will to achieve, to carry on when failure seems certain, come from?

We don't know. All we can do is observe the results; there's no way of predicting someone's success or failure before they achieve it. Let's suppose, for instance, that you're somebody who doesn't stand a chance of succeeding. Say you're just a college kid, maybe 21 years old, and you're female. Let's pretend that your father died suddenly of a heart attack, and you and your older sister inherit a trucking company that your father spent 20 years building. Let's suppose that before he died, you and your father had agreed that you weren't suited to the family business, and that after his death, your mother advised you to sell out. And let's suppose that your sister, who owned the other half of the company, tried to sell out behind your back because she thought you'd blow it all if you tried to run the company, and she wanted to get something from her half.

And just to give you confidence, let's say the company's banker is very unhappy with the idea of having you take over. He tells you he thinks you should be running a dress shop, not a trucking company. Now let's make life difficult. Let's set this all in the middle of the worst recession since the 1930s. And let's say that the person who was your father's second-in-command quits the company, exercises her stock options, and sells the stock back to the company, as was her right. In the process, she winds up with a big chunk of the company's working capital—and then uses the money to try to engineer a takeover. Suppose you arrive at work the first morning at 8 a.m., employing 27 drivers, an accountant, a receptionist, and a sales manager, and that by noon everyone has walked out except three drivers, the sales manager, and the receptionist. And, just to make life interesting, let's suppose that your ex-employee gives you 24 hours to sell the company to her, or lose it all.

Finally, let's suppose your name is Sherry Ruteck Orr, and you live in Calgary. But that's the point at which the make-believe stops, because all of these things really happened to Sherry—and she went ahead and rebuilt the company despite it all.

"If I had known what I was getting into..."

"I NEVER EVEN CONSIDERED SELLING OUT," says Sherry. "This company was my father's life, and he worked hard to build it.

"But if I had really known what I was getting into, I'm not sure I would have done it. As it was, there were long stretches when I worked seven days a week from 8 in the morning to midnight to do everything that had to be done.

"One of the hardest things I had to do was go to B.C. and visit Cominco, who was one of our biggest customers, and persuade them to let me keep the contract. They'd heard all the industry rumours, and they knew what was going on.

"When I walked into the room, there were six guys seated around the table waiting for some answers. And here I was, a 21-year-old girl in a business dominated by men my father's age, knowing nothing about the trucking business, trying to deal with some really tough questions about how I was going to service the contract. I don't remember what I said to them, but at the end of two hours, they gave me the go-ahead. Then I had to prove I could do it."

Today Sherry is 36 years old, and she's proven she can do it—and then some. She's also the sole owner and president, a member of the board of directors of the Alberta Trucking Association, and has a lifestyle that few of her peers will ever experience.

How did Sherry do it? Where did the inner resources come from that enabled someone to come through an impossible situation, and succeed despite it all? And how does this relate to whether you're the kind of person who can make it? Just this: your accomplishments, your past record, all of your feelings about your ability or lack of ability, your experience, your self-confidence, in fact, everything about you are in the past. If you, in your heart of hearts, have the desire for a better life, and the guts to work for it, and are prepared to go about it properly, then nothing else counts.

Yes, your fight will be easier if you have talent, if you are trained in doing certain things, and if you have the right connections and the right backing. But even if you lack any or all of these things, as Sherry Orr and Sandy Spicer did, you can still succeed. And if you're a nobody and you start from nothing, possessing nothing, and change your life into a classic rags-to-riches story, nobody will act surprised. People will look at you and say "I always knew she'd make it."

Although I don't know you personally, I can still say that, yes, you can do it. Human beings are incredibly complex—yet the inner differences between the tycoon in the limousine and the bum he passes on the street are so small as to be undetectable. But that's not the way we see things. We get blinded by someone's achievements and fail to see the person behind them.

Don't look at the label; check the contents

Labels are powerful tools. We label things to classify, order, arrange, and identify them. Think of how difficult it is to tell someone about another person if you don't know that person's name. You wind up inventing a very complicated label, like "the tall man wearing the pin-stripe suit with the gray hair and glasses" instead of saying "John Smith."

But like all powerful tools, labels are dangerous. In particular, they are dangerous to you in your pursuit of the life you really want, which we will label "success." To see the dangers that labels pose, remember that we attach expectations and limitations to things we label. If I tell you that someone is a chronic liar, for example, then you will tend to be on your guard against his or her lies. Your expectations will colour how you think, feel, and act towards this person, *even if I am wrong in applying the label.* Your expectations will affect your impressions of that individual.

But how do you label yourself? You are the most important thing in your world, so you have a variety of labels that your mind uses to work with all the aspects of you as you interact with the world. You may label yourself "strong," "young," "good-looking," "educated," "capable," or many other things. The danger comes when you are trying to accomplish something, and the labels you have in your head don't match the labels you think you will need.

For instance, if you would really like to be a professional pilot, and you imagine the labels for that kind of work are "physically fit, bright, well-educated, excellent eyesight, male, six-foot-two, blue eyes, steely gray hair, ice water for blood, sexually attractive, deserving of lots of admiration and attention," but your internal labels say "short, dumpy, has to be carried up a second flight of stairs, unable to read a menu unassisted, attracts snickers from pretty girls, grade three education at best, not bright enough to find way out of a paper bag," then you have a problem.

In fact, you have so much of a problem *with the labels* that you won't even consider trying to make yourself into someone who could be a professional pilot. I stress that your problem is first with the labels and only then with the qualifications. Why does the label problem come first? Because you may be wrong about how you think of yourself, or what the qualifications really are. Yet, if you accept your labels both for yourself and for the job at hand, you will give up without a fight. You're defeated before you even start.

H ow do we label success?

The problem with labels and success is that we usually define success as something like "a way of life that is so much better than mine that it bears no resemblance to what I've got or am capable of." In other words, we define success as something that is automatically out of our reach. It's like Groucho Marx's quip: "I wouldn't want to belong to any club that would have me as a member."

This kind of label carries the hidden assumptions that (a) success is a long, *long* way from where you are, and (b) even if it were possible to get there, *you* couldn't get there. These assumptions make it difficult to begin. Worse, if you believe you're going to fail, you probably won't even try. After all, it's safer to remain where you are.

"Success," then, as we define it in others, is something we probably can't reach. It's a double standard: success is only for the successful. Therefore, only a successful person can be successful. The result? We think we'd like to become wealthy, for example, if that's part of our label for success. But inside we know it's really all a waste of time because, after all, we're just not the type of person who becomes successful. I mean, if we were, wouldn't we already be successful? I mean, "if you're so smart, why ain't ya rich?" Right? And so, we subconsciously sabotage our own efforts.

W hat is it that makes people seem successful?

Think of someone you know who's successful. You may not know him or her personally, you may only have read about the person in a magazine. What is it about him or her that defines success to you? Is it money? Fame? The business he or she created from the ground up? What is it about this person that you wish you were or had or did? It may be more than one thing, so take some time now and think about them.

Another way of approaching this is to ask yourself, "If they didn't have _____, I wouldn't consider them successful." Then remove these things. For example, if Babe Ruth hadn't hit all those home runs in baseball, would you think of him as a great baseball player? If Lee Iaccoca had sunk with Chrysler instead of pulling it off the bottom, would he be a modern business hero? If John F. Kennedy had lost the presidential election instead of winning it, would he be a demigod today? What is it the successful person you chose has or did that makes them successful in your eyes?

Now think of the person you've chosen without their success suit—in their human underwear, as it were. What do you think you'd see? If you've followed me so far, suddenly this successful person stands before you as—a person. No more. They scratch themselves, have head colds, tell bad jokes, are ten pounds over-weight, and have all sorts of weird things wrong with them—just like the rest of us.

The problem is, we are so hypnotized by the sparkle from the success suits that we see them in, we no longer see them as human. And because we don't see them as human, we have a hard time see-ing ourselves in their places, or having or doing the things they do. So, part of our quest is to buy our own success suits, so that we, too, can be superhuman and dazzle everyone around us.

But before we finish with labels, let's look at one other thing. When you stripped off the success suit from the successful person you chose, what was it about the suit that made it the image of suc-cess? In other words, what caused you to consider that person to be successful? The answer is almost certain to be that the person did something exceptional. Note that I did not say that he or she was an exceptional person—just that he or she did something exceptional.

Now, doing exceptional things makes you exceptional—because if everybody did the same exceptional thing, it wouldn't *be* excep-tional. For example, the first time someone drove a car over 60 miles an hour, it was a big deal! Now, however, it's nothing special because we do it all the time. But doing something exceptional does *not* require you to become superhuman. It does, however, require three things:

1 the will to take action;

2 the desire to change your life from what it is to what you want it to be; and

3 the willingness to make the changes in yourself from who you are to who you need to become to succeed.

 he bottom line of success

So, when all is said and done, are you the kind of person who can make it? The following quiz may give you some idea of whether you're *more likely* to make it. But even that may be wrong, because the ultimate answer lies within you—and nowhere else.

 uiz

Have You Got What It Takes to Be Successful?

Answer "yes" or "no" to each of the following questions. Since this quiz is for your benefit, answer the questions as you honestly feel, not as you think they should be answered.

1) Can you visualize or feel what your life will be like when you're successful?

2) Have you written down all the things you want out of life, and when you want them?

3) Do you regularly reread your written goals?

4) Do you have a clear picture in your mind about the kind of person you will be when you've made it?

5) Do you know what skills you will need to succeed, and have you figured out either how to acquire them for yourself, or get someone on your team who has them?

6) Do you have a detailed, written business plan?

7) Have you arranged adequate financing, allowing a *generous* provision for unforeseen problems?

8) When you play games and find yourself in close, competitive situations, do you win more often than lose?

9) Write down a list of all your recognized achievements from age six on (awards, prizes, trophies, and so on). Would the list look impressive to someone interviewing you?

10) When you look in the mirror, do you like what you see?

11) If someone could hear you when you talk to yourself, even in your mind, would they think it sounded like you were encouraging yourself?

12) Are you good at maintaining your weight at what it should be, keeping your house picked up the way you like it, exercising as often as you should, and doing things that you dislike on time?

13) When things go wrong, is it often your fault?

14) When things go wrong, is it often someone else's fault?

15) When you've got a number of things to do, do you usually do those things you dislike first in order to get them out of the way?

16) Do you like making difficult decisions that can have a major impact on your life?

17) Do you enjoy a really tough challenge?

18) Do you work well under deadline pressure?

19) Do you avoid making excuses for mistakes you've made?

20) Do you enjoy preparing a carefully drawn out plan that you know will work?

21) Could you fire a close personal friend if they weren't doing their job?

22) Can you scream at people if the situation calls for it, even when you're not actually angry?

23) Can you lose a lot of money one day, and then put it out of your mind when the next day rolls around?

24) If it were necessary to cheat to keep your business afloat, would you resist cheating?

25) Do people call you stubborn?

26) Did you choose a business idea that is based on something you know a lot about and are an expert at?

27) Do people already spend money on the product or service you intend to sell?

28) Do you have a track record that shows that you're good at selling things?

29) Do you know what you're going to do if a major corporation jumps in and starts competing head-to-head with you?

30) Are the people around you, particularly those you live with, prepared to cheer you on through years of long working hours and little income?

31) Can you survive without a salary for six months or more if you have to?

32) Do you have a hobby or some form of recreation that you really enjoy, and indulge in regularly?

33) Do you absolutely love the business you're about to enter? Do you look forward to spending months and years working at it?

34) Do people like to spend time with you?

35) If you had to choose between having a lot of money or having a lot of control over your life, would you choose the control?

36) Would you say you were more of an anarchist than a team player?

37) Is there something specific you want to accomplish or be known for before you die?

38) Do you read more non-fiction than fiction?

39) Do you have an expert in finance and accounting on your team?

Note: Score 2½ points for each "yes" answer.
Your score is your probability of success—but is *only* an indication.

If your score is above 85, then you may be misleading yourself by answering the questions too optimistically. If you want the quiz to be of value to you, go back and carefully reconsider whether you're being honest in your answers.

12 Some Advice from Friends

As I interviewed entrepreneurs for this book, one question that I asked all of them was, "If a friend of yours was thinking about going into business for themselves, what advice would you give?" Some of their responses can be found throughout the book. But an awful lot of good, useful advice simply didn't fit within the structure of the book as I had defined it. Accordingly, I decided to add this chapter, which is devoted to the various bits of advice I collected from several of the entrepreneurs interviewed.

As a result, think of this chapter as being advice from a number of experienced friends, who have been where you are thinking of going and done what you're planning to do. I'll let them say it in their own words, then summarize the key points afterwards.

Snug Industries

GREG BLAGOEV, TONY ELSTON, AND Brent Micks are all in their twenties, and have carved out a niche for themselves in the fickle, cutthroat clothing industry by being very much in tune with their market and their customers. They had several things to say about their success.

"We didn't take any draws [salaries] for the first year-and-a-half," Tony told *Report on Business* magazine. "Nothing. We paid our rent and ate mashed potatoes to get our stuff out there. It's what we loved to do, so it wasn't like it was a big sacrifice in the sense that we weren't giving up this time and energy that was going to someone else's dream."

Now that they're successful, their friends all think they've got it made—but it ain't necessarily so.

"We were surprised by the capital that we needed," Greg told me, "and just with, like growth. The proper studio we needed, 'cause we started in my attic, right? It was just chaos with the fabrics being delivered up four flights of stairs. All these things that you never thought you needed, like a fax machine, a computer—just the expenses. We were really motivated to get our name out there, going to parties and going to stores and showing them what we were doing. Everything we were doing was being accepted by these stores in the market we were dealing with, and it just kind of grew from there.

"But the most difficult thing that we found when starting this small business was just how important the whole business aspect is. Like, you may have a great product or design, a concept, but you've got to know all the loopholes in business, and how not to, like, lose money. For us, one was sending orders C.O.D., because we never had credit on people, or anything like that. And also it's that you're getting credit from suppliers and the bank. That was probably the hardest thing.

"We've had very little help from banks. They know that this industry's very risky, so they just pushed us away for so long, we got our financing through family. And we just keep re-investing, even to this day, everything that we're earning, just so that we can keep growing. We're growing so fast, we need all the money we can get.

"People think we're loaded. It's funny because we just say that we're working for the future, and we say that our company is making the money. We just keep reinvesting, you know what I'm saying? We just take what we need to take home to pay our bills.

"We're very positive with what we've got going here. We're in it for the long run. We've had so many offers thrown at us that would help us be more successful quicker, but we have a schedule and timetable we're sticking to, and it's going really well. Financially, and in terms of marketing ourselves, it [the business] is getting stronger, and our relationship with the community [their market], everything that's kind of linked to our clothing. We're sticking to our guns, not just reacting to all the changes around us, because we're far ahead."

What kinds of tips do you give to people who ask you how to do what you've done?

"Mostly just how to be really careful with the money you have at the beginning. Really research your market. Understand how to price your products properly, and make sure you get paid. Just really be on the ball, and be very careful about avoiding losses.

"I'll admit that at the beginning all we thought about was design, like, 'Yah, wicked!' But the thing is you've got to understand the dinero and where it's all going.

"We learned most of our business stuff from Brent Micks and his uncle Gerry Smith. I mean, I took a couple of courses, but it's a good thing to be able to turn to people with questions rather than just going through all the mistakes or taking chances. We just don't believe in taking chances. We're really on top of financial things now.

"It's also very important to focus on the area where you

have input into the company, making sure that everything's on the ball, and that you're communicating very closely with everybody's that's involved in running the company."

 ummary

1 Run cheaply and don't take money out of the business in its early stages; make the sacrifices because it's the only way that the business will build up enough momentum and muscle to support you down the line.

2 You'll be surprised by how much capital you need, and how hard it is to find and manage it. Stay on top of money issues right from the start, or you can find yourself out of cash and out of business.

3 Make sure you have the business side handled as well as the creative. When you're not sure what to do, find someone who knows and ask advice.

4 Communicate clearly with everyone in your company what you want them to do. They can't read your mind, and although something may be obvious to you, it may not be to the people you work with.

 andy Spicer, NICs Garage

WHAT'S IT LIKE BEING AN employer instead of an employee?

"For the most part I really like it. There are definitely problem times when it's not so much fun, where you have to discipline an employee, or even question their approach. I have one employee who doesn't like change. In some ways I've made her change, and yet in others I've tried to allow her to resist change as well. Just to be able to approach things a little bit slower with her than with someone else, to try to take that into account.

"Of course, sometimes it's frustrating when you know that you could do the job a lot quicker yourself instead of waiting for someone else. But you have to allow that person to do it, because really your business is based on your employees. Once you grow so that your business is bigger than a single person, your business no longer will be a success or failure based solely on you. And as you grow, it becomes more and more evident that the success of the business is based on the employees."

What other qualities do you need to succeed?

"I think that one of the strongest personality traits that you have to have is persistence because there are so many times when things don't go exactly how you have them planned out, and you have to be persistent and look at other ways to get at your end goal.

"The ability to communicate—and to communicate effectively—is an incredible asset. I guess we weren't uncommon in our first year in that we ran into financial problems. The first thing that I did was to go talk to all of our suppliers to make sure they knew where we were at and what was happening, and that maybe we wouldn't be able to pay our bill on time, but we definitely had them in mind, and that we would send the money as we could. We had suppliers that supported us greatly through that period. We would be closed now if they hadn't supported us. A lot of that is just being able to be honest and open with people, and make sure that you're communicating with them.

"I think that honesty is one of your best qualities in business because if you're honest, your business is going to grow. It allows you to be able to solve problems. Sometimes they're not solved to the advantage of the business, but if they're solved the best for your employees and for your customers, it will work to your advantage in the long run. Like, we've had situations where it could have turned out really badly, and just to deal with it honestly and openly, and to say that a mistake was made, that, yes, it was our mistake, and yes, we will definitely cover it.

"I don't think that everybody can be a successful entrepreneur. I know some people that don't follow through on things, that don't see that time's important, and they procrastinate. I think those are the things that could hurt you quite quickly in business, especially in a business where you have a lot of customers. Customers get upset when you don't deliver when you said you would.

"Most people, if they were determined enough, and had clearly identified the goals they wanted, and worked really hard at it, they could succeed. But most people just don't have the determination, the drive, or aren't willing to give the hard work necessary to succeed."

 ummary

1 Once your business grows beyond what you can do by yourself, your future depends increasingly on your employees. You must adapt to your employees and their abilities, just as you expect them to adapt to the needs of the business.

2 Be persistent because things don't often work out the way you plan, so you have to find another way to get where you're going.

3 Honesty is one of the most important survival traits, because it allows you to solve problems and move on. If you've made a mistake, admit it, correct it, and build goodwill for the future.

4 Procrastination will upset your customers and kill your business.

5 Be persistent, determined, and willing to work hard.

S herry Orr, Trans-Mutual Trucking

SHERRY ORR HAS BEEN RUNNING her own trucking firm since her early twenties, and has learned most of her lessons the hard way. Today, she's not just the boss, but she's a wife and a mother of two small children.

"I think everybody has what it takes [to be an entrepreneur], it's just a matter of how they feel inside about choosing to go that way. I think my sister, for instance, would be wonderful in her own business, but she's got this little box that she wants to stay in because she feels comfortable and secure.

"I think as a small business owner, the first thing you've got to do is believe in yourself and what you can accomplish. Be honest with yourself. You've got be a little bit of everything. In my company, I've got to be dispatch, I've got to be accounting, I've got to be management, I've got to be sales, I've got to be a little bit of everything. Unfortunately, that didn't just happen, that took me a long, long, long time to do that.

"I do believe that you have to have a little bit of guts, be willing to be a bit of a risk-taker. How much of a risk-taker is up to the individual and the kind of business they're in, but I think you have to have that.

"Everybody has the potential, it's what you choose to make out of it. I see that all around me, like with drivers and things. They've got potential coming out of their ears, but they just don't do it. I think there's a fine line between either you are or you aren't suited to be an entrepreneur, but it's really whether you want to or not. Some people are very happy working for somebody else. Like I look at my sister and I say, 'Gee, you've got so many talents, just go do it!' But it's not going to happen."

And how would you maximize the odds of success?

"I think the best thing is, know what you're doing, know

what the market studies are, getting as much information as you can. That means if you've gone over it once, go over it 10 times. Being very, very prepared.

"Do not get yourself undercapitalized, that's probably the biggest problem. Do not expect to take a full salary. Initially, be prepared to live on the bare bones.

"Be prepared to do whatever it takes. If that includes cleaning the toilets, then that's what you do. The bottom line is to do whatever it takes, and don't whine about it. With hard work, a little bit of luck, and a good business, you'll do well.

"Get good support from your family. I think that's very important. Sit down with everybody and let them know what's going on. It's important because that's who you're going to lean on in rough times."

Sherry has young children, so I asked her what it was like running a business with young kids.

"It's stressful. It's very stressful, but in some respects we're very lucky because I'm in a position now where I can go and do volunteer work with the school and do some things with the kids.

"But there are days when, before you even come to work, you're stressed out because they won't eat, they won't get dressed, and you're coming to work in the car and you're just frazzled. It's very difficult.

"When they were babies, there were many days I came to work with just two, three hours sleep. The common perception is that you don't have to come in as the boss, but it's quite the opposite. You do come in, you have to be there.

"It just comes down to this: if you believe in yourself, and believe in what you do, just go for it. But be prepared, be very, very prepared. And have the people around you be prepared that are going to be supporting you on it, too."

S ummary

1 Anyone can be a successful entrepreneur, but many people won't because they don't want to or are afraid to.
2 Be honest with yourself, but believe in yourself, too.
3 Be willing to do whatever it takes to succeed, whether it's learning accounting or cleaning the toilets. And don't whine about it.
4 Get support from your family and keep them informed on what's happening, because you'll have to lean on them during the rough times.
5 Know the market; learn everything you can about it. Go over everything 10 times.
6 Don't start by being undercapitalized, and don't take a full salary until well past the time when the business can afford it. Your salary is your present; the business is your future.
7 Running your own business when you have kids is very stressful, there's no getting around it.

K onrad Tittler, Diacon Industries

KONRAD TITTLER IS A DOUBLE-DIPPER. He started a company in his thirties, built it up into the largest privately owned, specialty chemical company in the country, and sold it to a multinational. Then, in his sixties, he came out of retirement, bought back a portion of the company he had sold, increased its revenues fivefold, and will likely pass on the reins to his children when he retires for a second time. He offered a wide range of advice:

"My trouble with helping someone into business is that I did something that I thought was simple and obvious. I chose a work area that I knew, I continued in the business that I knew, but I continued now as an owner of a start-up company rather than as an employee of a large corporation. So my leap into business from a technical and a knowledge-base requirement was pretty minimal. I knew what I was getting into.

"I would advise that, if you can, go into a business you know something about rather than just going into business. I think a lot of people don't appreciate how much they know about the business that has provided them with a living. There are just hundreds and hundreds of details and things about a business that are not common knowledge, and yet the employee in that business assumes it's common knowledge because everyone around him seems to know what he knows. But it's only that group. You go outside of that boundary, and the world is mystified about that business, doesn't know how it works, and doesn't know the parts that make it work. So I say that you should go into a business you're already practised at, where someone else has funded your education in that business.

"I don't think age is a factor. I didn't have a message that now's the right time, or I'm the right age, and I'll never be the right age again. My experience underlines that in that I did it when I was in my late thirties, and I'm doing it again now in my mid-sixties, and it feels the same. Unless you're planning to go into the NHL, age doesn't matter.

"You don't have to have a new idea, or a completely different product, you just have to be able to say, 'But this is a benefit that no one else is offering you right now, and if you accept that this is a real benefit, and make the effort to do business with us, everyone will have to deliver the same benefit. If you reject it, then you will forever have to continue on the way you are going, because no one will have to offer this benefit. It was as simple as that.'

"I suppose that for every product line, for every idea, the entrepreneur has to have a vision of how he will be different, how he'll really be different. And it only has to be short-term. You don't have to be different forever. You can accept the fact that, yes, the competition will fill that gap, and will respond, but by that point, you're in business, and you've made a contribution to the marketplace, which is never forgotten. You're always then looked upon as an innovator.

"In my case, by the time my competitors woke up to what we were doing, it was too late because we had over 50% of the marketplace. By the time the whole thing settled down, we settled in at 70%, and everyone else came in at 30%. But that took a few years, that wasn't a few months."

What can you do to improve your chances of success?

"Have a supplemental income source—your own or your spouse's, or your partner's. This allows for a natural controlled learning-curve and a growth pattern, so that not everything needs to be perfected right from the start. 'Slow go' avoids sudden 'no go.' Don't put yourself in a situation where you have to succeed, or you have to have a certain growth level, don't get yourself in debt, and don't be beholden to a banker.

"If you don't have any supplemental income going into business, then all your decisions are driven by the need to create cash flow rather than the need to create a successful position in the marketplace. And those two things aren't always on the same time schedule.

"You have to be persistent. If you don't have persistence, stay employed [working for someone else]. Persistence is one of the key ingredients. In the first three or four years I was in business, my wife always tried to remind me that I had gone bankrupt each year, but I was the only guy that wasn't admitting it. But she knew it by our lifestyle. I think persistence is pretty important.

"Luck helps if it's good, but normally luck flows good and bad, so don't rely on it. I think it's very important to recognize good luck, and a lot of entrepreneurs don't. They attribute it to their own abilities, and just allow it to blow their egos a little larger. But in many, many cases, important building blocks in the success of a business were just there at the right time, and that wasn't necessarily planned by the entrepreneur, or some turn in the marketplace that happened to favour your position or your product.

"It's important to recognize those, because then you can deal with bad luck, because you can say, 'It was nothing to do with me. It was bad luck, I'm not a failure. This company is not a failure, these people are not failures, this was truly bad luck.' So if you can recognize when it was good luck and attribute it to that, you can also then deal with bad luck and attribute it correctly, and go on making sound business decisions.

"I've seen people who were very lucky, where everything worked, and they attributed it all to their own innate ability, and then later on went into even bigger ventures and found they weren't very good at business."

What are the major pitfalls to avoid?

"Impatience is the first. That impatience may come because there's a need to succeed quickly or you'll go bankrupt. You need somehow to structure the venture so that time is available to you, and that slow growth is one of the options you can tolerate. My current business didn't grow slowly, but then again, it didn't have to, I would have survived just fine if it hadn't.

"Another pitfall is that there has to be a willingness to postpone gratification, or else you go broke through your own greed.

"Probably the third one is if your primary measure of success is monetary. If you're in business, and the only reason you're in it is for money, then it's a higher-risk situation. If you're in the business because it's the kind of work you like to do, or this is a way you like to make a living, or you feel as though there is some worth to your existence in addition to making a living, that makes the venture a lot stronger than being in it solely to make a buck and make it fast.

"Another one is listening poorly. If you're determined that you have something that's worthwhile, and everyone's telling you you're wrong, there's a chance that you're the only one in the world that sees it correctly, but I wouldn't take that chance.

"I think that anyone that is highly selfish would have trouble getting a business off the ground. I suppose there's a greed factor there—there are some people who have made it to a high level in business and can attribute it to a high level of greed. I don't know if that's an important driving force. You can have some short-term successes, but I don't know if you can have long-term success. There has to be a willingness to share success with people, otherwise you should pretty well stay on your own."

Can anybody be a successful entrepreneur?

"No, because somewhere along the way, there has to be a level of discipline. In the early stages of the game, no one else is going to do the job, no one else is going to clean up after the parade. In other words, there has to be the discipline to apply yourself to anything that needs to be done. Things can be swept under a carpet in a corporation. Someone else will take that lump out and deal with it. But when you're in business for yourself, unless you have the discipline to deal with all the issues, and, one way or another resolve them, you're likely going to fail.

"If you can see around the corner to get a sense of what's coming, if you don't need a lot of money immediately, if you can postpone gratification, if you've got discipline, and you're getting some joy out of the business to get you through the lean times, then you're probably going to be all right."

 ummary

1 Go into a business you know something about.

2 Unless you're planning to play in the NHL, age doesn't matter; there's no right time to go into business.

3 You don't need a completely new idea or product, but you must be able to say that you're offering a real benefit that no one else is offering right now, and that if your customers make the effort to

deal with you, then the industry will have to respond, and the customer will wind up with the benefit. It doesn't have to be a long-term difference; just long enough for you to get established.

4   Have another source of income. Don't put yourself in a position where you have to succeed or go bankrupt, because the rhythm of the business may not match the timing of your financial needs. If you don't have any supplemental income, then all your decisions are driven by the need to create cash flow.

5   If you don't have persistence, stay employed.

6   Recognize that just as good luck is not due to your brilliance, bad luck is also not your fault. Knowing this will help you to make sound business decisions.

7   Be patient, and succeed slowly rather than fail quickly.

8   Be willing to postpone gratification. Rewards come later, not in the beginning.

9   Get joy out of the work itself, independent of your pay cheque. If the only reason you're in business is for the money, then you are putting yourself at risk, because you will try to hurry things along.

10   Listen carefully. If you're the only one who thinks you're right, it could be true, but the odds are against it.

11   You have to be willing to be disciplined about doing the work that needs to be done, whether you like it or not.

C larissa Desjardins and Lloyd Segal, Caprion Pharmaceutical

CLARISSA DESJARDINS, LLOYD SEGAL, AND Martin LeBlanc started with an idea, created a rapidly growing, highly successful biotech company, sold it out to a major pharmaceutical company, and are now starting again.

I asked Clarissa and Lloyd, what personality traits do you need to have to be successful, and which ones can destroy you?

"Our experience is that the worst thing you can do when

you're running a new business or an entrepreneurial business where by definition everything is new and the rules have yet to be written, is not to learn, not to be open to your mistakes, and other people's mistakes. We are notorious sponges. We'll suck the marrow out of anybody who will talk to us, because we figure that even people, or especially people who have failed, can teach us something. I think that that's the sign of a lot of great entrepreneurs. We don't get hung up on our own mistakes, of which we have made many. We euphemistically refer to a great big list of mistakes on the wall. Our only rule is: make each one once. Each time we make a mistake, we say, 'Well we can cross this one off, we've now made this mistake, we don't have to make it again. This is good, because we're further ahead now.'

"We meet a lot of people who just believe they're so smart they don't have to listen to anybody, so we're never surprised when they fail. And it doesn't in any way diminish your power and belief as an entrepreneur in what you're doing and how it flies in the face of what the industry is doing already.

"When our sales were $1000 a year, and people told us, 'You'll never do this,' or, 'You'll never sell more than $100,000 a year,' we knew they were wrong, but we wanted to know why they felt what they did. We listened intently to hear what their assumptions were, and we inevitably talked about it afterwards to make sure we understood why we thought they were wrong, and whether there was any insight that was instructive to us.

"We meet countless entrepreneurs, in our industry and others, and they don't want to listen to people. They don't want to listen to their customers, they don't want to listen to their competitors, they don't want to listen to people who've been in the business for 30 years, and we think they pay for it. There's hubris for a start-up company in not having very, very big ears.

"I think it's not just listening, it's internalizing, and putting it through a reasonable feedback loop. We learned as much from other industries as from our own industry. One of our board members is from the mining industry. There's a hell of a lot in the mining industry that's instructive for us in biotech. If you're not really listening, you would miss that. A lot of the core business processes are the same. You stake out some space, you tell everyone that there's gold in them thar hills, you beg people for money to let you start digging, and you essentially sell the gold before you actually hit any, and guess what I've just described? Biotechnology. It's all about how good were your royalties, and how good were you in getting someone to pay you upfront for the gold?

"A lot of people shouldn't be entrepreneurs. They're very risk-averse, and they'd be miserable in an entrepreneurial environment. They should recognize that within themselves, and they shouldn't do it. From my point of view, it's painful enough if you don't get to the finish line, and you don't reap the rewards, you can seriously hurt yourself. There's just people who are risk-averse, there are some people who are not optimistic or realistic, and you cannot do it that way. You can't go into business hesitantly, or backwards, it simply won't fly.

"Statistically, the day you start your company, the odds are against you. If you're not prepared to deal with that, then you probably ought not to be an entrepreneur.

"When we thought about this, we said, 'Okay, there's only a 20% chance of success. What are all the things we can do to increase the odds for us?' One was for us to be us. We didn't mind looking inside ourselves and saying that we were smarter than your average bear.

"We figure that you massively increase your odds if you get into an industry that's growing like gangbusters. All boats rise in a tide. If you choose an industry that's growing, then even inefficient or not great players tend to tail on some kind of success.

"We hired the best people. Hire great people, and involve great people in the company, and if they're not successful in the things you initially rely on them to do, they're smart enough to figure out something else. There's story after story about entrepreneurial companies that originally set out to do one thing, that thing wasn't successful, but they're smart, and that allowed them to do something completely different. They changed tack, and made money doing something else. That, we thought, increased our probability of success, and we used that as our guide when we hired people.

"A final one is that cash is king, and make sure you have a lot of it. Sure, there are people who think that if you have a lot of it, you can live too high on the hog. Even in the rare time when we had a lot of cash, we were acutely aware that cash was our lifeblood.

"But as long as we had cash, we could do things. Just after we did our major financing, someone came to us with a new technology for mad cow disease in veterinary practice. Only because we had a couple of hundred thousand dollars to commit to that project, and because we were living so frugally, were we able to commit and partner with McGill, and bring in the people to do the research. When we sold the company in November [1998], we didn't sell that piece of research, we spun that out as Caprion Pharmaceuticals, which is worth, today, far more than Bioconcept [the company they did sell].

"Cash provides you with all kinds of freedom from bankers, from new investors, but most importantly, it allows a small entrepreneurial company to do the one thing that big companies can't, which is turn on a dime, and rapidly embrace opportunities."

S ummary

1 Learn from your mistakes. Be willing to make mistakes, because they are unavoidable, but only make each mistake once. People who don't learn, fail.

2 Listen. Listen to your customers, your competitors, your employees. Listen to people who say you're doomed to fail. Find out why they are saying you'll fail, then decide for yourself whether there's any truth in what they say.

3 Learn from other industries, because many core business processes are the same.

4 If you are afraid of risk, don't start, because you will be miserable in an entrepreneurial environment. [I don't completely agree with this point, as I've said earlier. Fear is inevitable, but can be managed.—RW]

5 Don't go into business hesitantly or backwards; it simply won't work.

6 The day you start, the odds are against you, so do everything you can to improve the odds of your success.

7 Hire great people, and involve great people in other ways as well, such as a board of directors or a board of advisors. They will help you find an unexpected way of succeeding even if your original plans don't work out.

8 Cash is king, cash is your lifeblood. If you have enough cash, and use it frugally, then it gives you freedom from bankers or new investors. It also allows you to do the one thing big companies can't: turn on a dime and rapidly embrace new opportunities.

aureen Maclachlan,
Age Matters Communications Group, Inc.

MAUREEN MACLACHLAN, AGE 50, RUNS what may be a unique organization in Canada: one devoted to helping organizations serve and market to the mature Canadians. Not only does Maureen fit this category, but she has also studied gerontology, demographics, marketing, and business. She's worked for other people as well as herself, and I started by asking her to discuss what it's like working for herself:

"I always have to be on my toes 100%—or more. There's no slack. You know, in a company, if you don't feel really great one day, you can cut yourself a little slack sometimes, but when you're running your own show, and have people working for you, you've always got to be on your toes.

"You have to exercise a great deal of flexibility and initiative, and you have the ability to exercise it, whereas in large organizations there's often inertia and layers of other people to go through to make decisions. You just don't have that escape any more.

"Now, that flexibility can be kind of scary at times, too. It's like, 'Oh my God, I've got this decision, and I've got this, and this, and that choice. Which one's going to be the best?' Whereas if you're in a big company, somebody says, 'That's the decision, that's what you've got to do.'

"The most nerve-wracking part of working for myself was committing to do it, and wondering if it was going to succeed or fail. But it was making that commitment that was hard, and that was the point where I decided if I was going to incorporate, because that, to me, was a significant commitment, and to right away hire someone to work with me. And the fact that I was starting off cold-turkey, with no contracts, to build a business.

"You need to have a product or a service, and somebody that wants to buy it, and you need to identify those things up front. You need to have a particular skill set to be self-employed, and to work on your own. You need some basic business understanding of how money works. You need to be highly organized. You need to have some sales and marketing ability somewhere in your bones, because if you can't sell your company, nobody else can. And when you're starting off on your own, you really need to believe that this is good and worth buying. If you don't believe that, then how can you convince anybody else?

"You need to be self-sustaining, meaning that the buck stops at you, there are times when you have to bolster yourself. When you're sort of feeling down, and you think, 'Oh, have I made a big mistake? What am I doing here?' you have to be able to pull yourself up by the bootstraps and keep going, and say, 'Yup, I've made the decision, and it's going to be good.' If you haven't the ability to hire somebody to work with you, or you haven't organized it to bring in a partner, it can be really isolating, and very lonely. You're just out there by yourself.

"I find it particularly interesting when people in large companies say, 'Oh, I think it would be fascinating, it would be great to work out of home.' I think there are a ton of myths around working out of home. It's so easy to get distracted and go do something else if you're not disciplined. Lots of times your network outside of work, your family, friends, and so on, don't always understand that just because you're at home doesn't mean that they can phone you up, that you're trying to make a business go.

"And then there's the issue of children. I defy anyone to have little kids and work out of home unless they have a nanny or unless they have daycare outside the home. It's just really hard to separate that. Yesterday, for instance, I came back from being on the road, I had a 13-year-old who was sick, I had a cat that was sick, and I was trying to get my work done! You're too available lots of times, because you're not going out to the office. It has all sorts of challenges that people who have never tried it think it must be wonderful, but it takes a lot of discipline.

"The hours are long, but then I worked long hours when I worked in the corporate sector.

"I find it particularly difficult, and I think that a lot of self-employed people do, in defining the boundaries between work and family, particularly if you have an office in-home. Your work is always there, you can't walk away from it. When you decide to do your own work, the family needs to know what this is going to mean to you, because lots of times the evenings aren't free, the weekends aren't free, you're working. It can really take its toll. Your family has to be committed to that as well. There are going to be some sacrifices. So the family stuff can be important, and we're all trying to reach some kind of balance, which in some ways is a sort of a myth. I don't know about other people, but I tend to go from one end of the spectrum to the other. I'm either all on holidays, or I'm all at work.

"Being able to manage your finances is really important. Once you start out with a contract or a widget, there's going to be that time when you're building a business where there's not any money coming in. After a few years, you know when the lean times are, and the good times, so you figure out when you really need to bank it, and when you can spend it.

"That's really important. When you're starting off there's a kind of sense that I need this, and this, and this, and I've got the money in the door right now, but you really have to know how to manage your cash flow so that you've got it when you need it.

"The difference between having a client and a boss is that with a client, you're there to please and to get along with your clients, there's nobody running interference for you. This is where the buck stops; you either make it with your client or you don't. The other thing, too, is the autonomy to say, 'This contract will work for me,' or 'This contract won't.' I've walked away from a good contract because it just wasn't going to work. When you're working for someone in a big organization, you can't always do that.

"It's not less stressful than working in a major corporation, it's a different kind of stress, and it's always there. Sometimes you're only as good as the next contract that comes in, or the next widget that gets sold. That can be kind of nerve-wracking. But when it's all clicking, and the work is coming to you, it feels really good.

"The thing that's surprising me right now is the work that's coming to me, and where it's coming from. I have positioned myself in the for-profit sector, but there's work coming from the not-for-profit sector. The tricky side is that if work comes to me that I'm not sure I've really got the time to do, I find I'm trying to squeeze it in. It may be slightly out of the realm of what I and my company are focused on, and I think, 'Oh yes, but I can still stretch things to do that.' That's a challenge. A contract will come to me, and I really haven't got time to do all that, or it's beyond what I do but I still would like to do it because it PAYS! It PAYS! That's a tough one.

"The ability to see the opportunities is tough, because people who have been employed in a corporate environment are used to having people tell them what to do. Or having been in a long-term job, they don't think outside the box.

"I get up and get dressed, put my jewellery on, do all those things as if I was going to go to the office. I never know at a moment's notice that I could have a meeting here, or at a client's office outside. But also what it does is it puts me in the mindset of going to work. I laugh when people say, 'It must be nice, you can get up and just put your track suit on, or stay in your pajamas and your slippers.' They think that, and it's not that way—at least, not for me."

 ummary

1   Be on your toes 100% of the time; there's no slack.
2   The most nerve-wracking part of working for yourself is committing to doing it.
3   Have some basic understanding of business and how money works.
4   Be highly organized.

5 Have some sales and marketing ability because if you can't sell yourself, nobody else can, either. You must also believe that what you're selling is good, and worth buying, or you won't be able to convince anyone else.

6 Be able to pick yourself up when you get down.

7 Be very disciplined about your work and your working hours, especially if you work at home. Defining the boundaries of home and work is particularly hard.

8 Know how to manage your money. There will be times when you have money, but you can't spend it because there will be lean times in the future, and you have to prepare for them.

9 Know when to walk away from a contract that won't work for you, even if you need the money.

10 Dress as if you were going to the office; it puts you in the mindset you need to work.

Jonathan Strauss, Strauss Publishing

NINETEEN-YEAR-OLD JONATHAN STRAUSS bought a struggling computer publication when he was still in high school, and changed it into a successful publishing and event-planning organization. He has temporarily suspended his education, planning eventually to go to university, but finds the rigours of running a business to be both intriguing and an education in itself.

In seeking advice for people about to embark on their own business ventures, I started by asking Jonathan what he thought about the importance of luck in running a business:

"I'm not sure that luck has anything to do with anything. You could say that timing is important. I've never considered myself a lucky person. I mean, my younger brother wins every draw he enters. He's a lucky person. Could he run his own successful business? I don't know.

"Sure you get lucky sometimes, but I think it really comes down to timing is absolutely everything. In real estate, it's location, location, location. In business I think it's timing, timing, timing.

"Most convention facilities have a policy that they will not book a competing event anywhere from 30 to 60 days either side. We were booking an event that was very time-sensitive, and we were lucky enough that we booked it in the Winnipeg Convention Centre, the only facility that could host it in the city, 48 hours before a competitor tried to.

"Sure we were lucky to book it, but we knew there was potential in this event in this market. Does that mean other people knew it? Probably. So I mean, is it luck, is it timing, is it skill? I don't know.

"You need a little bit of luck in anything you do, whether it's driving your car, or running your own business, or going on vacation. You gotta have some luck somewhere. But I don't think it's a prime factor in our success, and I only say that because of how hard we work around the office. If everything we did came easily, and everyone was working four hours a day, four days a week, then I would probably tell you it was luck. But when you work very hard at what you do, I don't think that luck has anything to do with your success. And if it does, then I guess I'm very lucky.

"But if you think you're lucky, and that's the only way you work, then I wouldn't want to be your partner."

Do you ever get depressed?

"Sure, sometimes, when events don't work, or when an idea that you think might be great doesn't come to fruition, it's very frustrating. But then you just try to come up with a better idea, or a better concept. I have a mandate to myself of how many events I want to be doing, and if I can't fulfil my mandate with one idea, then it's a matter of let's go back to the drawing board and figure out what the next one is.

"Now that I employ six people full time, I have a responsibility to keep them employed. I would have to lay somebody off because we didn't have the work to keep them busy if I let one mishap stop us. If something doesn't work, then it's sort of,'Okay, how do we either make it better and make it work, or what else can we do? Where else is there opportunity?'"

And the keys to success?

"The key to success is asking a lot of questions, and don't be afraid to ask the stupid questions. What's the old quote, 'There are no stupid questions, only stupid answers.' I had a teacher in junior high who yelled at me for questioning something, and I said, 'Well, I don't know the answer, that's the only reason I'm asking. I mean, I don't care if it's a stupid question. I'm only asking it because I think it's relevant. I'm not asking it to waste your time.' I don't ask questions to waste time."

What do you say to your friends who say, "Gee, I wish I could do what you've done?"

"Well, what's your idea? People who say they want to be an entrepreneur say it because they have an idea they want to take to fruition. I think that most people who say that they want to work for themselves don't say they just want to work for themselves, they say they want to work for themselves because they want to do X, Y, or Z. I've had lots of friends say, 'Hey, I'm thinking of doing this, what do you think of it?' And sometimes I say, 'Well, I think you're better off not trying,' or I say, 'Call Bob or Bill over at XYZ company, and ask them what they think, if this would fit, or if this makes sense, or whether there's a market for it.' I would never discourage any of my friends. If anything, I would try to help them make their idea work. And I think now I'm in a sort of position where I can do that."

ummary

1 You need a little bit of luck in everything you do, but it's not a prime factor of success. Hard work is. But if you think you're lucky, and that's what you're depending on, I wouldn't want to be your partner.

2 When things don't work, try to come up with a way to do it better or a better idea. Look for another opportunity instead of wasting time being depressed.

3 The key to success is asking a lot of questions. And don't be afraid to ask questions that sound stupid if that's what you need to know.

4 People hardly ever want to go into business just to go into business. It's almost always because there's something they want to do.

13 Who Owns Tomorrow?

Do you want to depend on others for security, and hope that everything turns out all right? Or do you want to create your own security by creating your own work? This seems like a simple question, but, ironically, you may not have that choice, because the world is tending to move away from employment and towards something very like free agency for all.

As a futurist, I hear a lot of anxiety about tomorrow. One of the questions I get asked on a regular basis is: "Will the big, multinationals end up ruling the world?" Surprisingly, the answer is no, they won't. In fact, the trend in business and society is away from the power of corporations and governments, and towards the power of the individual.

With one exception, there are no longer any advantages to being big. The only exception involves industries that require an enormous amount of capital—industries that need a lot of plant and equipment to produce their products, as is the case with the car manufacturers, or industries that must do an enormous amount of advertising to convince consumers that, for example, their brand of cola is better than someone else's.

Yet, even this exception is starting to fade. It may well be in the future that you will buy your car from a one-person car designer, who subcontracts the manufacture to a car factory. And the Internet is changing all the rules about advertising, and may well mean that the company with the biggest bucks no longer gets the most attention.

So, if bigger isn't necessarily better any more, what will the corporate world look like? It will look a lot more like the film production business. A person will get an idea for a project, or a business opportunity. They will then go out seeking the financing for the project, enlisting partners as needed. Once they've secured the financing (assuming they don't have it themselves), they'll contract services from all the people they need to make their project a reality. Together, they'll accomplish the desired goal, market the hell out of it, have a wrap party, disband and then either wait for the next project to appear, or go out and create it.

Perhaps a particular project will turn out to be wildly successful, and they'll turn it into spin-offs and add-ons, marketing opportunities, and sequels. But there will be few permanent relationships, and no guarantees that being included with one project will lead to inclusion in later projects.

Not all companies will act this way, and not all employment will be this way. But this is the direction that the business world is clearly heading, and whether you receive a pay cheque from someone you call your employer, or are paid for working under a contract, the relationship between worker and payer is far more tenuous now than in the past. Which leads us back to where we started: Where can anyone find a secure job? There is no job security. When you accept this, it can be very liberating, because you can stop wasting your time looking for one and instead start investing your time in creating your own future.

Taking a job is entering into a bargain. You give up the value of what you create for a guarantee of a regular income over the period of your employment. If you create less than you are paid, you are harming your employer, and when they figure that out, you're gone.

Zig Ziglar is one of the best-known sales trainers in North America. For many years he has told people that everyone works on commission, but sales people know it. The job bargain means that the commissions you earn are paid to you in a regular flow, but you are still working on commission. What's different today is that employees no longer have as long a grace period to produce before their income is cut off.

But if you are going to create that kind of value for someone else, and still not have security, then why not keep all the value you create? Whether you do it through the Internet, through a franchise, through a distributorship, or by creating a new business from the ground up, the result will be both more security and greater satisfaction.

T he way it's going to be

If the world is changing so that individuals are becoming more powerful, and corporations and governments are becoming less powerful, then who owns the future? Anyone who goes out and creates it.

When people ask me how I predict the future, I tell them that I don't because I can't—no one can. It's impossible to predict the future accurately and consistently. However, one of the great technological visionaries of our time, a man named Alan Kay, disagrees with me. He says that the best way to predict the future is to invent it.

Now, we cannot control the world around us; that's not within our ability. But we can absolutely control how we respond to the world around us, so it is up to us to invent the kind of future we would like for ourselves, for our families, for our communities, for this country, and for the human race as a whole.

A sk the right question

One of the oldest questions in philosophy is "What's the purpose of life?" I don't have an answer, and I also think it's a bad question. You may recall earlier when we were discussing inspiration and ingenuity, we talked about "good" questions versus "bad" questions. A good question is one that suggests possible answers. A bad one leaves you facing a blank wall, with no idea of what to do next. In my opinion, "What is the purpose of life?" is a bad question. Fortunately, there is a way of framing a much better question. In fact, it leads to one of the best questions I've ever heard.

I came across this question in a slim volume by Dr. Viktor Frankl. Dr. Frankl was a Viennese psychiatrist who, because he was a Jew, spent most of World War II interned in the Auschwitz death camp. The death camps, as you probably know, were designed to exterminate the people imprisoned, either directly, through gas, bullets, or beatings; or indirectly, through starvation, cruelty, overwork, or disease. As a survivor and a psychiatrist, Dr. Frankl observed many people surrender to the horrors of the camp and die, and many others defy the ghastly odds against them and live. What separated one group from the other? Why did one person struggle and live, and another beside him die? Frankl remarks:

> The prisoner who had lost faith in the future—his future—was doomed. With his loss of belief in the future, he also lost his spiritual hold; he let himself decline and became subject to mental and physical decay . . . He was soon lost. The typical reply with which such a man rejected all encouraging argument was 'I have nothing to expect from life any more.' What sort of answer can one give to that?

What was really needed was a fundamental change in our attitude toward life. We had to learn ourselves and, furthermore, we had to teach the despairing men, that *it did not really matter what we expected from life, but rather what life expected from us.* . . . Our answer must consist, not in talk and meditation, but in right action and in right conduct.[1]

We don't need to be in such dire straits to benefit from that kind of advice, and a terrific question pops out of Dr. Frankl's experience: *What can life expect of you?* This question, if faced squarely, can provide many of the answers you may have been seeking. But the focus is inward, not outward. You won't find your purpose in an examination of the world, or the economy, or your responsibilities or position. You'll find it inside yourself. And that brings me to the ultimate point of this book.

You are at an age and stage of life where you are thinking about working for yourself, or at least considering it as an alternative. By getting this far through this book, you've proven that something within you wants to do this. So let me encourage you to start. Perhaps you'll turn back, just before you take the leap and commit yourself. But, having come this far, you should at least reach the edge and look. Whether or not you leap, you will learn an awful lot about yourself.

I haven't covered everything, and you will need to read and learn much more before you succeed. You will, in fact, have to stay in a constant state of learning for the rest of your life, so you might as well get to like it. But this book is enough to start.

In order to start, you must act. Dr. Rollo May, in his seminal book *Love and Will*, says, "The degree of intentionality can define the aliveness of the person." This is high-fallutin' talk, but it boils down to mean the same thing as Dr. Frankl said of his experience in a concentration camp: "Our answer [to life] must consist, not in talk and meditation, but in right action and in right conduct." Of the intentions that you have for your life, the more of them you act on, the more alive you are. The fewer of them you act on and the more you follow the wishes and goals of others, the less life you have. The living death consists of doing only that which is safe, expected, ordered by others, and about which you care nothing. "To cease wishing is to be dead," says Dr. Rollo May.

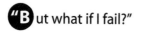ut what if I fail?"

And what of the possibility of failure? From where you are, can you afford to give up security to try the uncertainties of entrepreneurship? Listen to Vancouver entrepreneur Konrad Tittler, president of Diacon Industries: "I've never seen any security in a big corporate job, and the recent recessions have proven that. Worse, being in a corporate job gives you very little control over what's going to happen to you. A merger or takeover could wipe out your job tomorrow, and there'd be nothing you could do about it."

Or hear what Marci Lipman says about the risks of being in business: "A lot of business is a gamble, and you're never going to know what will happen until you take the next step. But I know a lot of my friends with good jobs who are sitting behind desks and hating it. 'I wish I'd done what you did!' they tell me.

"God! I could *never* work for someone else now. I'd be the most unemployable person in the world if I was out there. I don't even have a partner, I don't have to go to a committee, if it's not in the budget, I spend it anyway, just to get the thing done!

"Entrepreneurs have more control over their lives."

Life comes from being true to yourself, and *acting* on that truth. And for you, that truth includes the freedom to be your own boss, seek your own rewards, and create your own security. That's what you're here for. And that's why you read the book.

"The journey *is* the reward."

In the palmy days of Apple Computer's greatest success, their motto was: "The journey is the reward."

This may not be important to you now. But after you've reached the level that you now think of as your ultimate goal, when you've attained the cars, and the money, and the lifestyle, let me warn you of what has been called the "curse of the Buddha." You will find that the things you dreamed of are not enough. The euphoric "high" that you get from any achievement, from any possession, from any position or recognition seeps away after you've had it for a few years and have become used to it. That is why all the entrepreneurs I know, without exception, stay in the battle when they could retire for life at an early age.

"The journey is the reward." The experience of doing, of creating, of staying in the struggle and winning again and again, is more important than the prizes you win. The joy comes in the process of winning the game, not in possessing the trophies—although the trophies are certainly nice to have.

So approach the struggle with anticipation and joy, and stay in it to live your life to the fullest.

When should you start?

This is the end of the book, but, perhaps, the beginning of your career as an entrepreneur. When should you start?

Bob Shoniker, who was an entrepreneur and who now raises funding for other people's businesses, volunteered a remark that has stayed with me over the months that I've laboured over this book. It's a challenging statement that may provoke you to thought, so let me pass it on:

"Tell people either to do it within 48 hours of reading your book, or give it up forever."

That's pretty stark. I believe that people reach a certain degree of ripeness that allows them to go and do what they couldn't do before. If you've reached that ripeness, then Bob's advice is smack on the money—so go thou and do likewise. But if you're not ready, if the time is not right now, then ask yourself: What stands between me and entrepreneurship? Find out what's holding you back, then look for ways of overcoming such barriers. You *can* start this in the next 48 hours.

And keep this book on a handy bookshelf, for I have a feeling that, having read this far, you're a lot closer to ripeness than you think. Pick up the book whenever the urge hits, and read the passages that interest you the most. And when the time is right, go.

I wish you all the joys of the game. Go in peace.

When You're Rich and Famous . . .

Nobody's perfect, not even me. I'm sure I've screwed up somewhere along the way in trying to provide you with a blueprint to success. Despite this, some of you will succeed.

Win or lose, if you set out to be an entrepreneur, I'd like to hear how you got on. I'd love to hear about your triumphs and disasters. I know that nothing is easy, and nothing is simple, and I consider a temporary failure the same way as I think of success—as a change in the weather.

Let me know what I should tell the next person who wants to break free and go into business for themselves. Tell me what to tell them. *You* are the pioneer; send a message back from the frontier.

You can reach me care of Key Porter Books by writing me a letter addressed to:

Richard Worzel
c/o Key Porter Books
70 The Esplanade
Toronto, Ontario M5E 1R2

Yes, I have e-mail, but if you *write*, I'll know you mean it.

If you'd like to know more about my company, Futuresearch, and the work that I do, you can find my website on the Internet at: www.futuresearch.com

If you want me to speak for your group, either about the future, or about the business of entrepreneurship, contact my agent:

The David Lavin Agency
24 Duncan Street, 4th floor
Toronto, Ontario M5V 2B8
416-979-7979 / 800-265-4870

I speak to high school students for free when my schedule permits. All other groups fall under my agreement with the Lavin Agency as a commercial engagement.

Thank you.

otes

Chapter 1

1 "How the economy is changing far faster than people are," *The Globe and Mail*, April 20, 1996.

2 *Labour Force Update*, 2nd quarter, 1998, Statistics Canada, "Economy has been dishing up very good jobs, indeed," *The Globe and Mail*, August 31, 1998, p. A6.

3 "An overview of permanent layoffs," Garnett Picot, Zhengxi Lin, and Wendy Pyper, *Perspectives*, Autumn 1997, Statistics Canada, p. 46.

Chapter 4

1 Sawyer, Deborah C., "When creating jobs doesn't work," *The Globe and Mail*, January 27, 1993, p. A20.

Chapter 7

1 May, Rollo, Dr., *Love and Will*. (W.W. Norton & Company, 1969)

Chapter 13

1 Frankel, Viktor, *Man's Search for Meaning*. (Washington Square Press, 1984)

Index